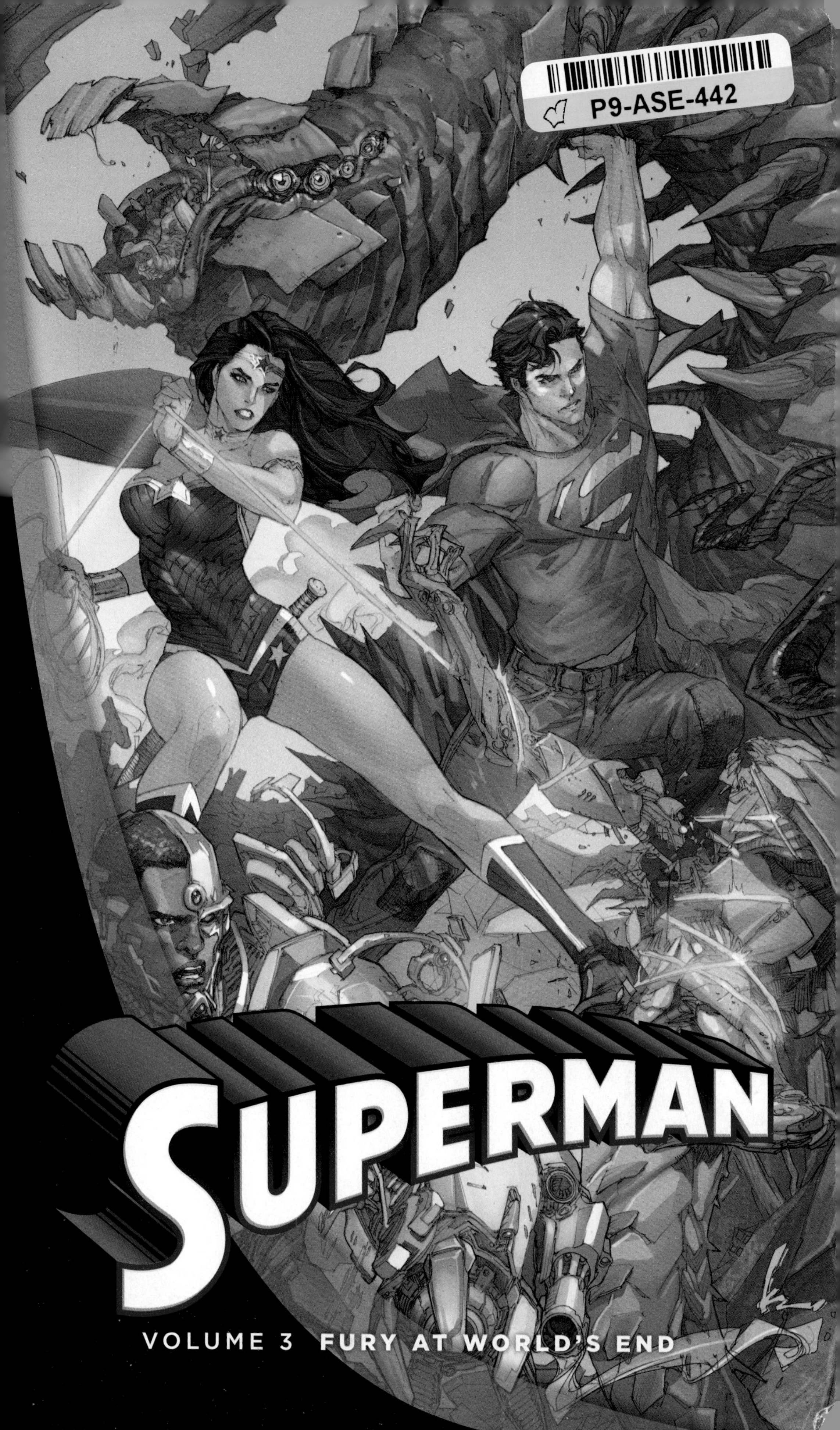

SUPERMAN

VOLUME 3 FURY AT WORLD'S END

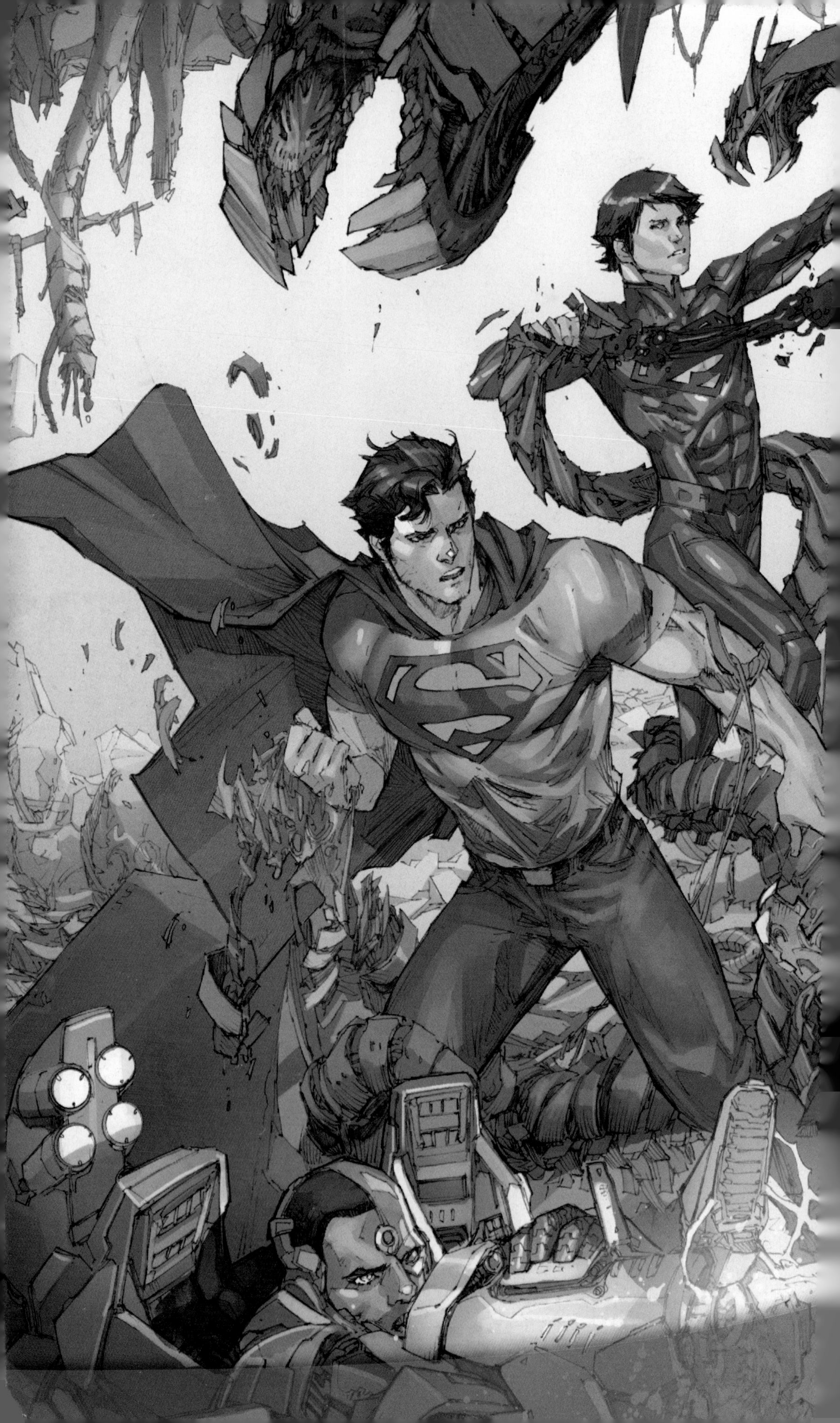

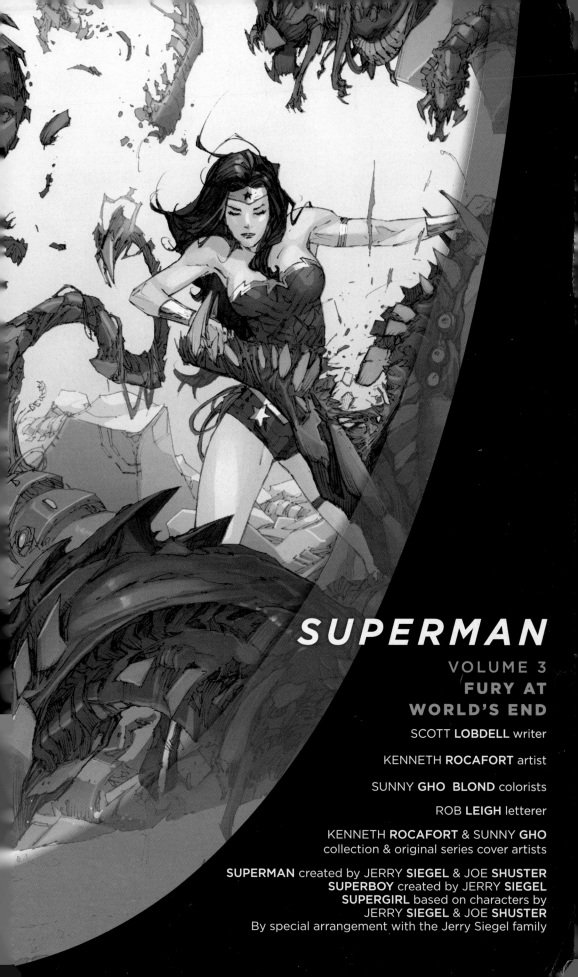

SUPERMAN

VOLUME 3
FURY AT
WORLD'S END

SCOTT **LOBDELL** writer

KENNETH **ROCAFORT** artist

SUNNY **GHO** **BLOND** colorists

ROB **LEIGH** letterer

KENNETH **ROCAFORT** & SUNNY **GHO**
collection & original series cover artists

SUPERMAN created by JERRY **SIEGEL** & JOE **SHUSTER**
SUPERBOY created by JERRY **SIEGEL**
SUPERGIRL based on characters by
JERRY **SIEGEL** & JOE **SHUSTER**
By special arrangement with the Jerry Siegel family

EDDIE BERGANZA Editor - Original Series DARREN SHAN ANTHONY MARQUES Assistant Editors - Original Series
ROWENA YOW Editor ROBBIN BROSTERMAN Design Director - Books ROBBIE BIEDERMAN Publication Design

BOB HARRAS Senior VP - Editor-in-Chief, DC Comics

DIANE NELSON President DAN DIDIO and JIM LEE Co-Publishers GEOFF JOHNS Chief Creative Officer
AMIT DESAI Senior VP - Marketing and Franchise Management
AMY GENKINS Senior VP - Business and Legal Affairs NAIRI GARDINER Senior VP - Finance
JEFF BOISON VP - Publishing Planning MARK CHIARELLO VP - Art Direction and Design
JOHN CUNNINGHAM VP - Marketing TERRI CUNNINGHAM VP - Editorial Administration
LARRY GANEM VP - Talent Relations and Services ALISON GILL Senior VP - Manufacturing and Operations
HANK KANALZ Senior VP - Vertigo and Integrated Publishing JAY KOGAN VP - Business and Legal Affairs, Publishing
JACK MAHAN VP - Business Affairs, Talent NICK NAPOLITANO VP - Manufacturing Administration SUE POHJA VP - Book Sales
FRED RUIZ VP - Manufacturing Operations COURTNEY SIMMONS Senior VP - Publicity BOB WAYNE Senior VP - Sales

SUPERMAN VOLUME 3: FURY AT WORLD'S END

DC Comics, 1700 Broadway, New York, NY 10019
A Warner Bros. Entertainment Company.
Printed by RR Donnelley, Owensville, MO, USA. 7/14/14. First Printing.

ISBN: 978-1-4012-4622-8

Library of Congress Cataloging-in-Publication Data

Lobdell, Scott, author.
Superman Volume 3 : Fury at World's End / Scott Lobdell ; [illustrated by Kenneth Rocafort].
pages cm. — (The New 52!)
"Originally published in single magazine form as SUPERMAN 0, 13-17"—T.p. verso
"Superman created by Jerry Siegel and Joe Shuster."
ISBN 978-1-4012-4622-8
1. Graphic novels. I. Rocafort, Kenneth, illustrator. II. Title. III. Title: Fury at World's End.
PN6728.S9L585 2014
741.5'973—dc23
201303592

SUSTAINABLE FORESTRY INITIATIVE
Certified Chain of Custody
20% Certified Forest Content,
80% Certified Sourcing
www.sfiprogram.org
SFI-01042
APPLIES TO TEXT STOCK ONLY

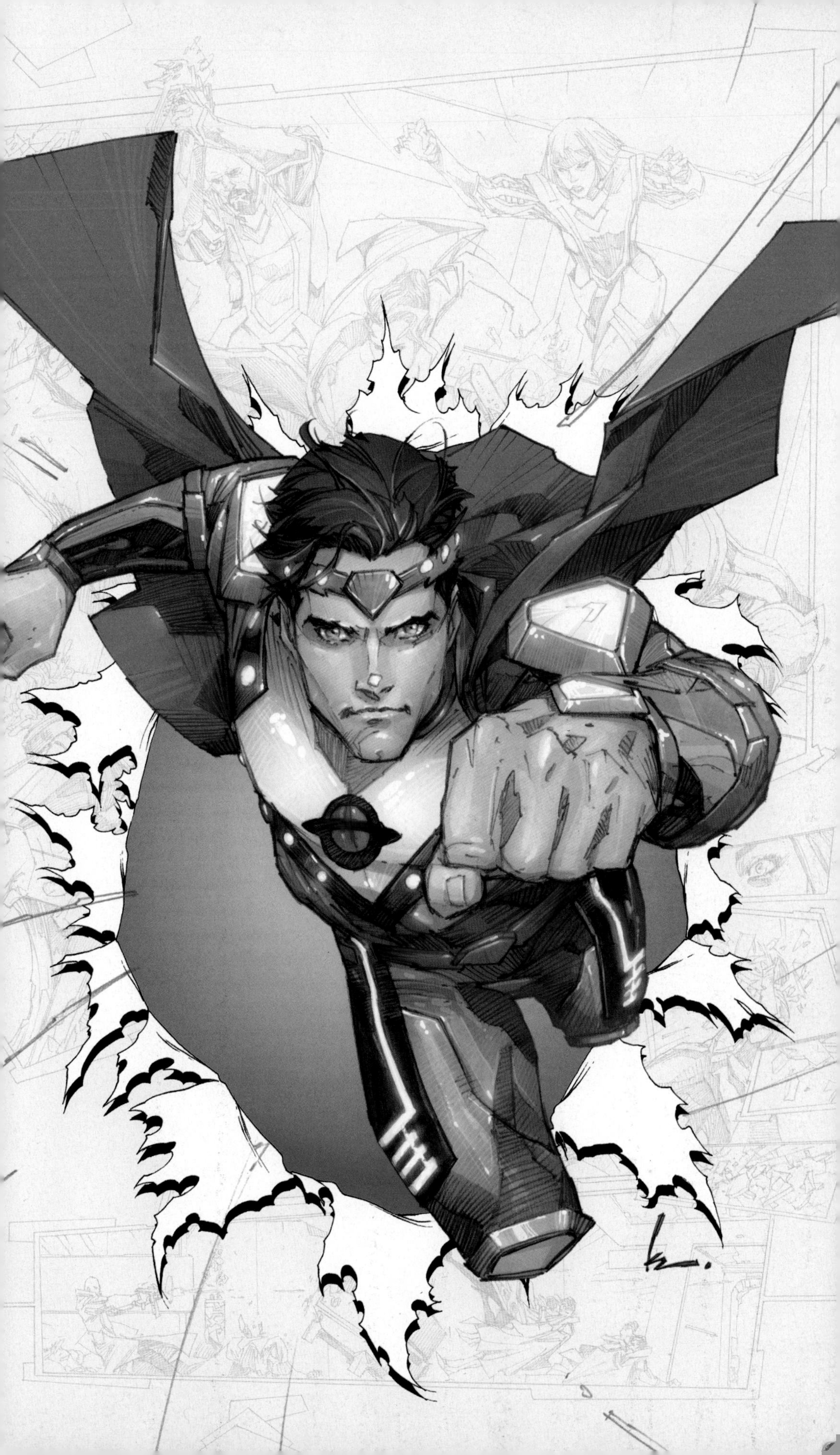

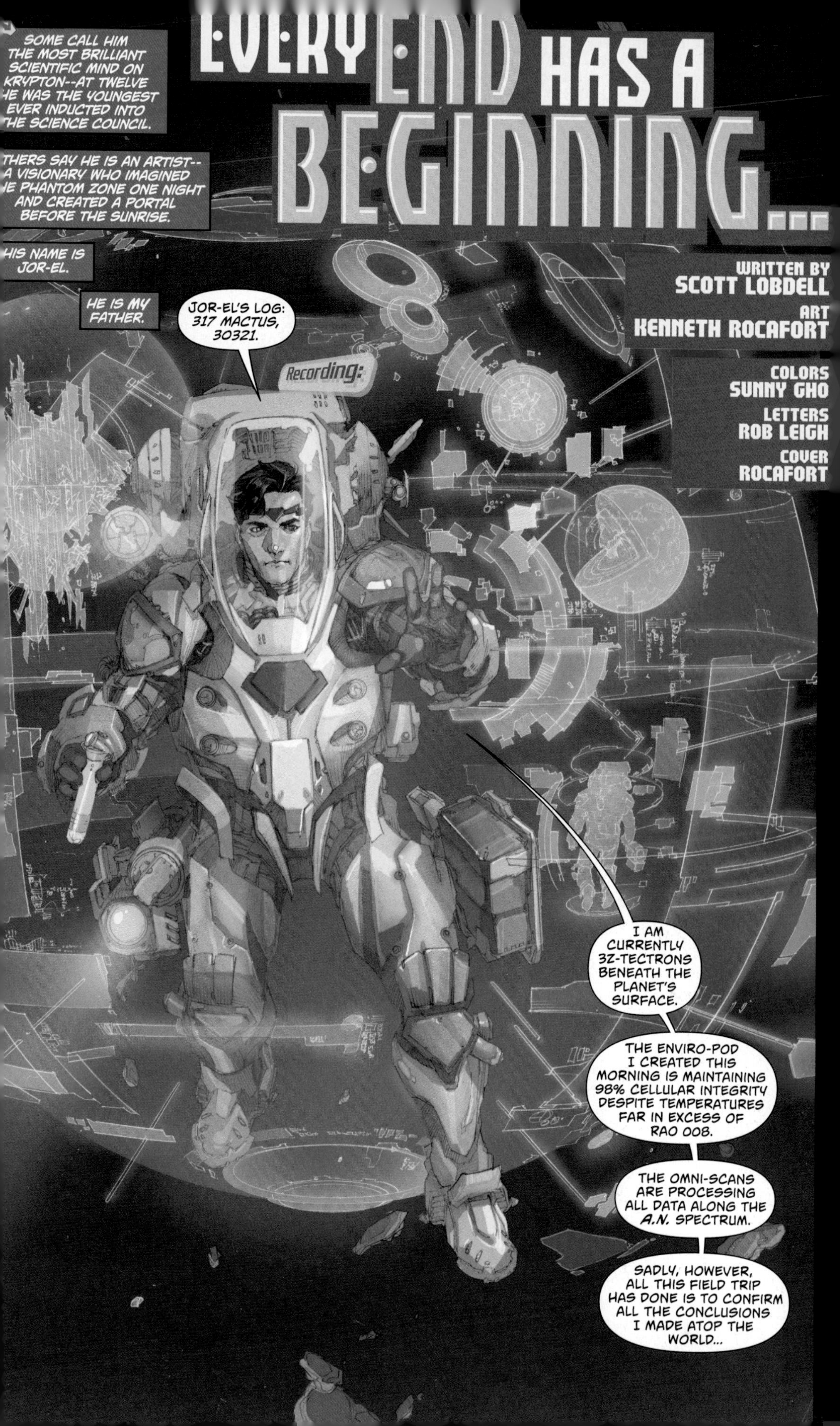

SOME CALL HIM THE MOST BRILLIANT SCIENTIFIC MIND ON KRYPTON--AT TWELVE HE WAS THE YOUNGEST EVER INDUCTED INTO THE SCIENCE COUNCIL.
EVERY END HAS A BEGINNING...
OTHERS SAY HE IS AN ARTIST--A VISIONARY WHO IMAGINED THE PHANTOM ZONE ONE NIGHT AND CREATED A PORTAL BEFORE THE SUNRISE.
HIS NAME IS JOR-EL.
HE IS MY FATHER.
WRITTEN BY SCOTT LOBDELL
ART KENNETH ROCAFORT
COLORS SUNNY GHO
LETTERS ROB LEIGH
COVER ROCAFORT
JOR-EL'S LOG: 317 MACTUS, 30321.
Recording:
I AM CURRENTLY 3Z-TECTRONS BENEATH THE PLANET'S SURFACE.
THE ENVIRO-POD I CREATED THIS MORNING IS MAINTAINING 98% CELLULAR INTEGRITY DESPITE TEMPERATURES FAR IN EXCESS OF RAO 008.
THE OMNI-SCANS ARE PROCESSING ALL DATA ALONG THE A.N. SPECTRUM.
SADLY, HOWEVER, ALL THIS FIELD TRIP HAS DONE IS TO CONFIRM ALL THE CONCLUSIONS I MADE ATOP THE WORLD...

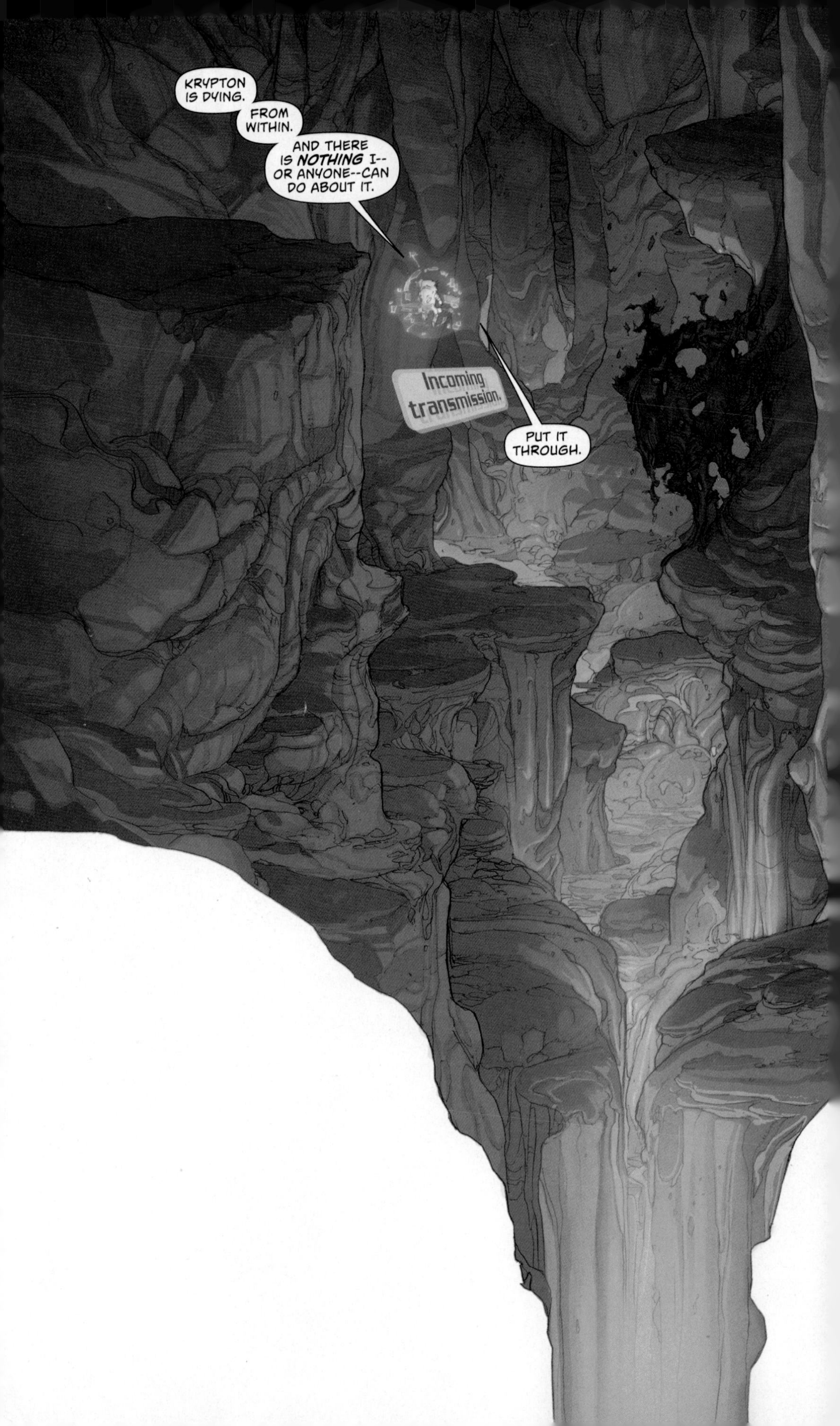
KRYPTON IS DYING.
FROM WITHIN.
AND THERE IS **NOTHING** I--OR ANYONE--CAN DO ABOUT IT.
Incoming transmission.
PUT IT THROUGH.

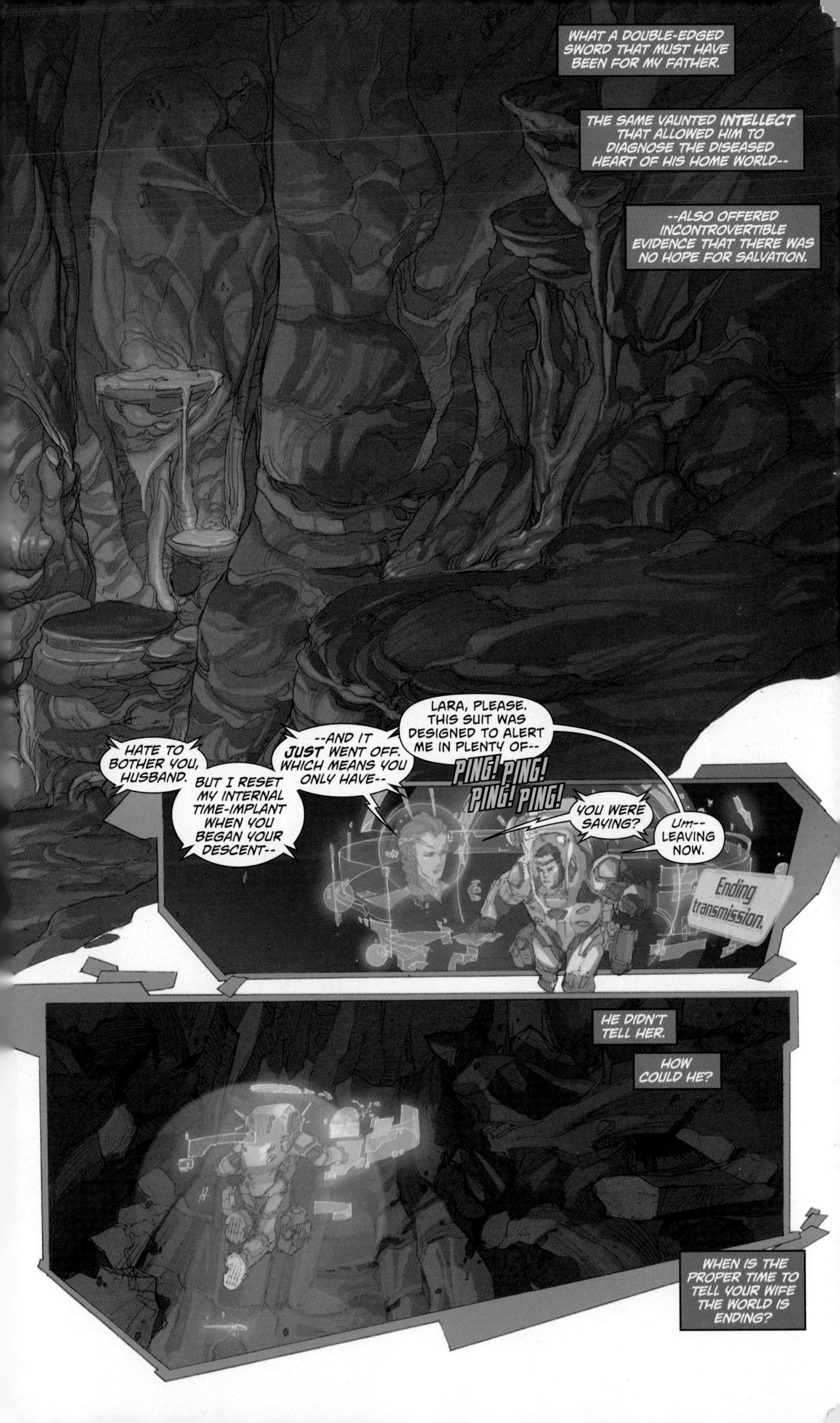
WHAT A DOUBLE-EDGED SWORD THAT MUST HAVE BEEN FOR MY FATHER.
THE SAME VAUNTED INTELLECT THAT ALLOWED HIM TO DIAGNOSE THE DISEASED HEART OF HIS HOME WORLD--
--ALSO OFFERED INCONTROVERTIBLE EVIDENCE THAT THERE WAS NO HOPE FOR SALVATION.
HATE TO BOTHER YOU, HUSBAND.
BUT I RESET MY INTERNAL TIME-IMPLANT WHEN YOU BEGAN YOUR DESCENT--
LARA, PLEASE. THIS SUIT WAS DESIGNED TO ALERT ME IN PLENTY OF--
--AND IT JUST WENT OFF. WHICH MEANS YOU ONLY HAVE--
PING! PING! PING! PING!
YOU WERE SAYING?
UM-- LEAVING NOW.
Ending transmission.
HE DIDN'T TELL HER.
HOW COULD HE?
WHEN IS THE PROPER TIME TO TELL YOUR WIFE THE WORLD IS ENDING?

NOTE TO SCIENCE COUNCIL:
EVEN THE CORE-WAY IS DETERIORATING.
REPAIRS WILL BE NECESSARY IF WE'RE TO HAVE ANY CHANCE--NO MATTER HOW SLIM--
--OF TREATING THE GEO-MOLECULAR DAMAGE TO KRYPTON'S TECTONIC STRUCTURE.
RED SON!
HE HAD NEVER SEEN ANYTHING LIKE IT.
NO ONE HAD.
ANYWHERE.

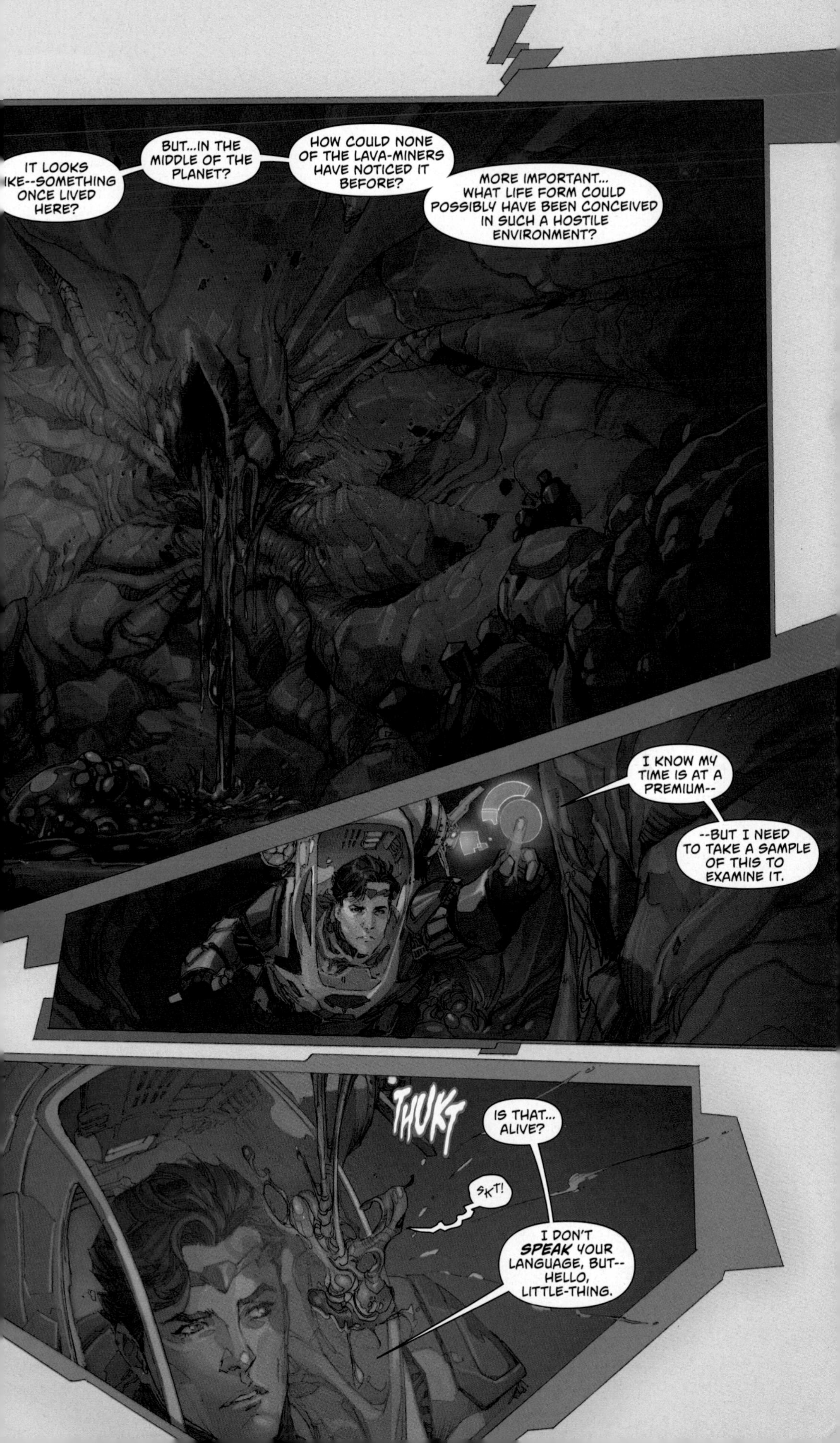
IT LOOKS
LIKE--SOMETHING ONCE LIVED HERE?
BUT...IN THE MIDDLE OF THE PLANET?
HOW COULD NONE OF THE LAVA-MINERS HAVE NOTICED IT BEFORE?
MORE IMPORTANT... WHAT LIFE FORM COULD POSSIBLY HAVE BEEN CONCEIVED IN SUCH A HOSTILE ENVIRONMENT?
I KNOW MY TIME IS AT A PREMIUM--
--BUT I NEED TO TAKE A SAMPLE OF THIS TO EXAMINE IT.
THUKT
IS THAT... ALIVE?
SKT!
I DON'T SPEAK YOUR LANGUAGE, BUT-- HELLO, LITTLE-THING.

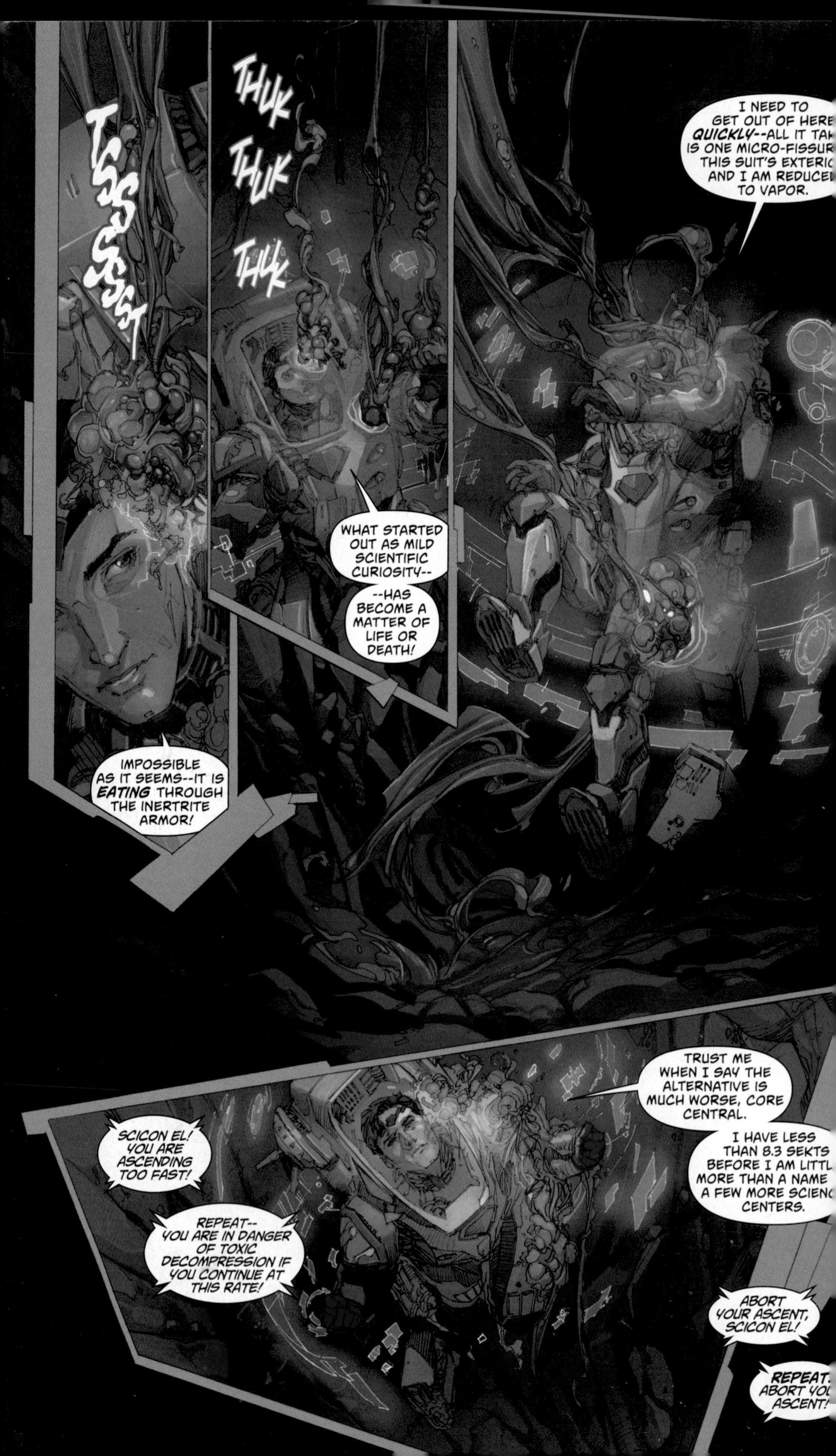
TSSSSSST
THUK THUK THUK
WHAT STARTED OUT AS MILD SCIENTIFIC CURIOSITY--
--HAS BECOME A MATTER OF LIFE OR DEATH!
IMPOSSIBLE AS IT SEEMS--IT IS EATING THROUGH THE INERTRITE ARMOR!
I NEED TO GET OUT OF HERE QUICKLY--ALL IT TAK IS ONE MICRO-FISSUR THIS SUIT'S EXTERIC AND I AM REDUCE TO VAPOR.
SCICON EL! YOU ARE ASCENDING TOO FAST!
REPEAT-- YOU ARE IN DANGER OF TOXIC DECOMPRESSION IF YOU CONTINUE AT THIS RATE!
TRUST ME WHEN I SAY THE ALTERNATIVE IS MUCH WORSE, CORE CENTRAL.
I HAVE LESS THAN 8.3 SEKTS BEFORE I AM LITTL MORE THAN A NAME A FEW MORE SCIENC CENTERS.
ABORT YOUR ASCENT, SCICON EL!
REPEAT: ABORT YOU ASCENT!

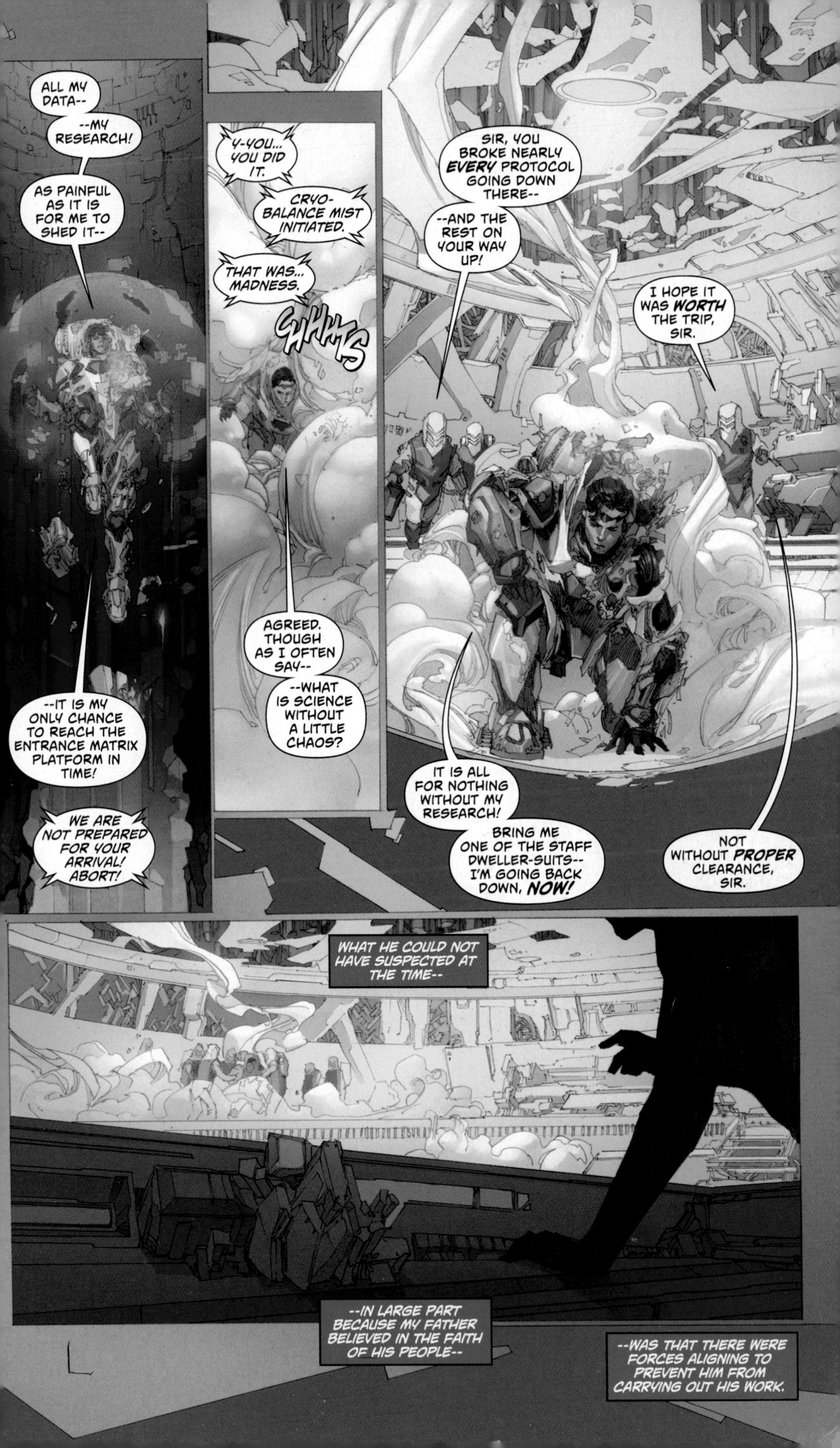

ALL MY DATA--
--MY RESEARCH!
AS PAINFUL AS IT IS FOR ME TO SHED IT--
--IT IS MY ONLY CHANCE TO REACH THE ENTRANCE MATRIX PLATFORM IN TIME!
WE ARE NOT PREPARED FOR YOUR ARRIVAL! ABORT!
Y-YOU... YOU DID IT.
CRYO-BALANCE MIST INITIATED.
THAT WAS... MADNESS.
CHHHTS
AGREED. THOUGH AS I OFTEN SAY--
--WHAT IS SCIENCE WITHOUT A LITTLE CHAOS?
SIR, YOU BROKE NEARLY EVERY PROTOCOL GOING DOWN THERE--
--AND THE REST ON YOUR WAY UP!
I HOPE IT WAS WORTH THE TRIP, SIR.
IT IS ALL FOR NOTHING WITHOUT MY RESEARCH!
BRING ME ONE OF THE STAFF DWELLER-SUITS--I'M GOING BACK DOWN, NOW!
NOT WITHOUT PROPER CLEARANCE, SIR.
WHAT HE COULD NOT HAVE SUSPECTED AT THE TIME--
--IN LARGE PART BECAUSE MY FATHER BELIEVED IN THE FAITH OF HIS PEOPLE--
--WAS THAT THERE WERE FORCES ALIGNING TO PREVENT HIM FROM CARRYING OUT HIS WORK.

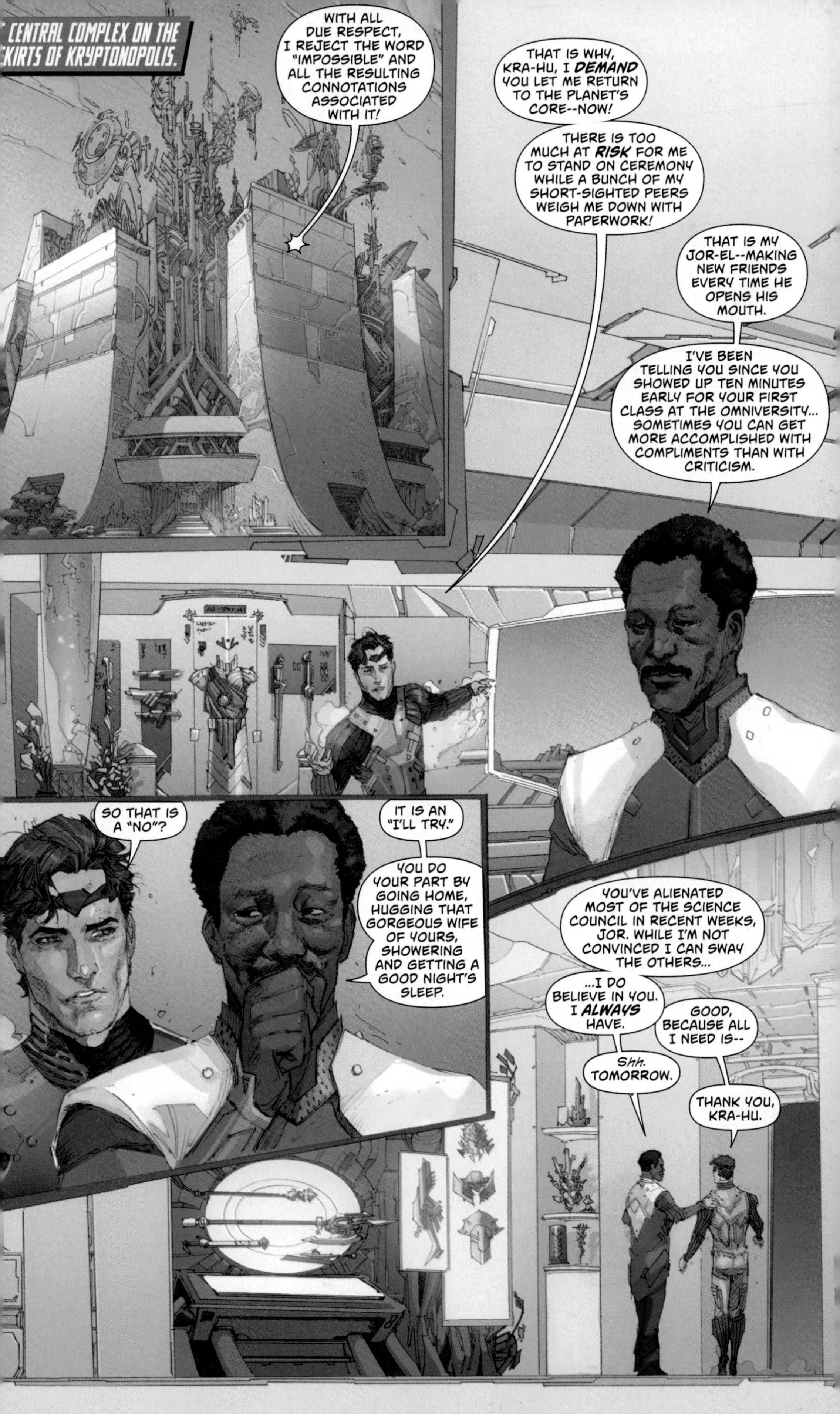

...CENTRAL COMPLEX ON THE ...KIRTS OF KRYPTONOPOLIS.
WITH ALL DUE RESPECT, I REJECT THE WORD "IMPOSSIBLE" AND ALL THE RESULTING CONNOTATIONS ASSOCIATED WITH IT!
THAT IS WHY, KRA-HU, I *DEMAND* YOU LET ME RETURN TO THE PLANET'S CORE--NOW!
THERE IS TOO MUCH AT *RISK* FOR ME TO STAND ON CEREMONY WHILE A BUNCH OF MY SHORT-SIGHTED PEERS WEIGH ME DOWN WITH PAPERWORK!
THAT IS MY JOR-EL--MAKING NEW FRIENDS EVERY TIME HE OPENS HIS MOUTH.
I'VE BEEN TELLING YOU SINCE YOU SHOWED UP TEN MINUTES EARLY FOR YOUR FIRST CLASS AT THE OMNIVERSITY... SOMETIMES YOU CAN GET MORE ACCOMPLISHED WITH COMPLIMENTS THAN WITH CRITICISM.
SO THAT IS A "NO"?
IT IS AN "I'LL TRY."
YOU DO YOUR PART BY GOING HOME, HUGGING THAT GORGEOUS WIFE OF YOURS, SHOWERING AND GETTING A GOOD NIGHT'S SLEEP.
YOU'VE ALIENATED MOST OF THE SCIENCE COUNCIL IN RECENT WEEKS, JOR. WHILE I'M NOT CONVINCED I CAN SWAY THE OTHERS...
...I DO BELIEVE IN YOU. I *ALWAYS* HAVE.
GOOD, BECAUSE ALL I NEED IS--
Shh. TOMORROW.
THANK YOU, KRA-HU.

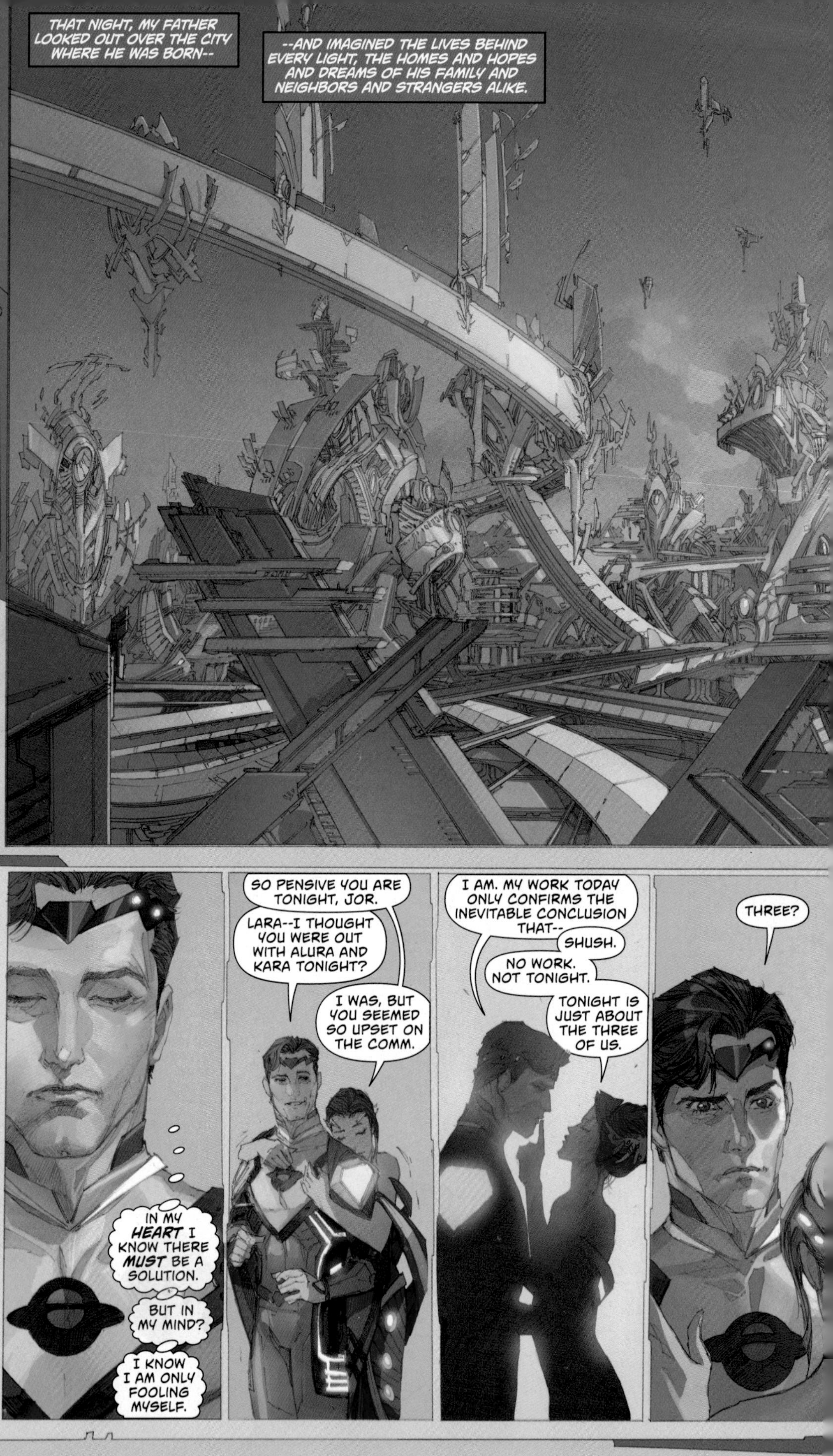

THAT NIGHT, MY FATHER LOOKED OUT OVER THE CITY WHERE HE WAS BORN--
--AND IMAGINED THE LIVES BEHIND EVERY LIGHT, THE HOMES AND HOPES AND DREAMS OF HIS FAMILY AND NEIGHBORS AND STRANGERS ALIKE.
IN MY *HEART* I KNOW THERE *MUST* BE A SOLUTION.
BUT IN MY MIND?
I KNOW I AM ONLY FOOLING MYSELF.
SO PENSIVE YOU ARE TONIGHT, JOR.
LARA--I THOUGHT YOU WERE OUT WITH ALURA AND KARA TONIGHT?
I WAS, BUT YOU SEEMED SO UPSET ON THE COMM.
I AM. MY WORK TODAY ONLY CONFIRMS THE INEVITABLE CONCLUSION THAT--
SHUSH.
NO WORK. NOT TONIGHT.
TONIGHT IS JUST ABOUT THE THREE OF US.
THREE?

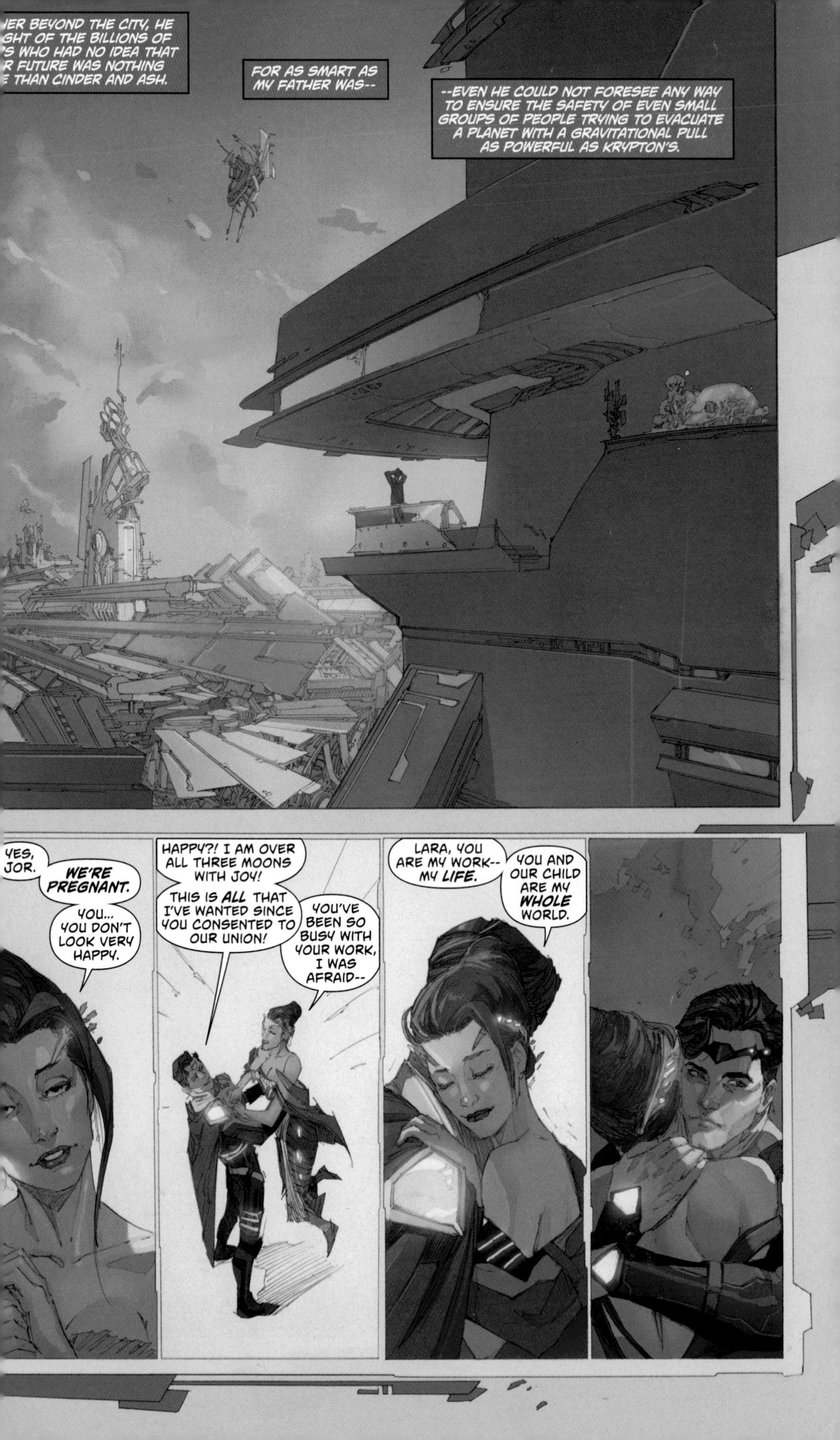

ER BEYOND THE CITY, HE
GHT OF THE BILLIONS OF
'S WHO HAD NO IDEA THAT
R FUTURE WAS NOTHING
E THAN CINDER AND ASH.
FOR AS SMART AS MY FATHER WAS--
--EVEN HE COULD NOT FORESEE ANY WAY TO ENSURE THE SAFETY OF EVEN SMALL GROUPS OF PEOPLE TRYING TO EVACUATE A PLANET WITH A GRAVITATIONAL PULL AS POWERFUL AS KRYPTON'S.
YES, JOR.
WE'RE PREGNANT.
YOU... YOU DON'T LOOK VERY HAPPY.
HAPPY?! I AM OVER ALL THREE MOONS WITH JOY!
THIS IS ALL THAT I'VE WANTED SINCE YOU CONSENTED TO OUR UNION!
YOU'VE BEEN SO BUSY WITH YOUR WORK, I WAS AFRAID--
LARA, YOU ARE MY WORK-- MY LIFE.
YOU AND OUR CHILD ARE MY WHOLE WORLD.

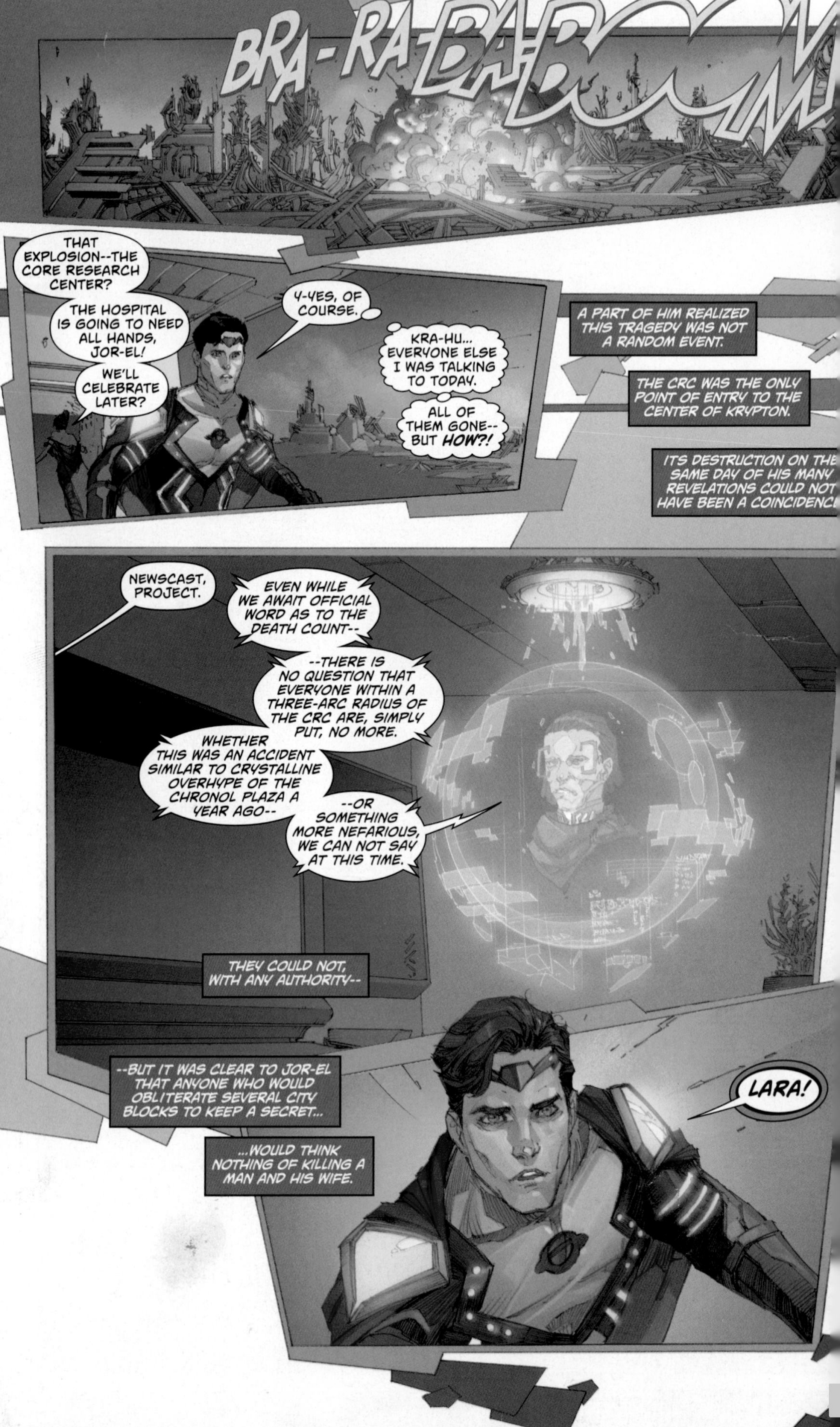
BRA-RA-BADOOM
THAT EXPLOSION--THE CORE RESEARCH CENTER?
THE HOSPITAL IS GOING TO NEED ALL HANDS, JOR-EL!
WE'LL CELEBRATE LATER?
Y-YES, OF COURSE.
KRA-HU... EVERYONE ELSE I WAS TALKING TO TODAY.
ALL OF THEM GONE-- BUT HOW?!
A PART OF HIM REALIZED THIS TRAGEDY WAS NOT A RANDOM EVENT.
THE CRC WAS THE ONLY POINT OF ENTRY TO THE CENTER OF KRYPTON.
ITS DESTRUCTION ON THE SAME DAY OF HIS MANY REVELATIONS COULD NOT HAVE BEEN A COINCIDENCE.
NEWSCAST, PROJECT.
EVEN WHILE WE AWAIT OFFICIAL WORD AS TO THE DEATH COUNT--
--THERE IS NO QUESTION THAT EVERYONE WITHIN A THREE-ARC RADIUS OF THE CRC ARE, SIMPLY PUT, NO MORE.
WHETHER THIS WAS AN ACCIDENT SIMILAR TO CRYSTALLINE OVERHYPE OF THE CHRONOL PLAZA A YEAR AGO--
--OR SOMETHING MORE NEFARIOUS, WE CAN NOT SAY AT THIS TIME.
THEY COULD NOT, WITH ANY AUTHORITY--
--BUT IT WAS CLEAR TO JOR-EL THAT ANYONE WHO WOULD OBLITERATE SEVERAL CITY BLOCKS TO KEEP A SECRET...
...WOULD THINK NOTHING OF KILLING A MAN AND HIS WIFE.
LARA!

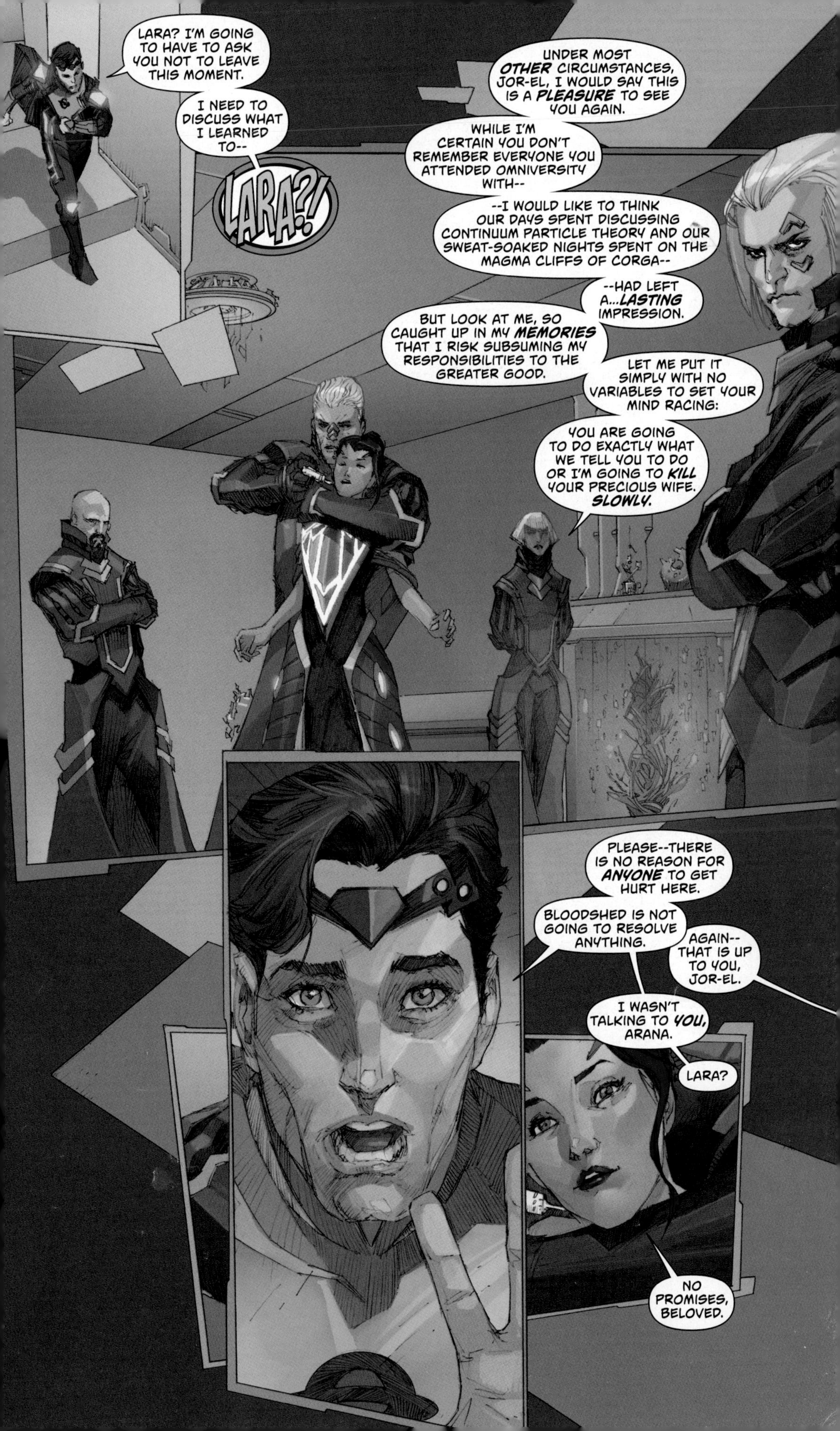
LARA? I'M GOING TO HAVE TO ASK YOU NOT TO LEAVE THIS MOMENT.
I NEED TO DISCUSS WHAT I LEARNED TO--
LARA?!
UNDER MOST OTHER CIRCUMSTANCES, JOR-EL, I WOULD SAY THIS IS A PLEASURE TO SEE YOU AGAIN.
WHILE I'M CERTAIN YOU DON'T REMEMBER EVERYONE YOU ATTENDED OMNIVERSITY WITH--
--I WOULD LIKE TO THINK OUR DAYS SPENT DISCUSSING CONTINUUM PARTICLE THEORY AND OUR SWEAT-SOAKED NIGHTS SPENT ON THE MAGMA CLIFFS OF CORGA--
--HAD LEFT A...LASTING IMPRESSION.
BUT LOOK AT ME, SO CAUGHT UP IN MY MEMORIES THAT I RISK SUBSUMING MY RESPONSIBILITIES TO THE GREATER GOOD.
LET ME PUT IT SIMPLY WITH NO VARIABLES TO SET YOUR MIND RACING:
YOU ARE GOING TO DO EXACTLY WHAT WE TELL YOU TO DO OR I'M GOING TO KILL YOUR PRECIOUS WIFE. SLOWLY.
PLEASE--THERE IS NO REASON FOR ANYONE TO GET HURT HERE.
BLOODSHED IS NOT GOING TO RESOLVE ANYTHING.
AGAIN--THAT IS UP TO YOU, JOR-EL.
I WASN'T TALKING TO YOU, ARANA.
LARA?
NO PROMISES, BELOVED.

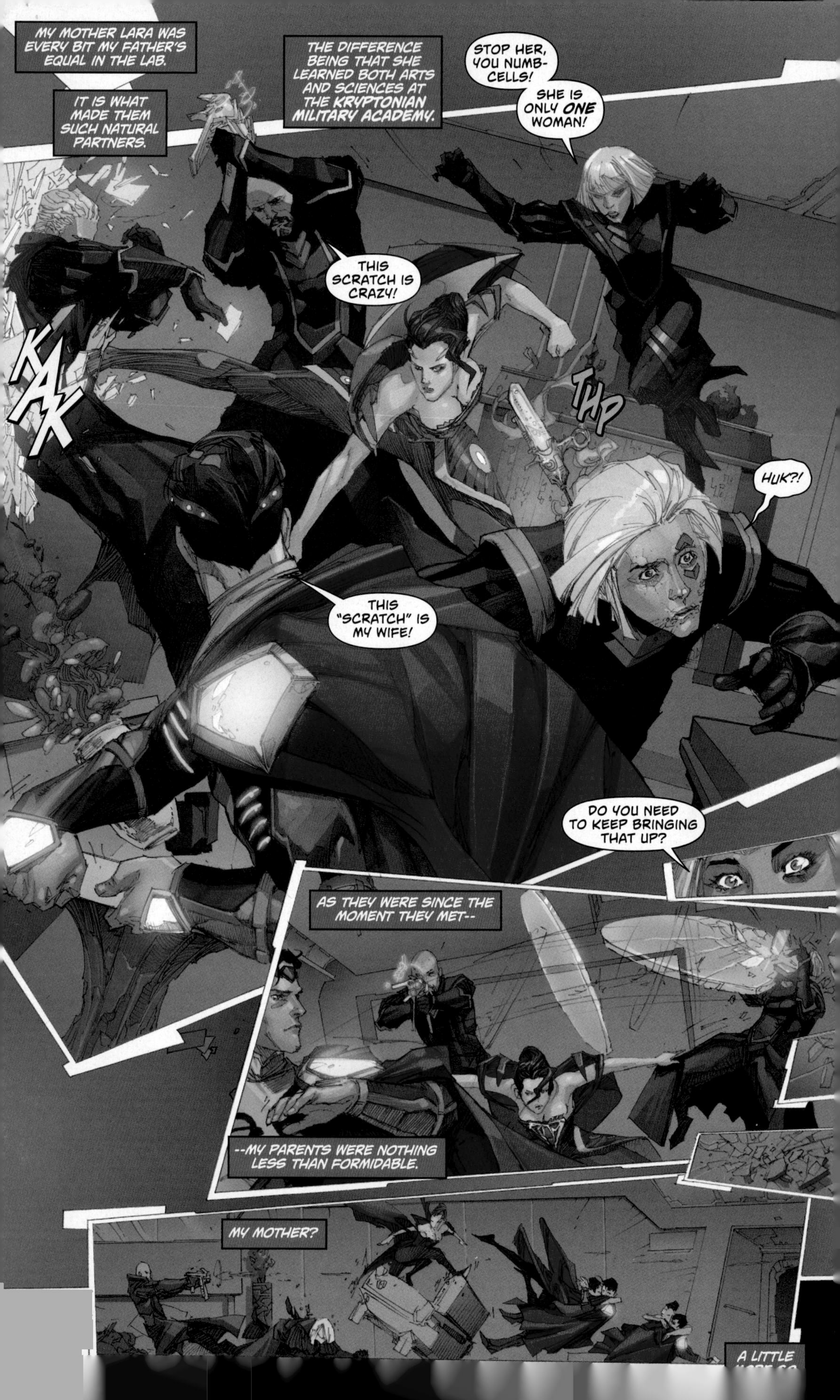
MY MOTHER LARA WAS EVERY BIT MY FATHER'S EQUAL IN THE LAB.
IT IS WHAT MADE THEM SUCH NATURAL PARTNERS.
THE DIFFERENCE BEING THAT SHE LEARNED BOTH ARTS AND SCIENCES AT THE KRYPTONIAN MILITARY ACADEMY.
STOP HER, YOU NUMB-CELLS!
SHE IS ONLY ONE WOMAN!
THIS SCRATCH IS CRAZY!
KAK
THP
HUK?!
THIS "SCRATCH" IS MY WIFE!
DO YOU NEED TO KEEP BRINGING THAT UP?
AS THEY WERE SINCE THE MOMENT THEY MET--
--MY PARENTS WERE NOTHING LESS THAN FORMIDABLE.
MY MOTHER?
A LITTLE

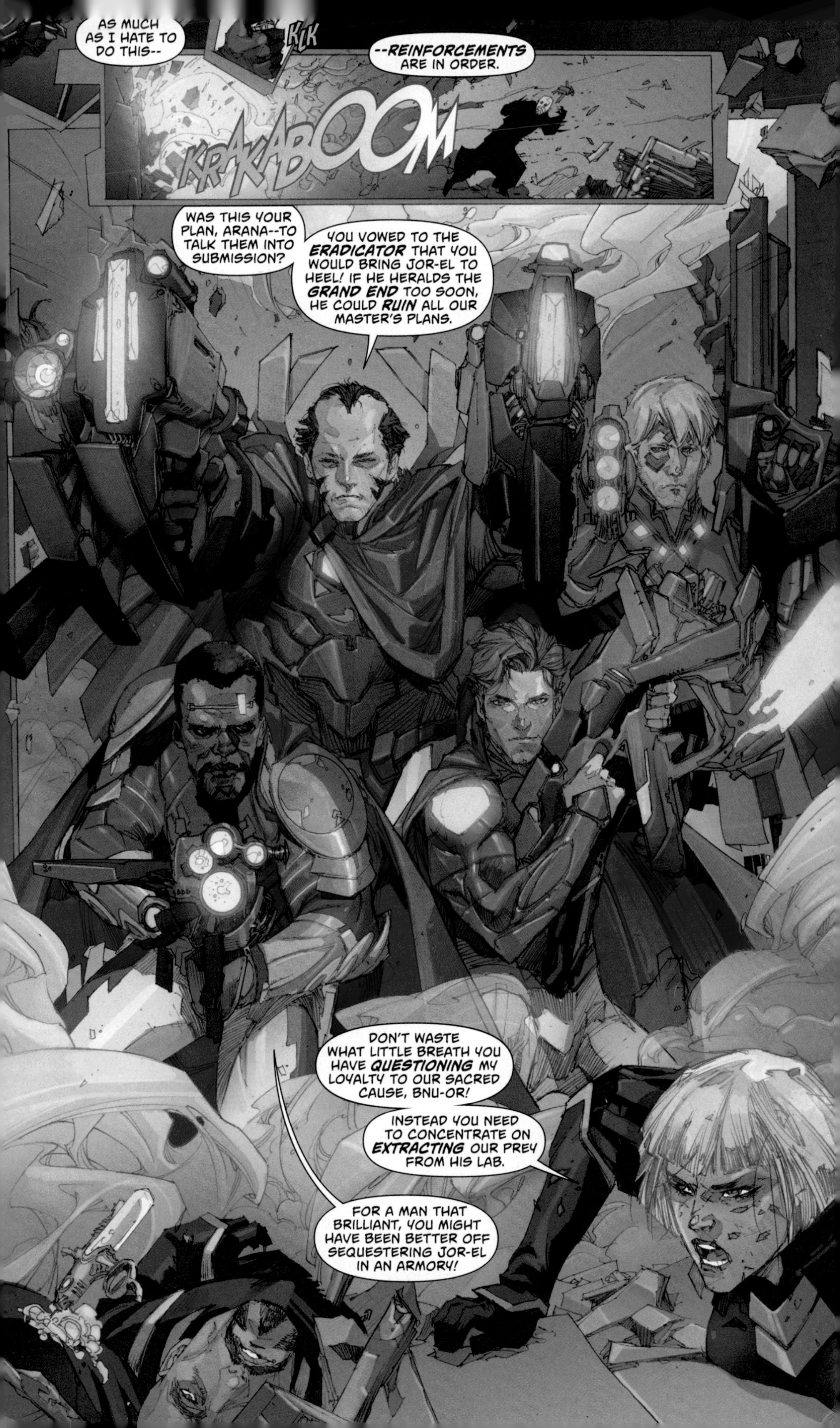
AS MUCH AS I HATE TO DO THIS--
KLIK
--REINFORCEMENTS ARE IN ORDER.
KRAKABOOM
WAS THIS YOUR PLAN, ARANA--TO TALK THEM INTO SUBMISSION?
YOU VOWED TO THE ERADICATOR THAT YOU WOULD BRING JOR-EL TO HEEL! IF HE HERALDS THE GRAND END TOO SOON, HE COULD RUIN ALL OUR MASTER'S PLANS.
DON'T WASTE WHAT LITTLE BREATH YOU HAVE QUESTIONING MY LOYALTY TO OUR SACRED CAUSE, BNU-OR!
INSTEAD YOU NEED TO CONCENTRATE ON EXTRACTING OUR PREY FROM HIS LAB.
FOR A MAN THAT BRILLIANT, YOU MIGHT HAVE BEEN BETTER OFF SEQUESTERING JOR-EL IN AN ARMORY!

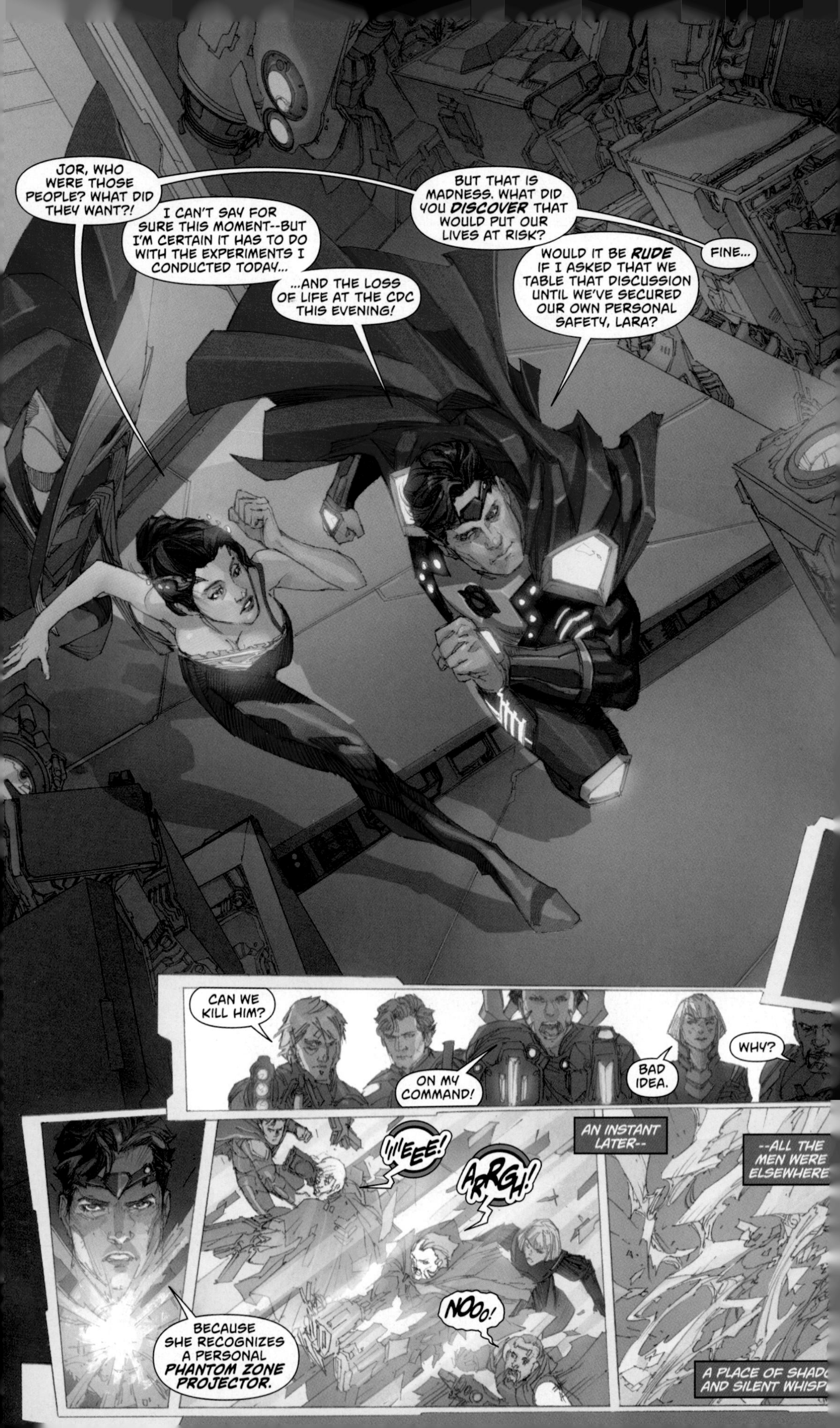
JOR, WHO WERE THOSE PEOPLE? WHAT DID THEY WANT?!
I CAN'T SAY FOR SURE THIS MOMENT--BUT I'M CERTAIN IT HAS TO DO WITH THE EXPERIMENTS I CONDUCTED TODAY...
...AND THE LOSS OF LIFE AT THE CDC THIS EVENING!
BUT THAT IS MADNESS. WHAT DID YOU **DISCOVER** THAT WOULD PUT OUR LIVES AT RISK?
WOULD IT BE **RUDE** IF I ASKED THAT WE TABLE THAT DISCUSSION UNTIL WE'VE SECURED OUR OWN PERSONAL SAFETY, LARA?
FINE...
CAN WE KILL HIM?
ON MY COMMAND!
BAD IDEA.
WHY?
BECAUSE SHE RECOGNIZES A PERSONAL **PHANTOM ZONE PROJECTOR.**
IIIEEEE!
ARRGH!
NOOo!
AN INSTANT LATER--
--ALL THE MEN WERE ELSEWHERE
A PLACE OF SHADO
AND SILENT WHISP

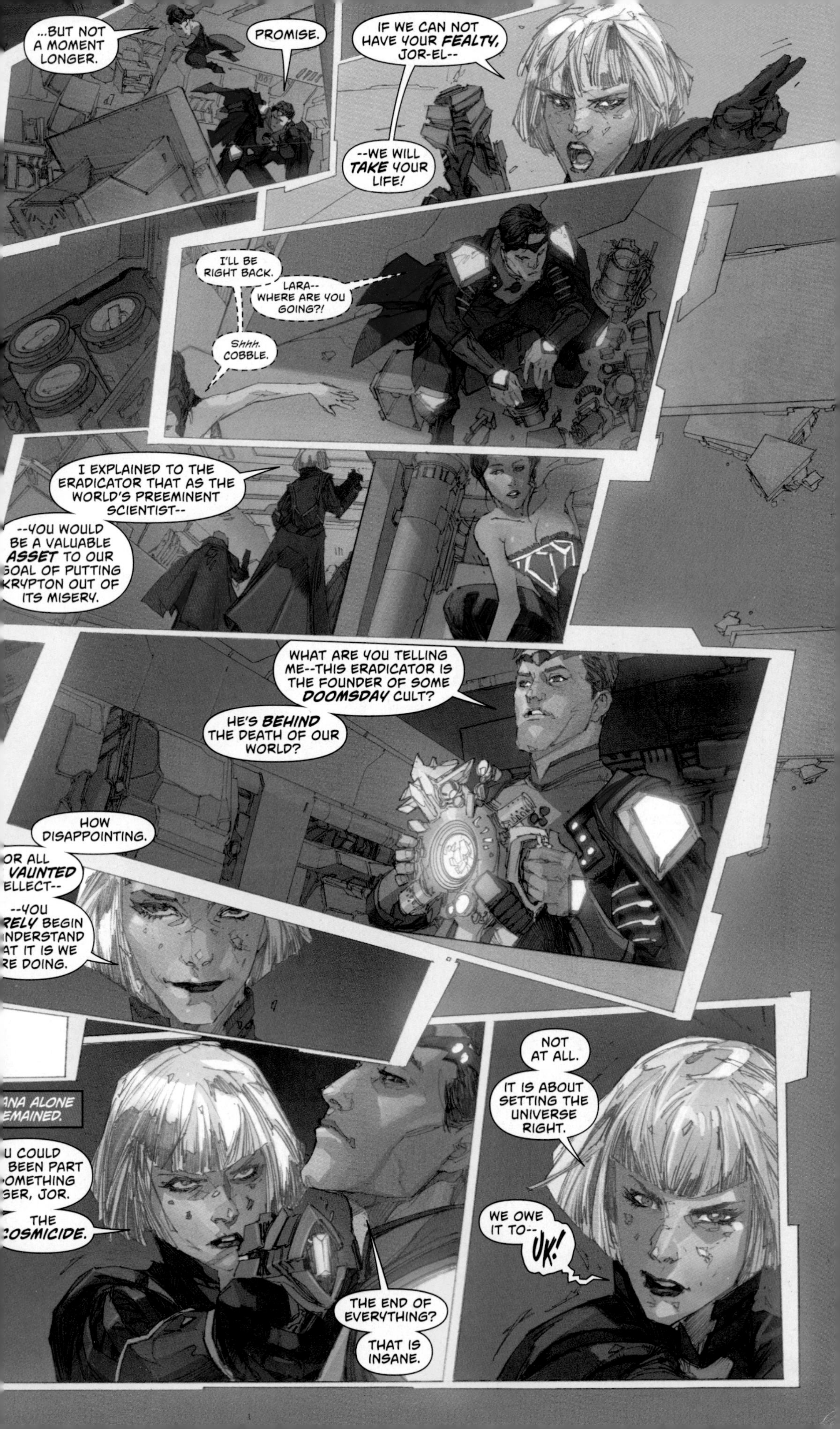
...BUT NOT A MOMENT LONGER.
PROMISE.
IF WE CAN NOT HAVE YOUR FEALTY, JOR-EL--
--WE WILL TAKE YOUR LIFE!
I'LL BE RIGHT BACK.
LARA-- WHERE ARE YOU GOING?!
Shhh. COBBLE.
I EXPLAINED TO THE ERADICATOR THAT AS THE WORLD'S PREEMINENT SCIENTIST--
--YOU WOULD BE A VALUABLE ASSET TO OUR GOAL OF PUTTING KRYPTON OUT OF ITS MISERY.
WHAT ARE YOU TELLING ME--THIS ERADICATOR IS THE FOUNDER OF SOME DOOMSDAY CULT?
HE'S BEHIND THE DEATH OF OUR WORLD?
HOW DISAPPOINTING.
OR ALL VAUNTED ELLECT--
--YOU RELY BEGIN NDERSTAND AT IT IS WE RE DOING.
ANA ALONE EMAINED.
U COULD BEEN PART OMETHING GER, JOR.
THE COSMICIDE.
THE END OF EVERYTHING?
THAT IS INSANE.
NOT AT ALL.
IT IS ABOUT SETTING THE UNIVERSE RIGHT.
WE OWE IT TO--
UK!

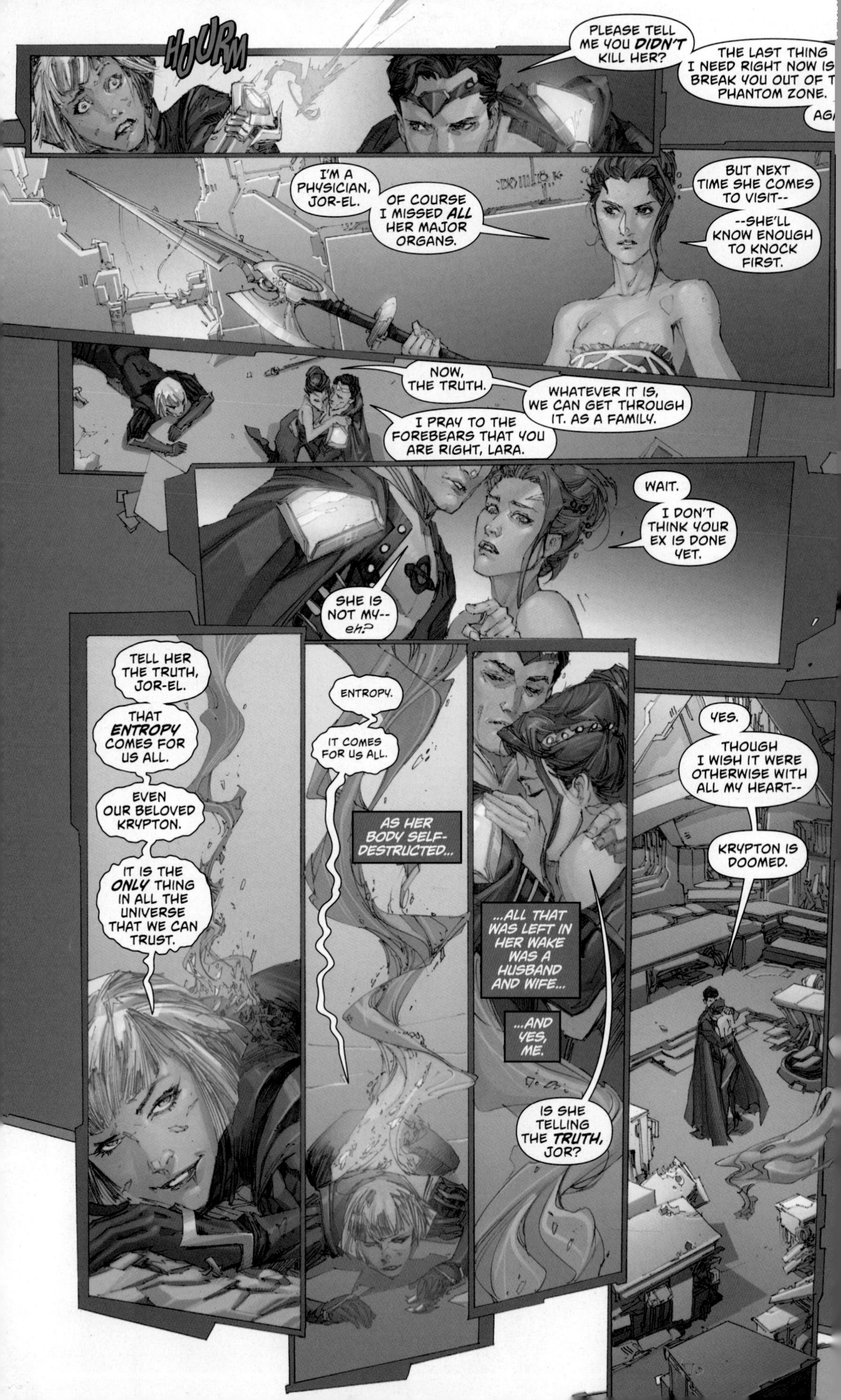

HUURM
PLEASE TELL ME YOU DIDN'T KILL HER?
THE LAST THING I NEED RIGHT NOW IS BREAK YOU OUT OF T PHANTOM ZONE.
AG
I'M A PHYSICIAN, JOR-EL.
OF COURSE I MISSED ALL HER MAJOR ORGANS.
BUT NEXT TIME SHE COMES TO VISIT--
--SHE'LL KNOW ENOUGH TO KNOCK FIRST.
NOW, THE TRUTH.
WHATEVER IT IS, WE CAN GET THROUGH IT. AS A FAMILY.
I PRAY TO THE FOREBEARS THAT YOU ARE RIGHT, LARA.
WAIT.
I DON'T THINK YOUR EX IS DONE YET.
SHE IS NOT MY-- eh?
TELL HER THE TRUTH, JOR-EL.
THAT ENTROPY COMES FOR US ALL.
EVEN OUR BELOVED KRYPTON.
IT IS THE ONLY THING IN ALL THE UNIVERSE THAT WE CAN TRUST.
ENTROPY.
IT COMES FOR US ALL.
AS HER BODY SELF-DESTRUCTED...
...ALL THAT WAS LEFT IN HER WAKE WAS A HUSBAND AND WIFE...
...AND YES, ME.
IS SHE TELLING THE TRUTH, JOR?
YES.
THOUGH I WISH IT WERE OTHERWISE WITH ALL MY HEART--
KRYPTON IS DOOMED.

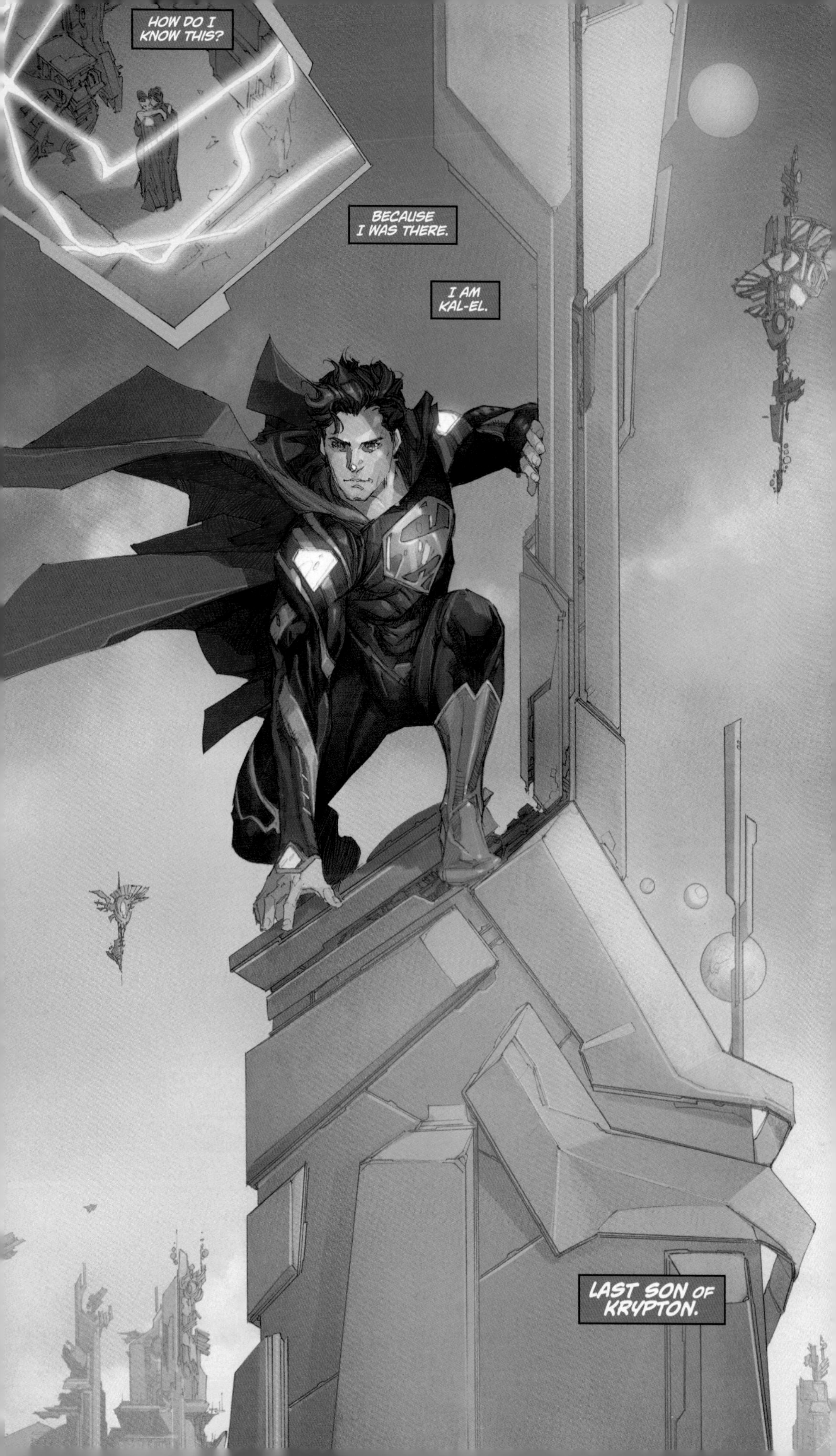
HOW DO I KNOW THIS?
BECAUSE I WAS THERE.
I AM KAL-EL.
LAST SON OF KRYPTON.

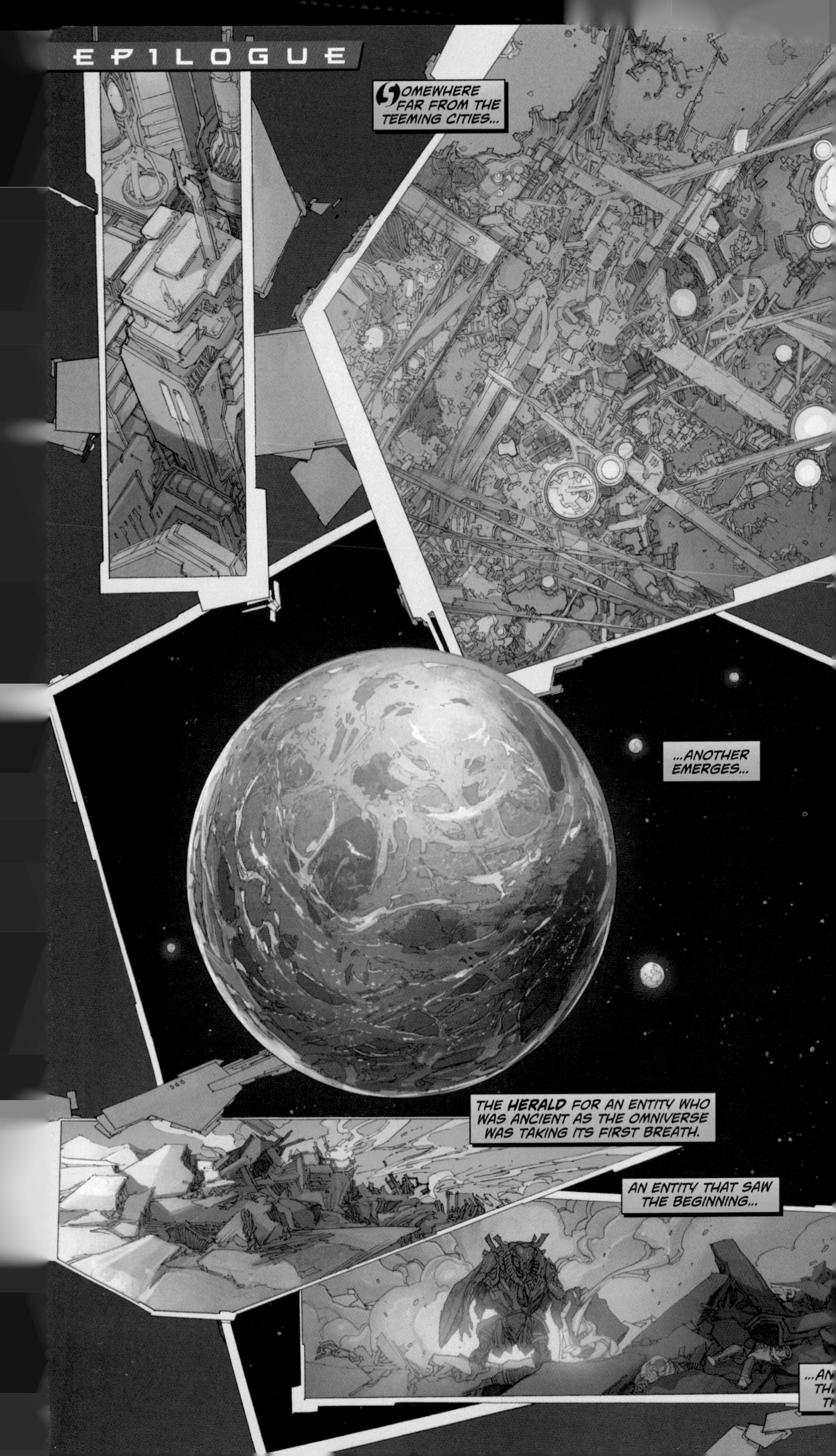
EPILOGUE
SOMEWHERE FAR FROM THE TEEMING CITIES...
...ANOTHER EMERGES...
THE HERALD FOR AN ENTITY WHO WAS ANCIENT AS THE OMNIVERSE WAS TAKING ITS FIRST BREATH.
AN ENTITY THAT SAW THE BEGINNING...

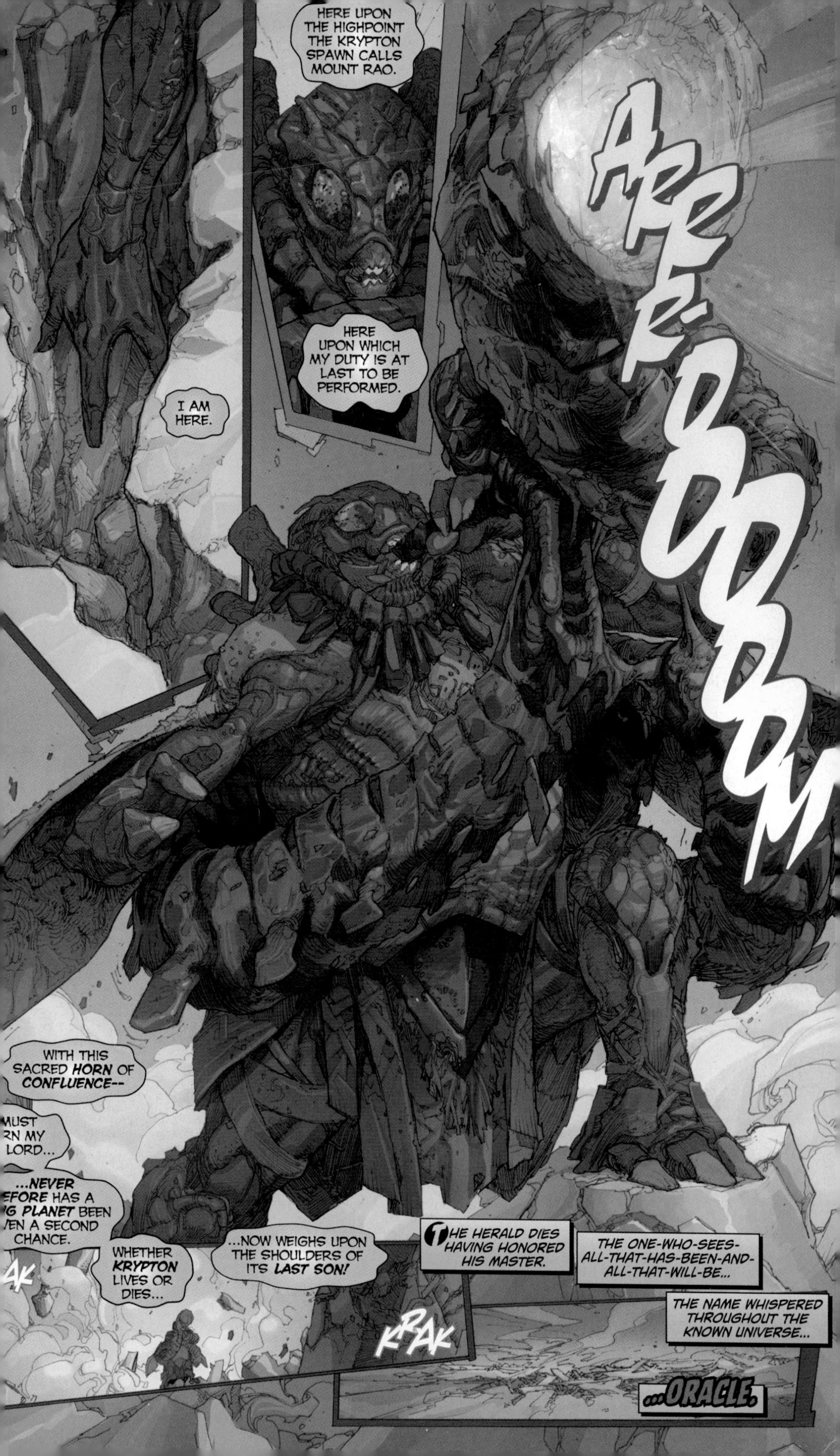
HERE UPON THE HIGHPOINT THE KRYPTON SPAWN CALLS MOUNT RAO.
HERE UPON WHICH MY DUTY IS AT LAST TO BE PERFORMED.
I AM HERE.
ARRRROOOOM
WITH THIS SACRED HORN OF CONFLUENCE--
MUST RN MY LORD...
...NEVER EFORE HAS A G PLANET BEEN VEN A SECOND CHANCE.
WHETHER KRYPTON LIVES OR DIES...
...NOW WEIGHS UPON THE SHOULDERS OF ITS LAST SON!
AK
KRAK
THE HERALD DIES HAVING HONORED HIS MASTER.
THE ONE-WHO-SEES-ALL-THAT-HAS-BEEN-AND-ALL-THAT-WILL-BE...
THE NAME WHISPERED THROUGHOUT THE KNOWN UNIVERSE...
...ORACLE.

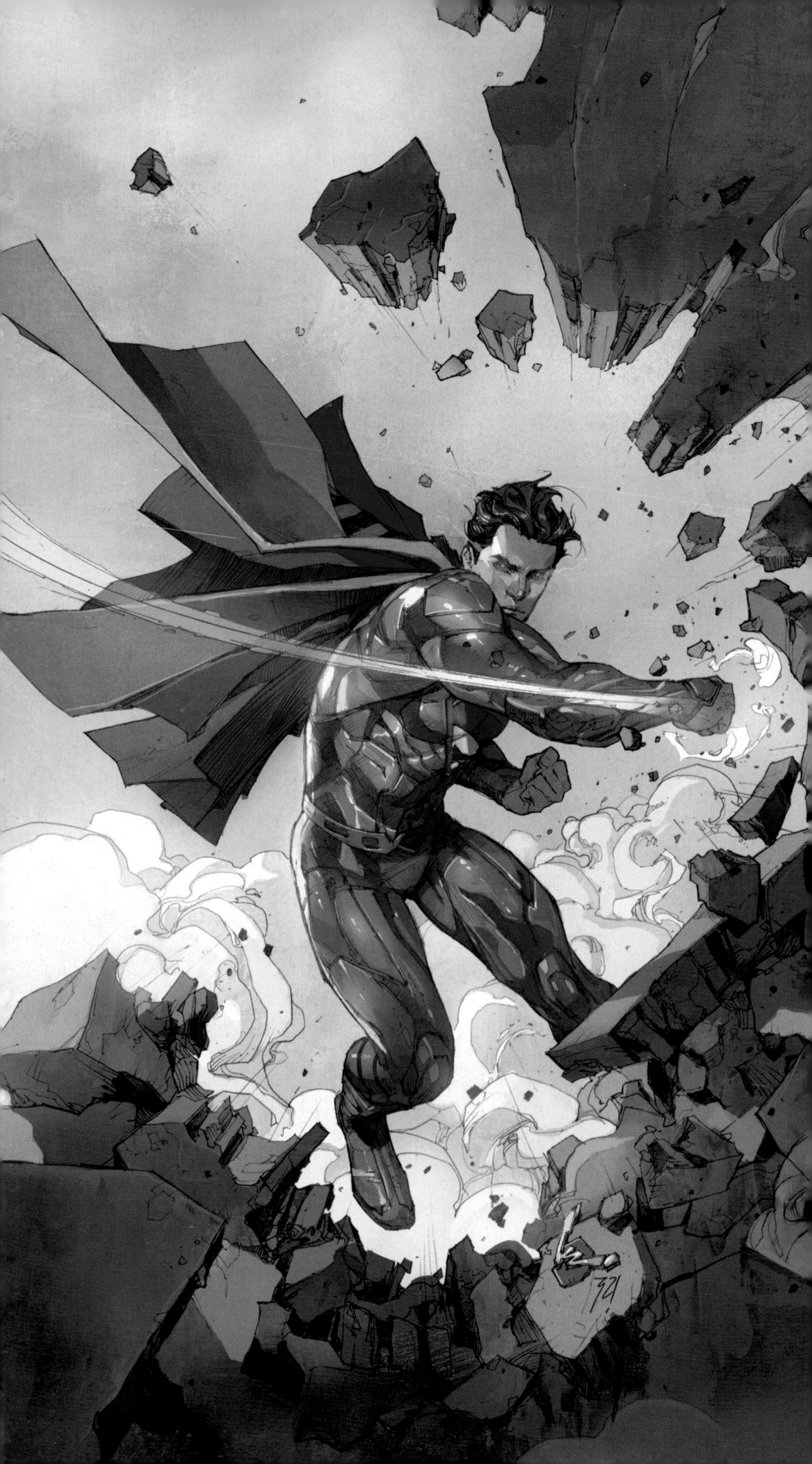

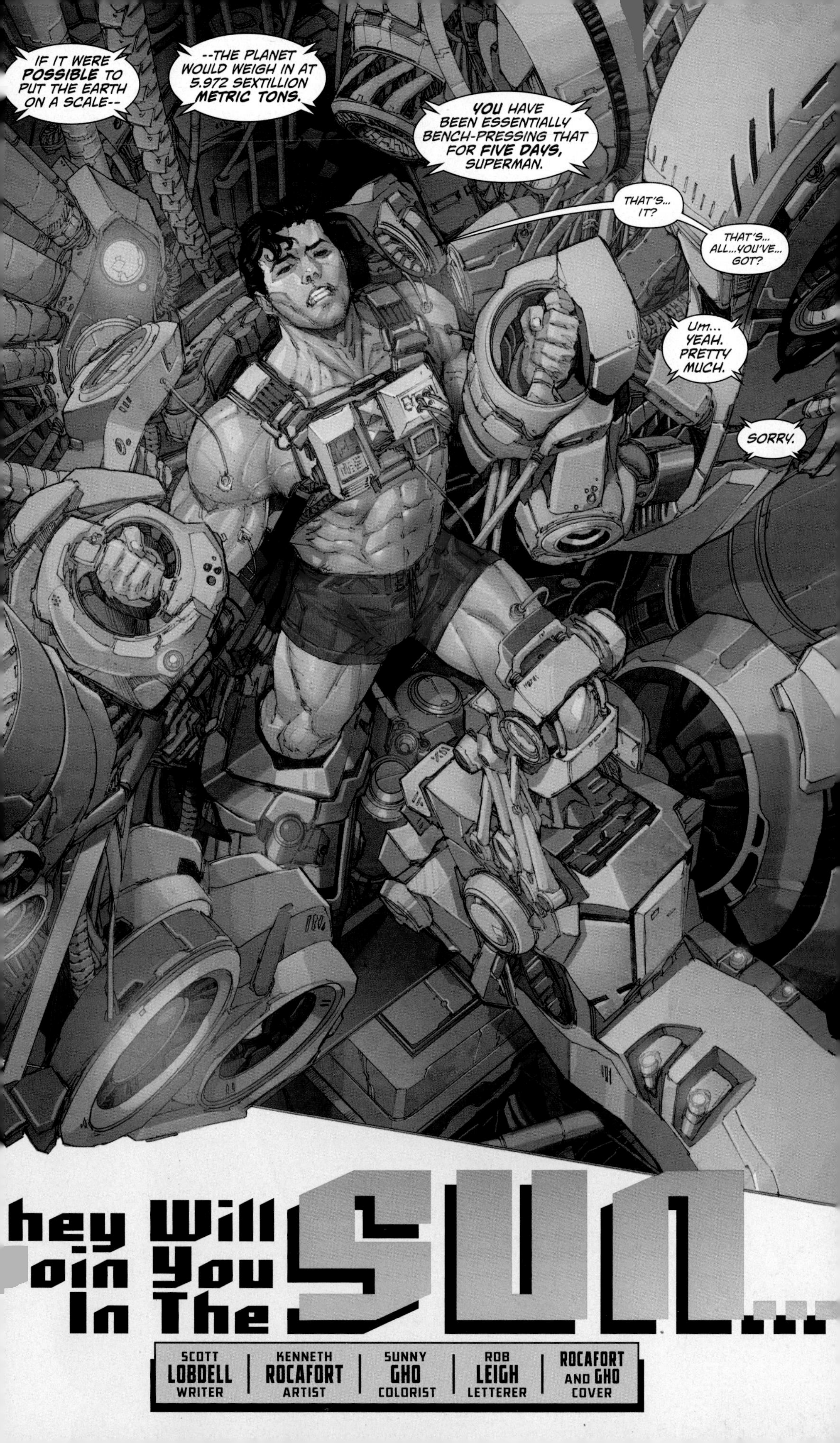
IF IT WERE POSSIBLE TO PUT THE EARTH ON A SCALE--
--THE PLANET WOULD WEIGH IN AT 5.972 SEXTILLION METRIC TONS.
YOU HAVE BEEN ESSENTIALLY BENCH-PRESSING THAT FOR FIVE DAYS, SUPERMAN.
THAT'S... IT?
THAT'S... ALL...YOU'VE... GOT?
Um... YEAH. PRETTY MUCH.
SORRY.
hey Will
oin You
In The SUN...
SCOTT LOBDELL WRITER
KENNETH ROCAFORT ARTIST
SUNNY GHO COLORIST
ROB LEIGH LETTERER
ROCAFORT AND GHO COVER

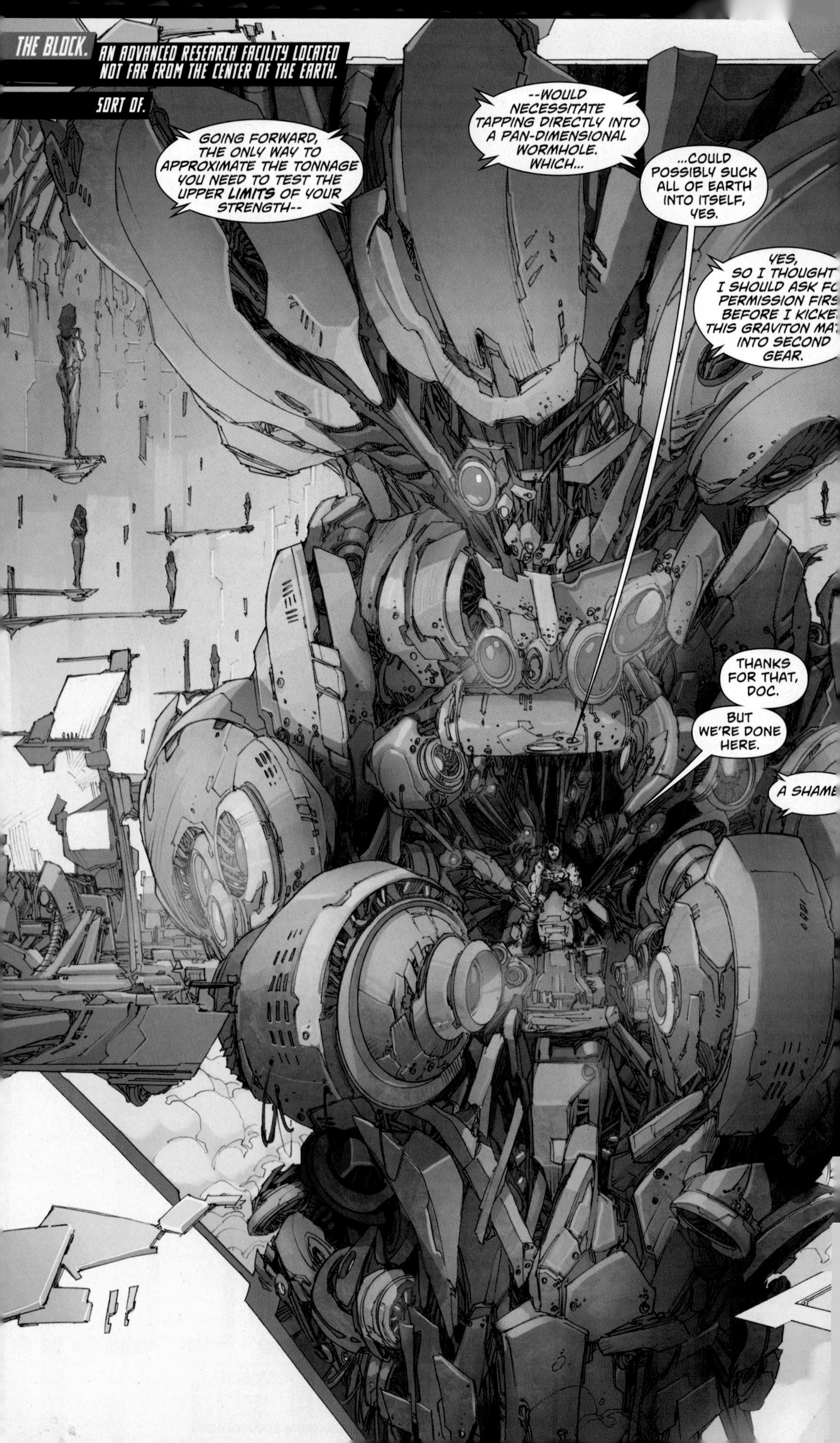
THE BLOCK. AN ADVANCED RESEARCH FACILITY LOCATED NOT FAR FROM THE CENTER OF THE EARTH.
SORT OF.
GOING FORWARD, THE ONLY WAY TO APPROXIMATE THE TONNAGE YOU NEED TO TEST THE UPPER LIMITS OF YOUR STRENGTH--
--WOULD NECESSITATE TAPPING DIRECTLY INTO A PAN-DIMENSIONAL WORMHOLE. WHICH...
...COULD POSSIBLY SUCK ALL OF EARTH INTO ITSELF, YES.
YES, SO I THOUGHT I SHOULD ASK FO PERMISSION FIRS BEFORE I KICKE THIS GRAVITON MA INTO SECOND GEAR.
THANKS FOR THAT, DOC.
BUT WE'RE DONE HERE.
A SHAME

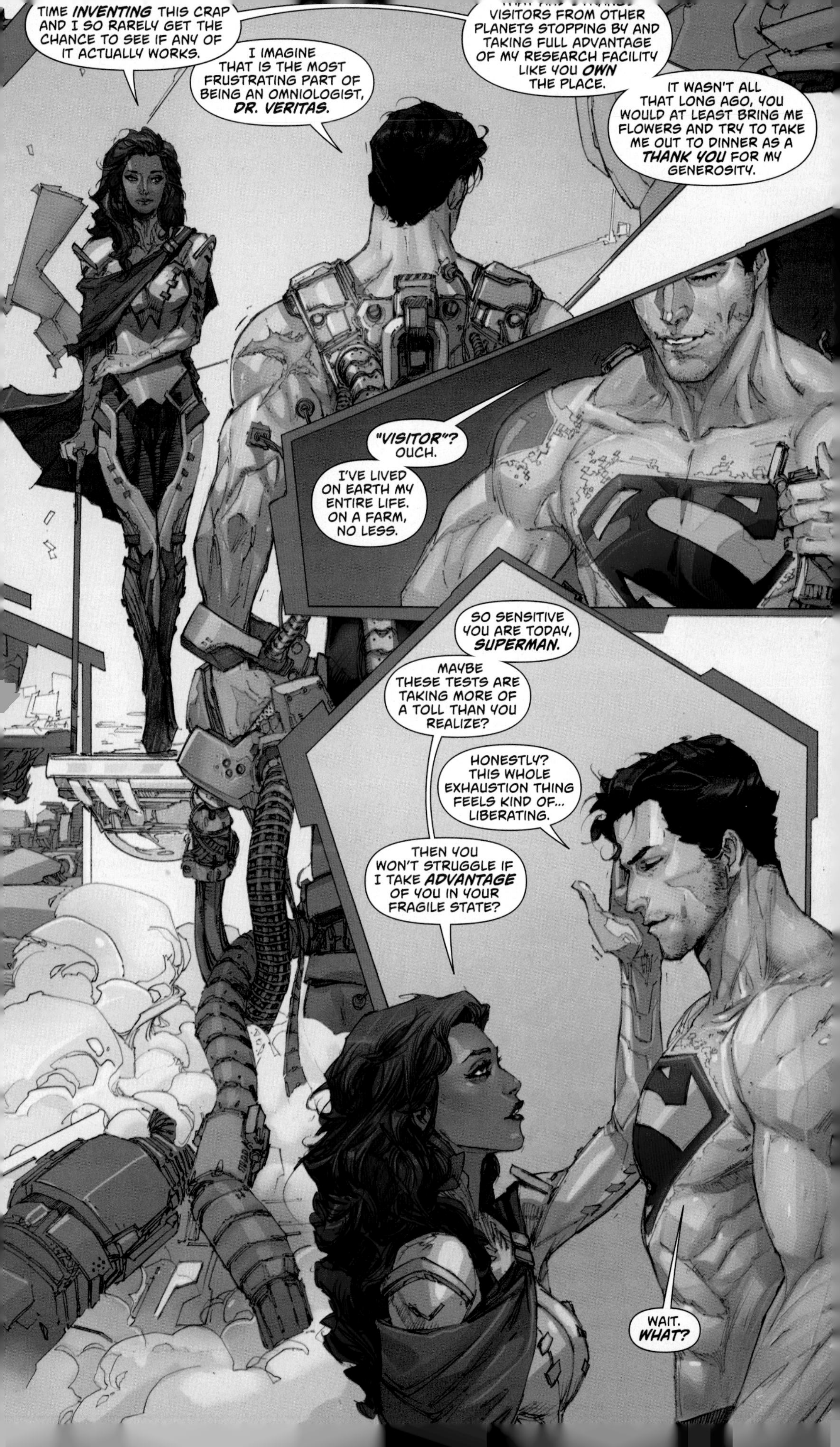
TIME INVENTING THIS CRAP AND I SO RARELY GET THE CHANCE TO SEE IF ANY OF IT ACTUALLY WORKS.
I IMAGINE THAT IS THE MOST FRUSTRATING PART OF BEING AN OMNIOLOGIST, DR. VERITAS.
VISITORS FROM OTHER PLANETS STOPPING BY AND TAKING FULL ADVANTAGE OF MY RESEARCH FACILITY LIKE YOU OWN THE PLACE.
IT WASN'T ALL THAT LONG AGO, YOU WOULD AT LEAST BRING ME FLOWERS AND TRY TO TAKE ME OUT TO DINNER AS A THANK YOU FOR MY GENEROSITY.
"VISITOR"? OUCH.
I'VE LIVED ON EARTH MY ENTIRE LIFE. ON A FARM, NO LESS.
SO SENSITIVE YOU ARE TODAY, SUPERMAN.
MAYBE THESE TESTS ARE TAKING MORE OF A TOLL THAN YOU REALIZE?
HONESTLY? THIS WHOLE EXHAUSTION THING FEELS KIND OF... LIBERATING.
THEN YOU WON'T STRUGGLE IF I TAKE ADVANTAGE OF YOU IN YOUR FRAGILE STATE?
WAIT. WHAT?

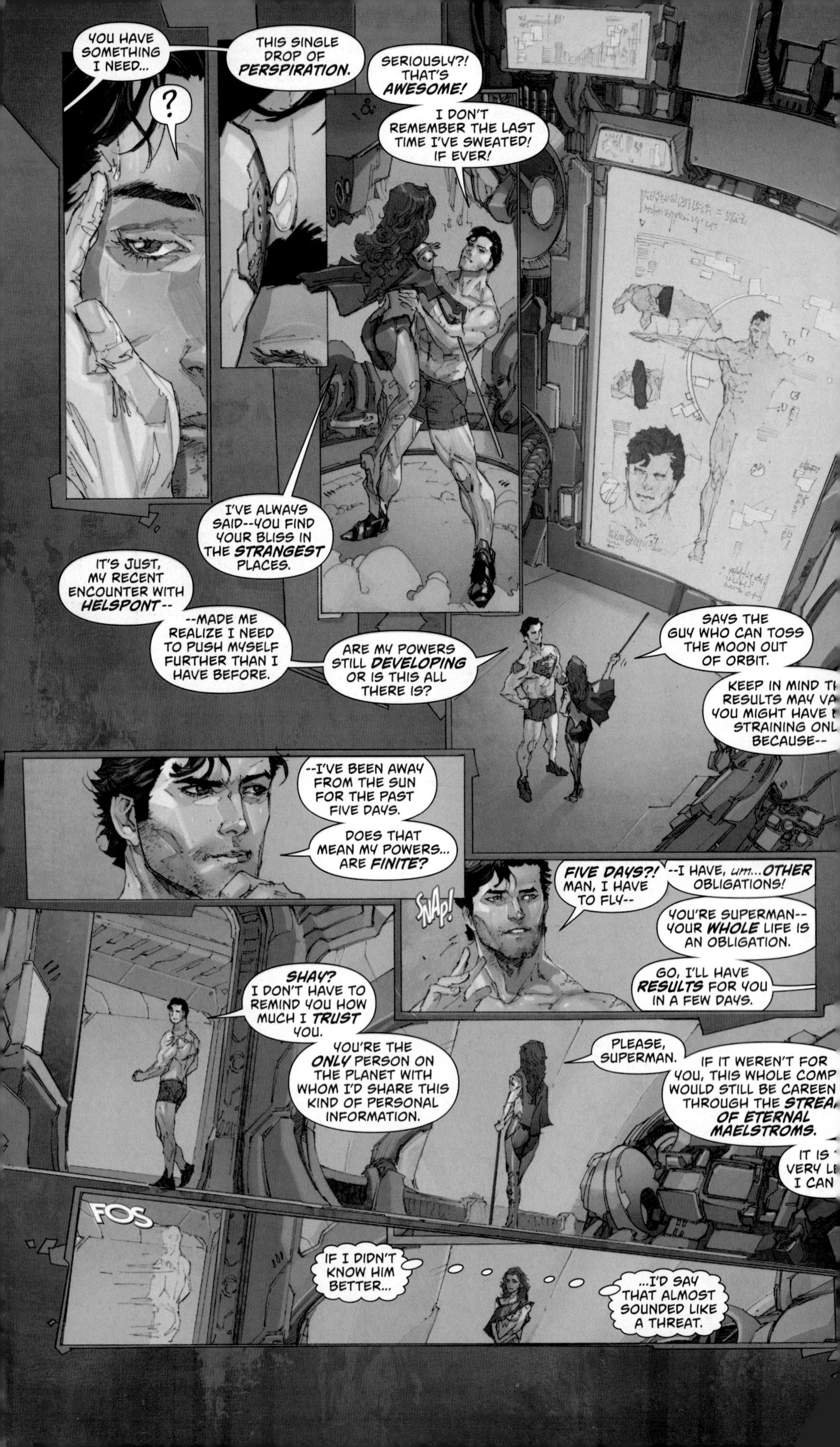

YOU HAVE SOMETHING I NEED...
?
THIS SINGLE DROP OF PERSPIRATION.
SERIOUSLY?! THAT'S AWESOME!
I DON'T REMEMBER THE LAST TIME I'VE SWEATED! IF EVER!
I'VE ALWAYS SAID--YOU FIND YOUR BLISS IN THE STRANGEST PLACES.
IT'S JUST, MY RECENT ENCOUNTER WITH HELSPONT--
--MADE ME REALIZE I NEED TO PUSH MYSELF FURTHER THAN I HAVE BEFORE.
ARE MY POWERS STILL DEVELOPING OR IS THIS ALL THERE IS?
SAYS THE GUY WHO CAN TOSS THE MOON OUT OF ORBIT.
KEEP IN MIND TH RESULTS MAY VA YOU MIGHT HAVE STRAINING ONL BECAUSE--
--I'VE BEEN AWAY FROM THE SUN FOR THE PAST FIVE DAYS.
DOES THAT MEAN MY POWERS... ARE FINITE?
SNAP!
FIVE DAYS?! MAN, I HAVE TO FLY--
--I HAVE, um...OTHER OBLIGATIONS!
YOU'RE SUPERMAN-- YOUR WHOLE LIFE IS AN OBLIGATION.
GO, I'LL HAVE RESULTS FOR YOU IN A FEW DAYS.
SHAY? I DON'T HAVE TO REMIND YOU HOW MUCH I TRUST YOU.
YOU'RE THE ONLY PERSON ON THE PLANET WITH WHOM I'D SHARE THIS KIND OF PERSONAL INFORMATION.
PLEASE, SUPERMAN.
IF IT WEREN'T FOR YOU, THIS WHOLE COMP WOULD STILL BE CAREEN THROUGH THE STREA OF ETERNAL MAELSTROMS.
IT IS VERY LE I CAN
FOS
IF I DIDN'T KNOW HIM BETTER...
...I'D SAY THAT ALMOST SOUNDED LIKE A THREAT.

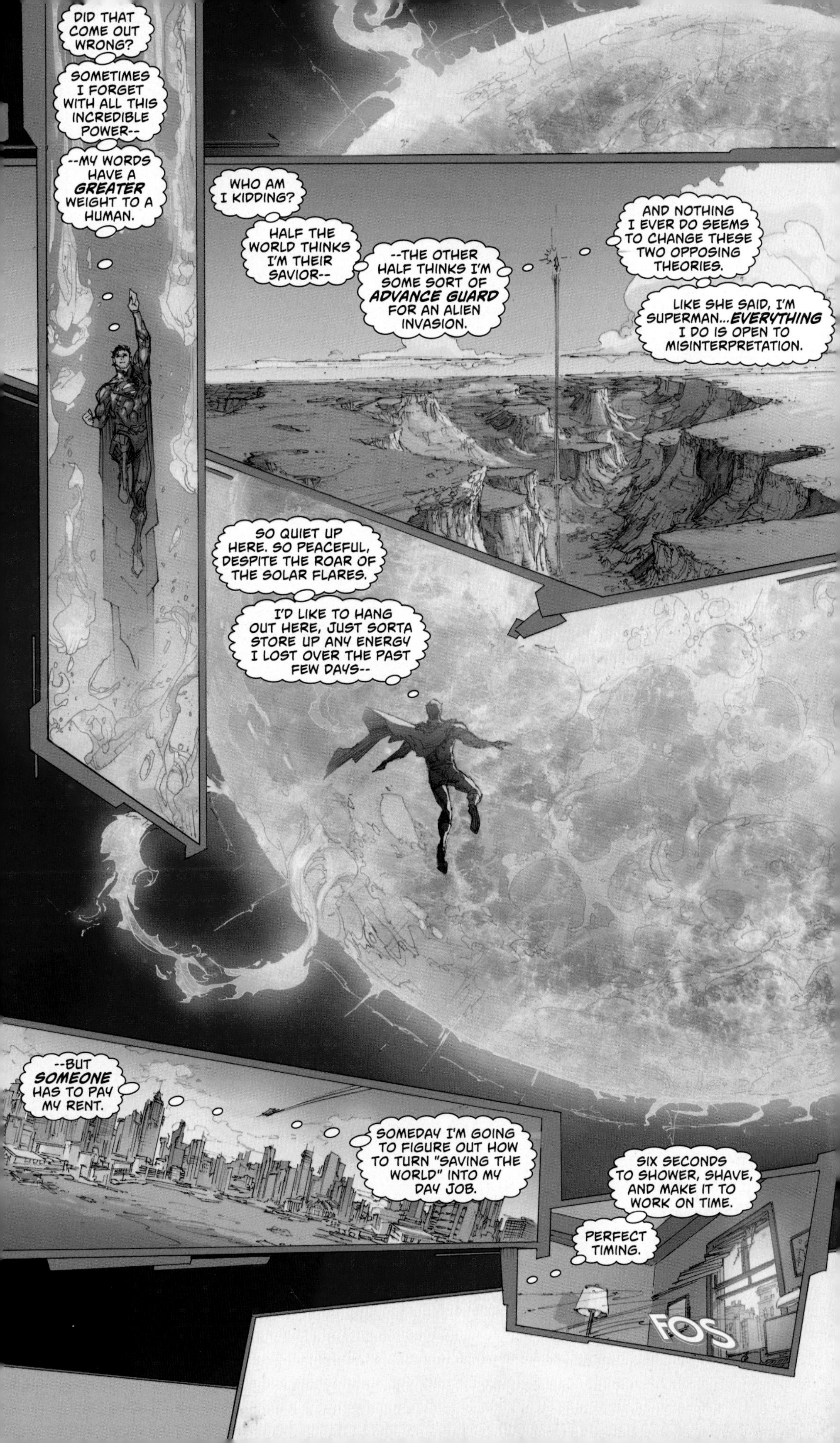
DID THAT COME OUT WRONG?
SOMETIMES I FORGET WITH ALL THIS INCREDIBLE POWER--
--MY WORDS HAVE A GREATER WEIGHT TO A HUMAN.
WHO AM I KIDDING?
HALF THE WORLD THINKS I'M THEIR SAVIOR--
--THE OTHER HALF THINKS I'M SOME SORT OF ADVANCE GUARD FOR AN ALIEN INVASION.
AND NOTHING I EVER DO SEEMS TO CHANGE THESE TWO OPPOSING THEORIES.
LIKE SHE SAID, I'M SUPERMAN...EVERYTHING I DO IS OPEN TO MISINTERPRETATION.
SO QUIET UP HERE. SO PEACEFUL, DESPITE THE ROAR OF THE SOLAR FLARES.
I'D LIKE TO HANG OUT HERE, JUST SORTA STORE UP ANY ENERGY I LOST OVER THE PAST FEW DAYS--
--BUT SOMEONE HAS TO PAY MY RENT.
SOMEDAY I'M GOING TO FIGURE OUT HOW TO TURN "SAVING THE WORLD" INTO MY DAY JOB.
SIX SECONDS TO SHOWER, SHAVE, AND MAKE IT TO WORK ON TIME.
PERFECT TIMING.
FOS

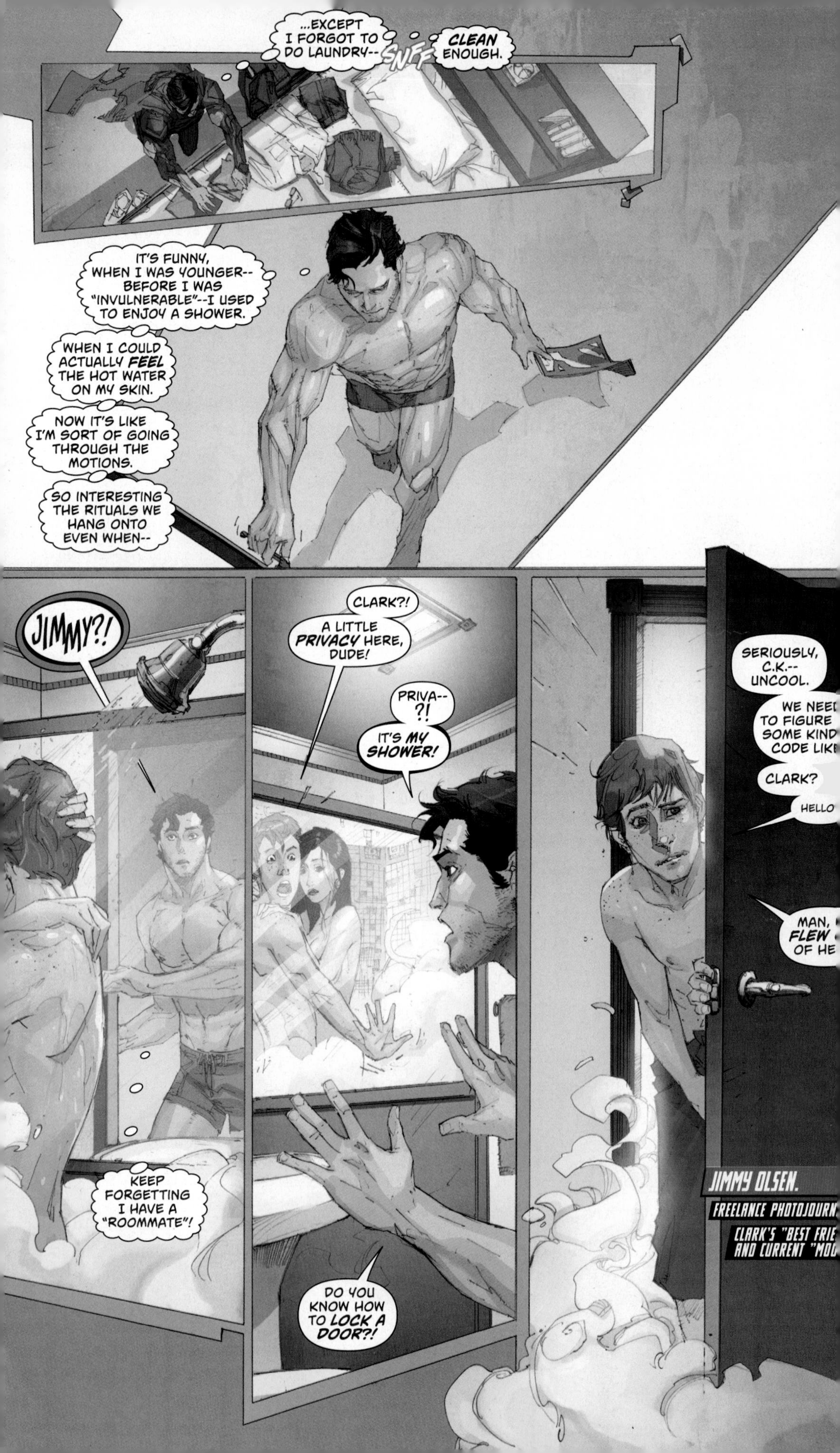
...EXCEPT I FORGOT TO DO LAUNDRY--
SNFF
CLEAN ENOUGH.
IT'S FUNNY, WHEN I WAS YOUNGER-- BEFORE I WAS "INVULNERABLE"--I USED TO ENJOY A SHOWER.
WHEN I COULD ACTUALLY FEEL THE HOT WATER ON MY SKIN.
NOW IT'S LIKE I'M SORT OF GOING THROUGH THE MOTIONS.
SO INTERESTING THE RITUALS WE HANG ONTO EVEN WHEN--
JIMMY?!
KEEP FORGETTING I HAVE A "ROOMMATE"!
CLARK?!
A LITTLE PRIVACY HERE, DUDE!
PRIVA-- ?!
IT'S MY SHOWER!
DO YOU KNOW HOW TO LOCK A DOOR?!
SERIOUSLY, C.K.-- UNCOOL.
WE NEED TO FIGURE SOME KIND CODE LIKE
CLARK?
HELLO
MAN, FLEW OF HE
JIMMY OLSEN.
FREELANCE PHOTOJOURN
CLARK'S "BEST FRIE AND CURRENT "MO

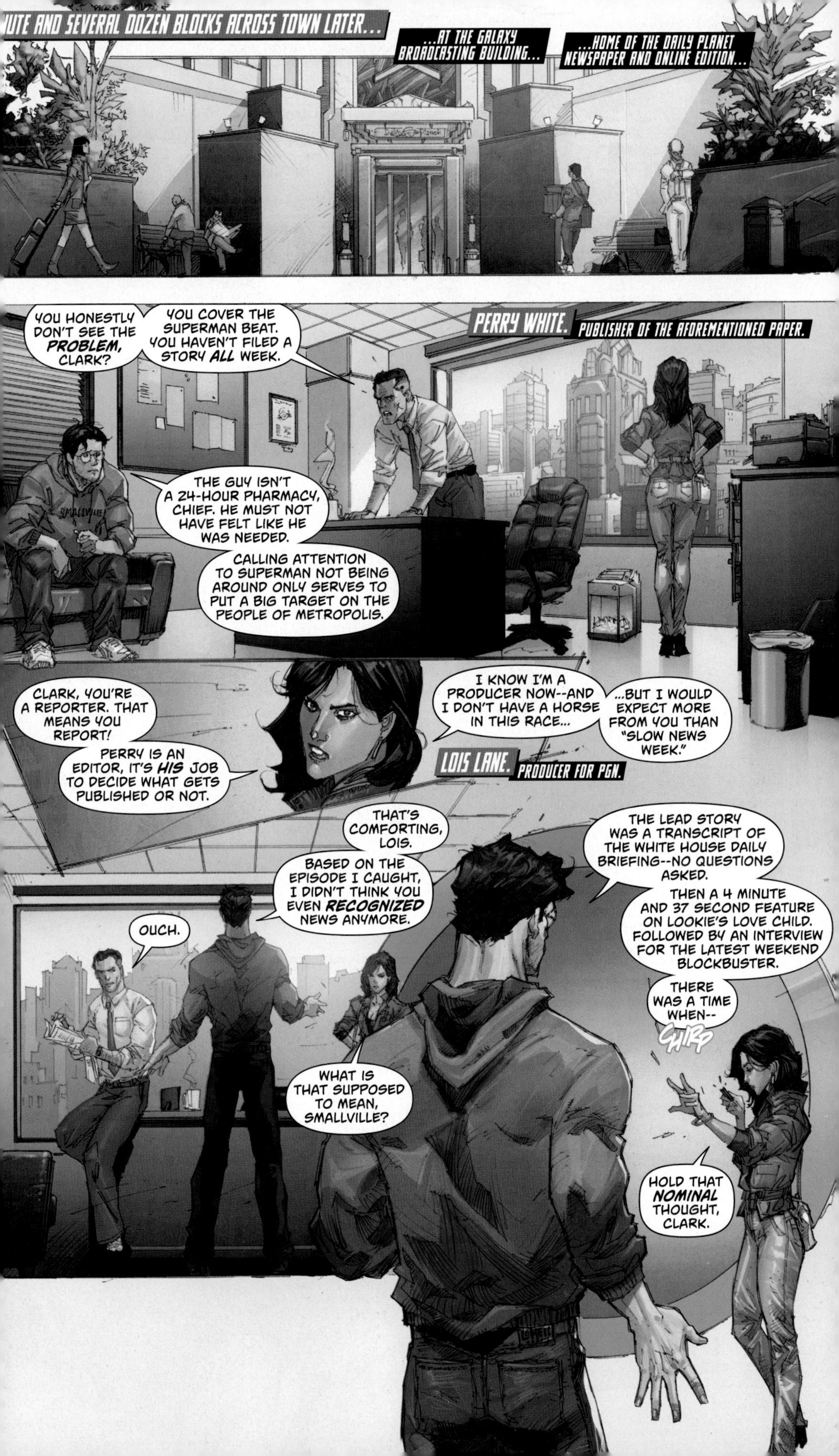
UTE AND SEVERAL DOZEN BLOCKS ACROSS TOWN LATER...
...AT THE GALAXY BROADCASTING BUILDING...
...HOME OF THE DAILY PLANET NEWSPAPER AND ONLINE EDITION...
YOU HONESTLY DON'T SEE THE PROBLEM, CLARK?
YOU COVER THE SUPERMAN BEAT. YOU HAVEN'T FILED A STORY ALL WEEK.
PERRY WHITE. PUBLISHER OF THE AFOREMENTIONED PAPER.
THE GUY ISN'T A 24-HOUR PHARMACY, CHIEF. HE MUST NOT HAVE FELT LIKE HE WAS NEEDED.
CALLING ATTENTION TO SUPERMAN NOT BEING AROUND ONLY SERVES TO PUT A BIG TARGET ON THE PEOPLE OF METROPOLIS.
CLARK, YOU'RE A REPORTER. THAT MEANS YOU REPORT!
PERRY IS AN EDITOR, IT'S HIS JOB TO DECIDE WHAT GETS PUBLISHED OR NOT.
I KNOW I'M A PRODUCER NOW--AND I DON'T HAVE A HORSE IN THIS RACE...
...BUT I WOULD EXPECT MORE FROM YOU THAN "SLOW NEWS WEEK."
LOIS LANE. PRODUCER FOR PGN.
THAT'S COMFORTING, LOIS.
BASED ON THE EPISODE I CAUGHT, I DIDN'T THINK YOU EVEN RECOGNIZED NEWS ANYMORE.
OUCH.
WHAT IS THAT SUPPOSED TO MEAN, SMALLVILLE?
THE LEAD STORY WAS A TRANSCRIPT OF THE WHITE HOUSE DAILY BRIEFING--NO QUESTIONS ASKED.
THEN A 4 MINUTE AND 37 SECOND FEATURE ON LOOKIE'S LOVE CHILD. FOLLOWED BY AN INTERVIEW FOR THE LATEST WEEKEND BLOCKBUSTER.
THERE WAS A TIME WHEN--
CHIRP
HOLD THAT NOMINAL THOUGHT, CLARK.

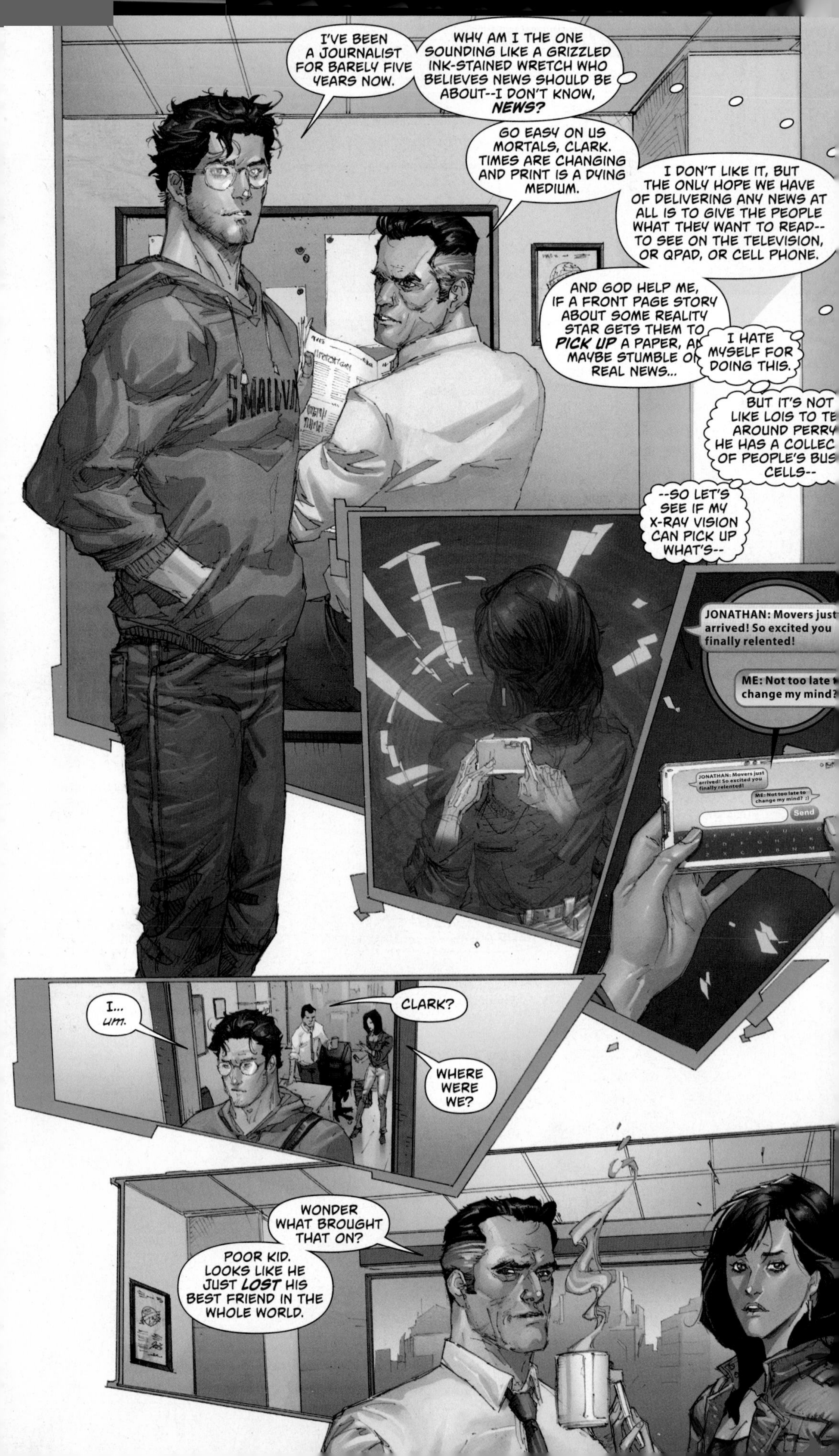

I'VE BEEN A JOURNALIST FOR BARELY FIVE YEARS NOW.
WHY AM I THE ONE SOUNDING LIKE A GRIZZLED INK-STAINED WRETCH WHO BELIEVES NEWS SHOULD BE ABOUT--I DON'T KNOW, NEWS?
GO EASY ON US MORTALS, CLARK. TIMES ARE CHANGING AND PRINT IS A DYING MEDIUM.
I DON'T LIKE IT, BUT THE ONLY HOPE WE HAVE OF DELIVERING ANY NEWS AT ALL IS TO GIVE THE PEOPLE WHAT THEY WANT TO READ-- TO SEE ON THE TELEVISION, OR QPAD, OR CELL PHONE.
AND GOD HELP ME, IF A FRONT PAGE STORY ABOUT SOME REALITY STAR GETS THEM TO PICK UP A PAPER, AN MAYBE STUMBLE ON REAL NEWS...
I HATE MYSELF FOR DOING THIS.
BUT IT'S NOT LIKE LOIS TO TE AROUND PERRY HE HAS A COLLEC OF PEOPLE'S BUS CELLS--
--SO LET'S SEE IF MY X-RAY VISION CAN PICK UP WHAT'S--
JONATHAN: Movers just arrived! So excited you finally relented!
ME: Not too late t change my mind?
I... um.
CLARK?
WHERE WERE WE?
WONDER WHAT BROUGHT THAT ON?
POOR KID. LOOKS LIKE HE JUST LOST HIS BEST FRIEND IN THE WHOLE WORLD.

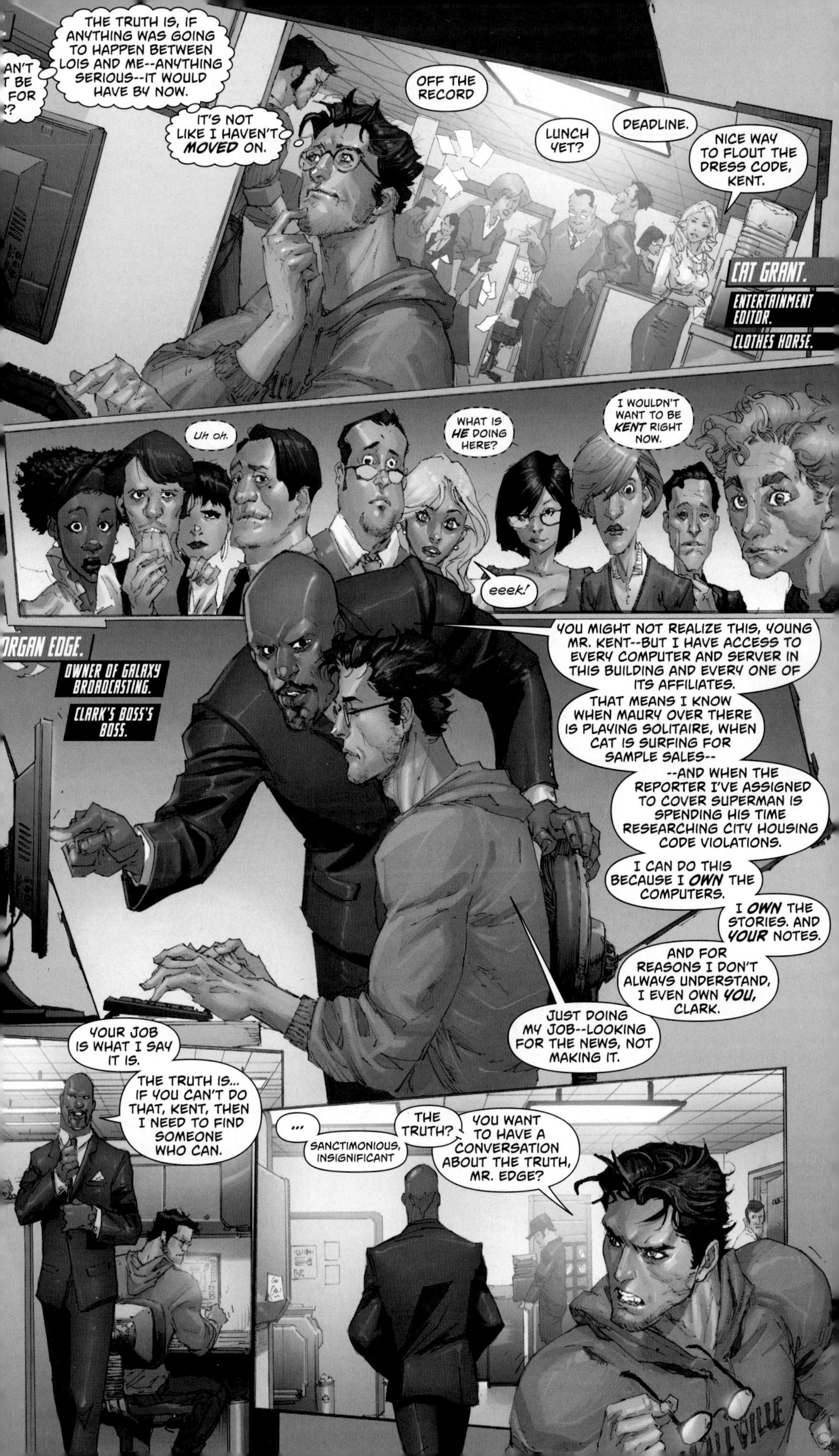

AN'T
T BE
FOR
?
THE TRUTH IS, IF ANYTHING WAS GOING TO HAPPEN BETWEEN LOIS AND ME--ANYTHING SERIOUS--IT WOULD HAVE BY NOW.
IT'S NOT LIKE I HAVEN'T MOVED ON.
OFF THE RECORD
LUNCH YET?
DEADLINE.
NICE WAY TO FLOUT THE DRESS CODE, KENT.
CAT GRANT.
ENTERTAINMENT EDITOR.
CLOTHES HORSE.
Uh oh.
WHAT IS HE DOING HERE?
I WOULDN'T WANT TO BE KENT RIGHT NOW.
eeek!
ORGAN EDGE.
OWNER OF GALAXY BROADCASTING.
CLARK'S BOSS'S BOSS.
YOU MIGHT NOT REALIZE THIS, YOUNG MR. KENT--BUT I HAVE ACCESS TO EVERY COMPUTER AND SERVER IN THIS BUILDING AND EVERY ONE OF ITS AFFILIATES.
THAT MEANS I KNOW WHEN MAURY OVER THERE IS PLAYING SOLITAIRE, WHEN CAT IS SURFING FOR SAMPLE SALES--
--AND WHEN THE REPORTER I'VE ASSIGNED TO COVER SUPERMAN IS SPENDING HIS TIME RESEARCHING CITY HOUSING CODE VIOLATIONS.
I CAN DO THIS BECAUSE I OWN THE COMPUTERS.
I OWN THE STORIES. AND YOUR NOTES.
AND FOR REASONS I DON'T ALWAYS UNDERSTAND, I EVEN OWN YOU, CLARK.
JUST DOING MY JOB--LOOKING FOR THE NEWS, NOT MAKING IT.
YOUR JOB IS WHAT I SAY IT IS.
THE TRUTH IS... IF YOU CAN'T DO THAT, KENT, THEN I NEED TO FIND SOMEONE WHO CAN.
...
SANCTIMONIOUS, INSIGNIFICANT
THE TRUTH?
YOU WANT TO HAVE A CONVERSATION ABOUT THE TRUTH, MR. EDGE?

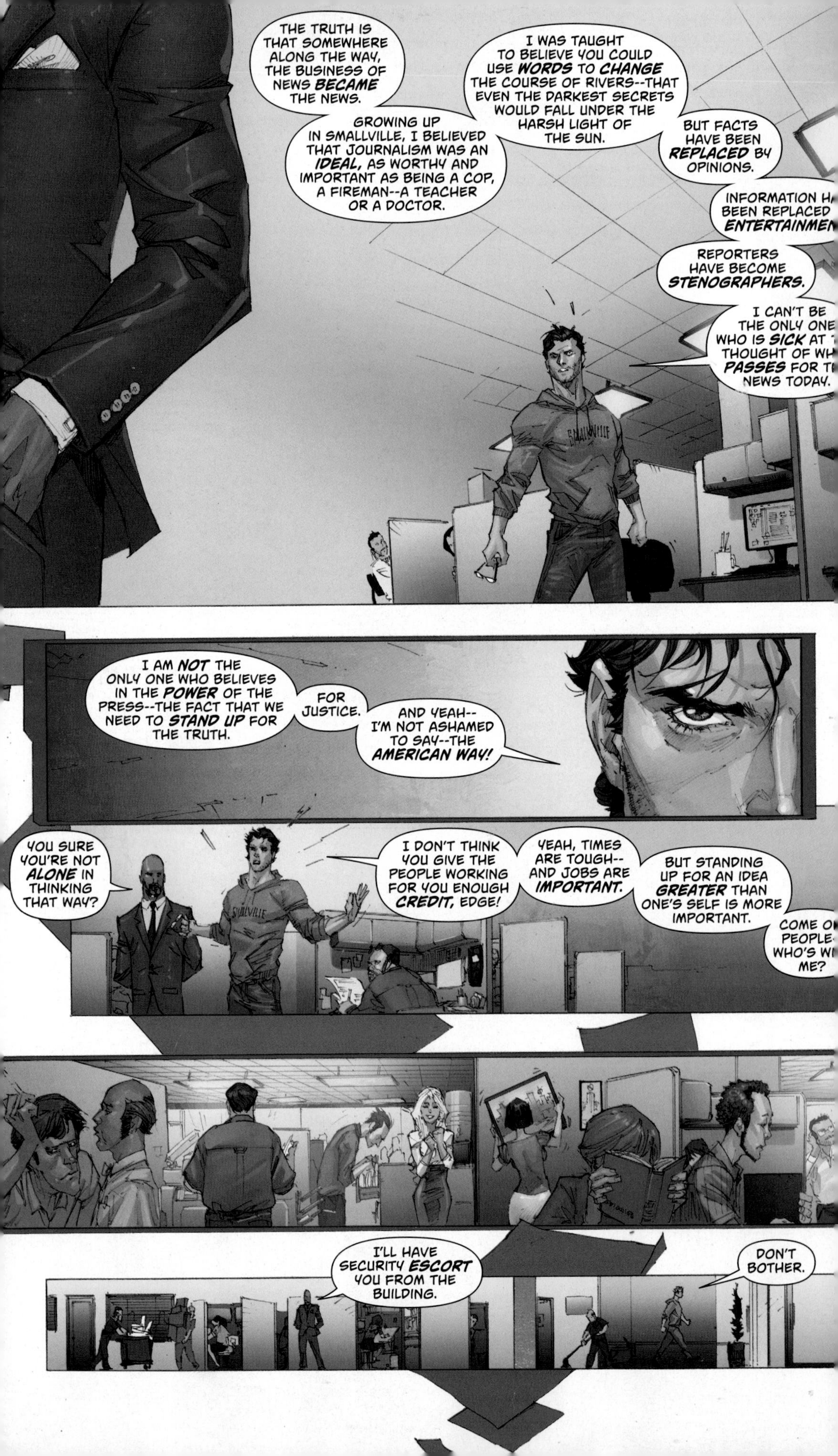
THE TRUTH IS THAT SOMEWHERE ALONG THE WAY, THE BUSINESS OF NEWS BECAME THE NEWS.
GROWING UP IN SMALLVILLE, I BELIEVED THAT JOURNALISM WAS AN IDEAL, AS WORTHY AND IMPORTANT AS BEING A COP, A FIREMAN--A TEACHER OR A DOCTOR.
I WAS TAUGHT TO BELIEVE YOU COULD USE WORDS TO CHANGE THE COURSE OF RIVERS--THAT EVEN THE DARKEST SECRETS WOULD FALL UNDER THE HARSH LIGHT OF THE SUN.
BUT FACTS HAVE BEEN REPLACED BY OPINIONS.
INFORMATION H BEEN REPLACED ENTERTAINME
REPORTERS HAVE BECOME STENOGRAPHERS.
I CAN'T BE THE ONLY ONE WHO IS SICK AT T THOUGHT OF WH PASSES FOR T NEWS TODAY.
SMALLVILLE
I AM NOT THE ONLY ONE WHO BELIEVES IN THE POWER OF THE PRESS--THE FACT THAT WE NEED TO STAND UP FOR THE TRUTH.
FOR JUSTICE.
AND YEAH-- I'M NOT ASHAMED TO SAY--THE AMERICAN WAY!
YOU SURE YOU'RE NOT ALONE IN THINKING THAT WAY?
I DON'T THINK YOU GIVE THE PEOPLE WORKING FOR YOU ENOUGH CREDIT, EDGE!
YEAH, TIMES ARE TOUGH-- AND JOBS ARE IMPORTANT.
BUT STANDING UP FOR AN IDEA GREATER THAN ONE'S SELF IS MORE IMPORTANT.
COME O PEOPLE WHO'S W ME?
I'LL HAVE SECURITY ESCORT YOU FROM THE BUILDING.
DON'T BOTHER.

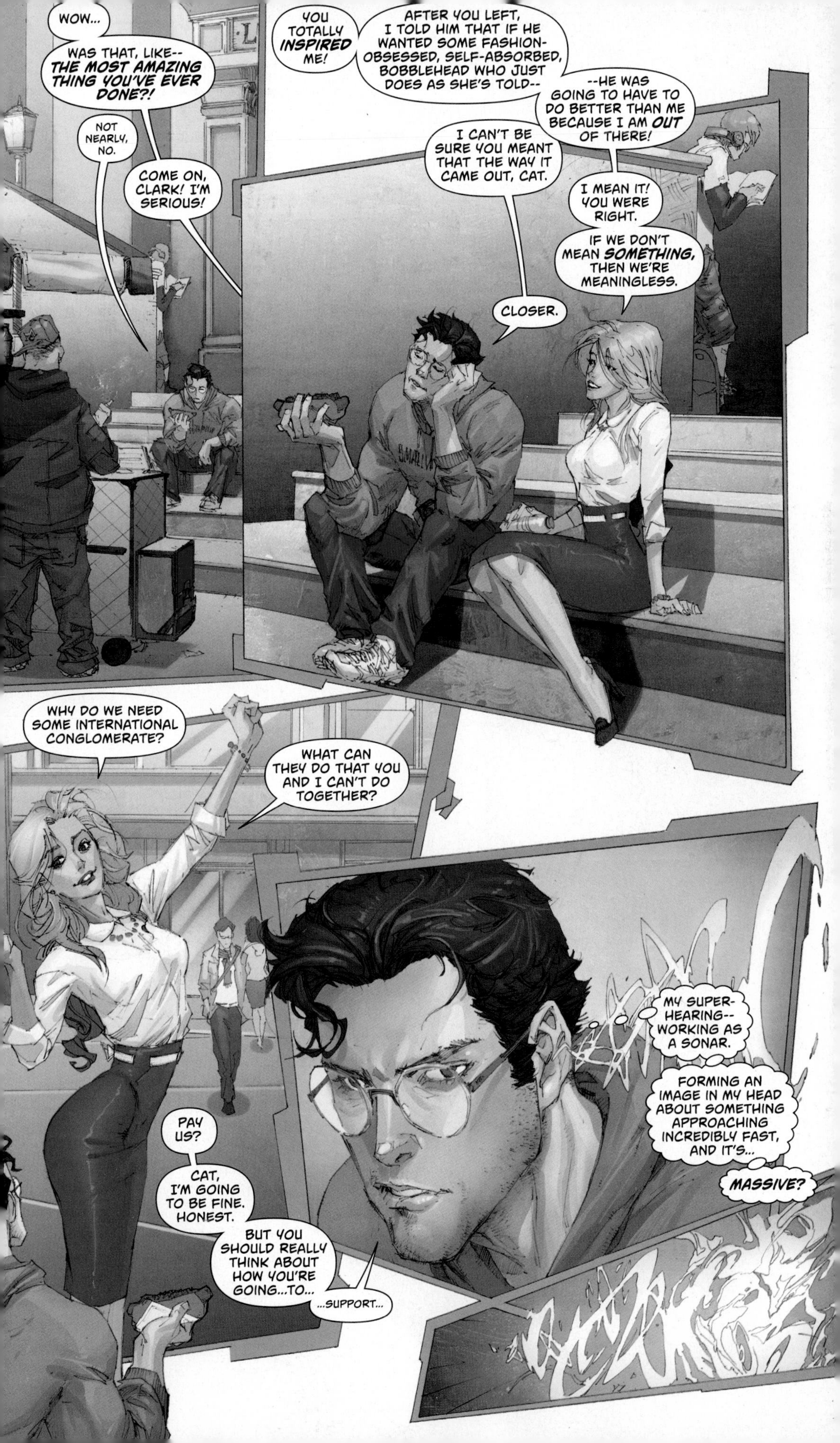

WOW...
WAS THAT, LIKE-- THE MOST AMAZING THING YOU'VE EVER DONE?!
NOT NEARLY, NO.
COME ON, CLARK! I'M SERIOUS!
YOU TOTALLY INSPIRED ME!
AFTER YOU LEFT, I TOLD HIM THAT IF HE WANTED SOME FASHION-OBSESSED, SELF-ABSORBED, BOBBLEHEAD WHO JUST DOES AS SHE'S TOLD--
--HE WAS GOING TO HAVE TO DO BETTER THAN ME BECAUSE I AM OUT OF THERE!
I CAN'T BE SURE YOU MEANT THAT THE WAY IT CAME OUT, CAT.
I MEAN IT! YOU WERE RIGHT.
IF WE DON'T MEAN SOMETHING, THEN WE'RE MEANINGLESS.
CLOSER.
WHY DO WE NEED SOME INTERNATIONAL CONGLOMERATE?
WHAT CAN THEY DO THAT YOU AND I CAN'T DO TOGETHER?
PAY US?
CAT, I'M GOING TO BE FINE. HONEST.
BUT YOU SHOULD REALLY THINK ABOUT HOW YOU'RE GOING...TO...
...SUPPORT...
MY SUPER-HEARING-- WORKING AS A SONAR.
FORMING AN IMAGE IN MY HEAD ABOUT SOMETHING APPROACHING INCREDIBLY FAST, AND IT'S...
MASSIVE?

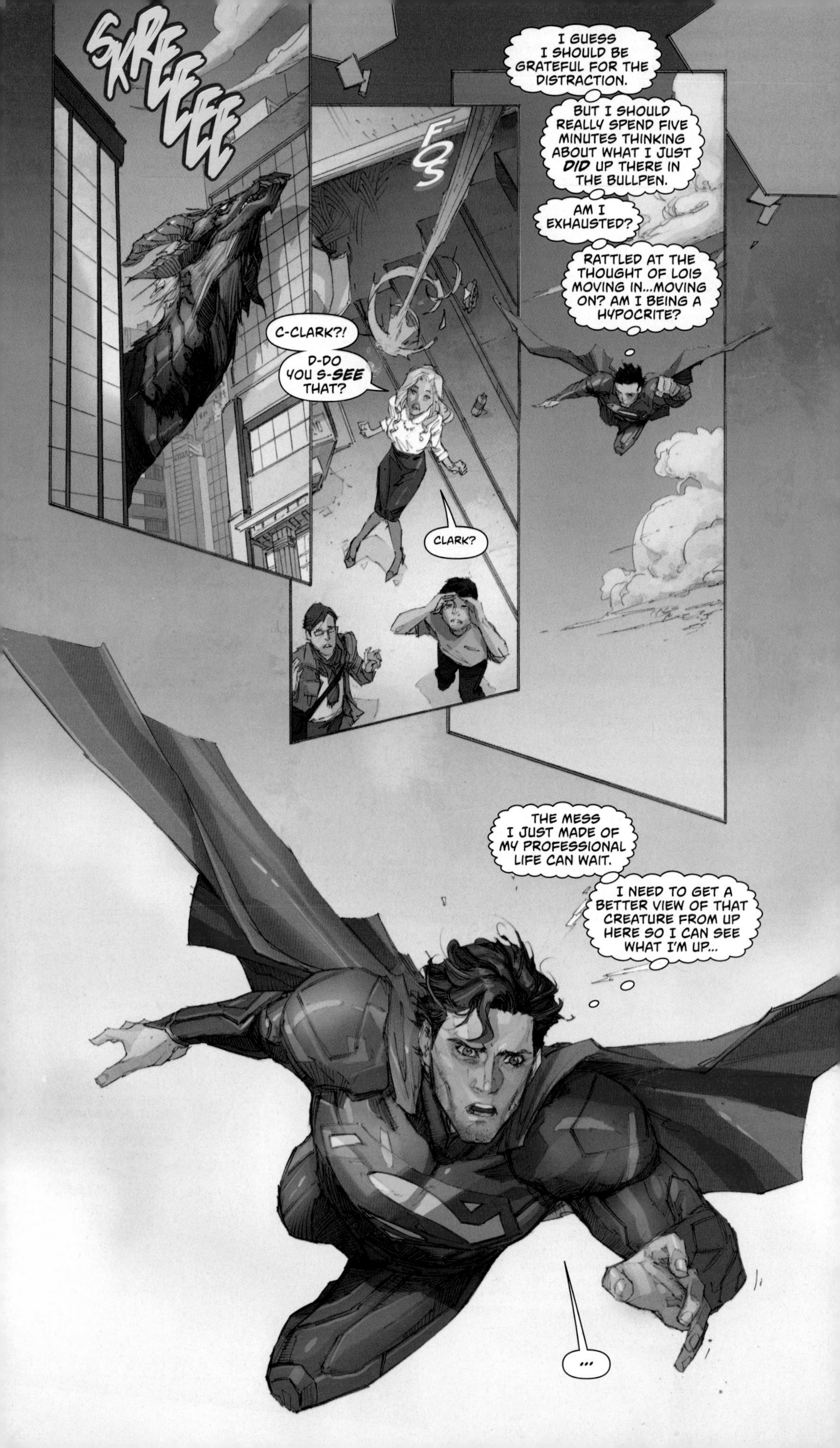
SKREEEEE
FOS
I GUESS I SHOULD BE GRATEFUL FOR THE DISTRACTION.
BUT I SHOULD REALLY SPEND FIVE MINUTES THINKING ABOUT WHAT I JUST DID UP THERE IN THE BULLPEN.
AM I EXHAUSTED?
RATTLED AT THE THOUGHT OF LOIS MOVING IN...MOVING ON? AM I BEING A HYPOCRITE?
C-CLARK?!
D-DO YOU S-SEE THAT?
CLARK?
THE MESS I JUST MADE OF MY PROFESSIONAL LIFE CAN WAIT.
I NEED TO GET A BETTER VIEW OF THAT CREATURE FROM UP HERE SO I CAN SEE WHAT I'M UP...
...

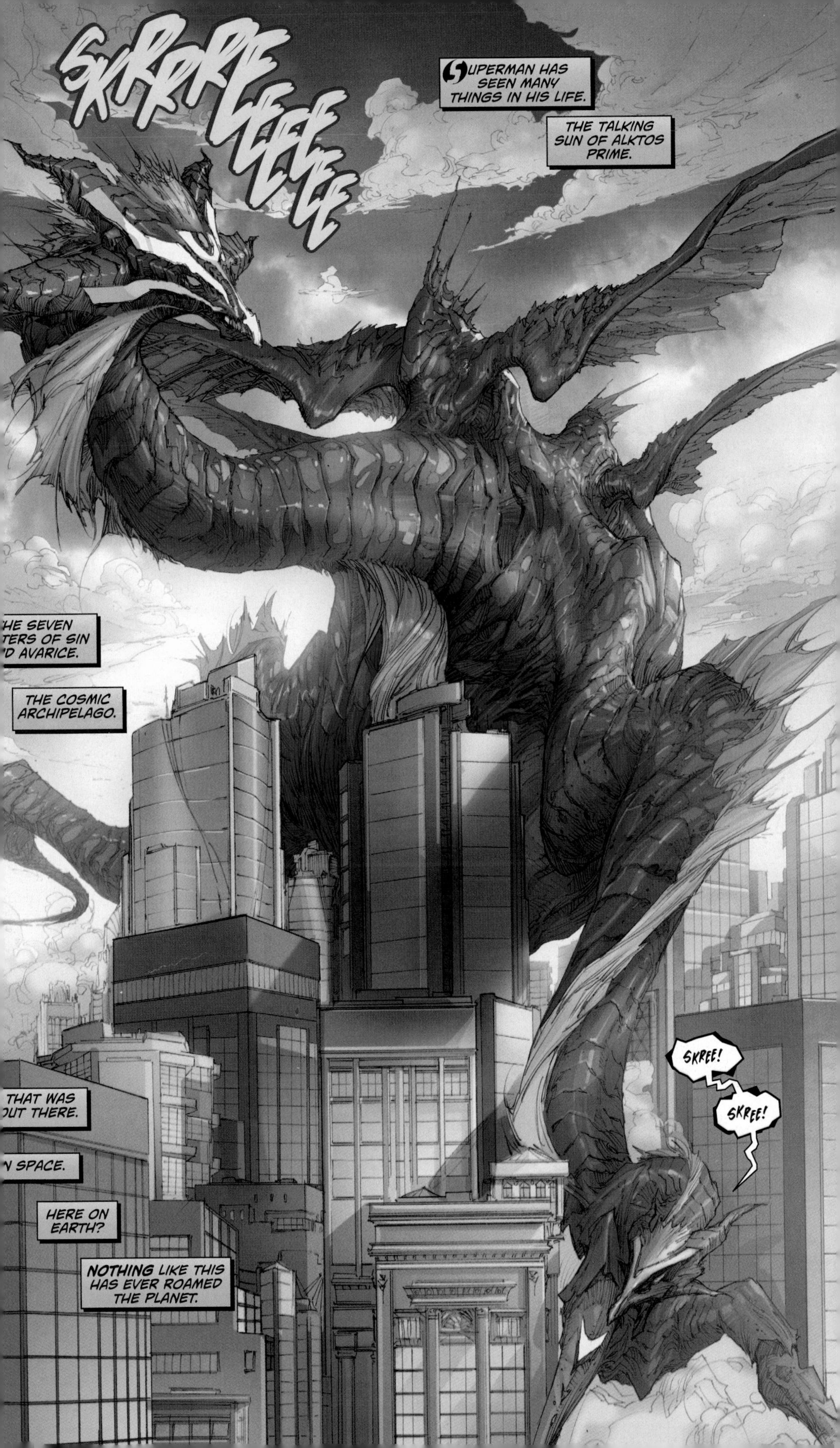
SUPERMAN HAS SEEN MANY THINGS IN HIS LIFE.
THE TALKING SUN OF ALKTOS PRIME.
HE SEVEN TERS OF SIN D AVARICE.
THE COSMIC ARCHIPELAGO.
THAT WAS OUT THERE.
N SPACE.
HERE ON EARTH?
NOTHING LIKE THIS HAS EVER ROAMED THE PLANET.
SKREE!
SKREE!

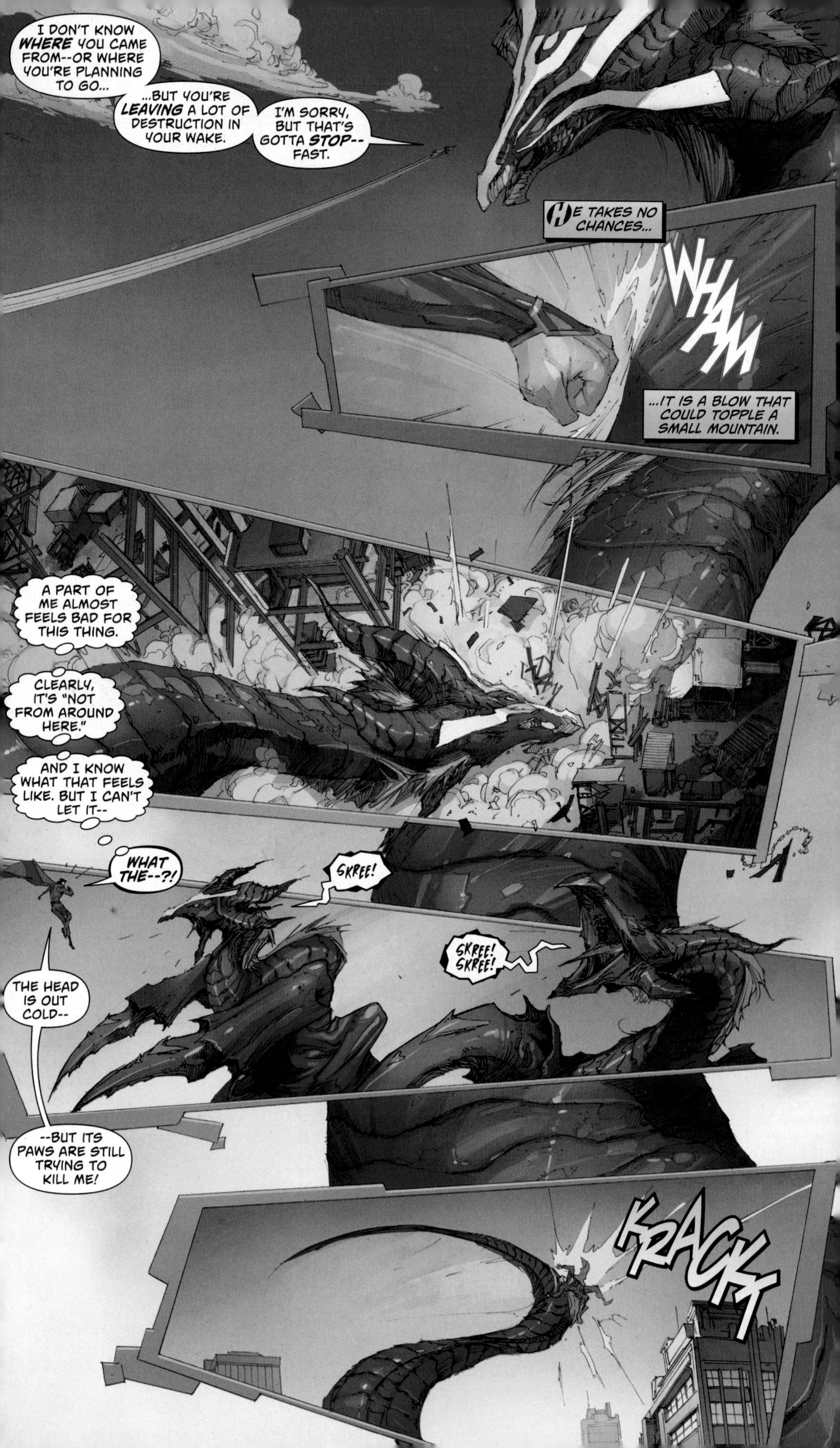
I DON'T KNOW WHERE YOU CAME FROM--OR WHERE YOU'RE PLANNING TO GO...
...BUT YOU'RE LEAVING A LOT OF DESTRUCTION IN YOUR WAKE.
I'M SORRY, BUT THAT'S GOTTA STOP--FAST.
HE TAKES NO CHANCES...
WHAM
...IT IS A BLOW THAT COULD TOPPLE A SMALL MOUNTAIN.
A PART OF ME ALMOST FEELS BAD FOR THIS THING.
CLEARLY, IT'S "NOT FROM AROUND HERE."
AND I KNOW WHAT THAT FEELS LIKE. BUT I CAN'T LET IT--
WHAT THE--?!
SKREE!
SKREE! SKREE!
THE HEAD IS OUT COLD--
--BUT ITS PAWS ARE STILL TRYING TO KILL ME!
KRACK

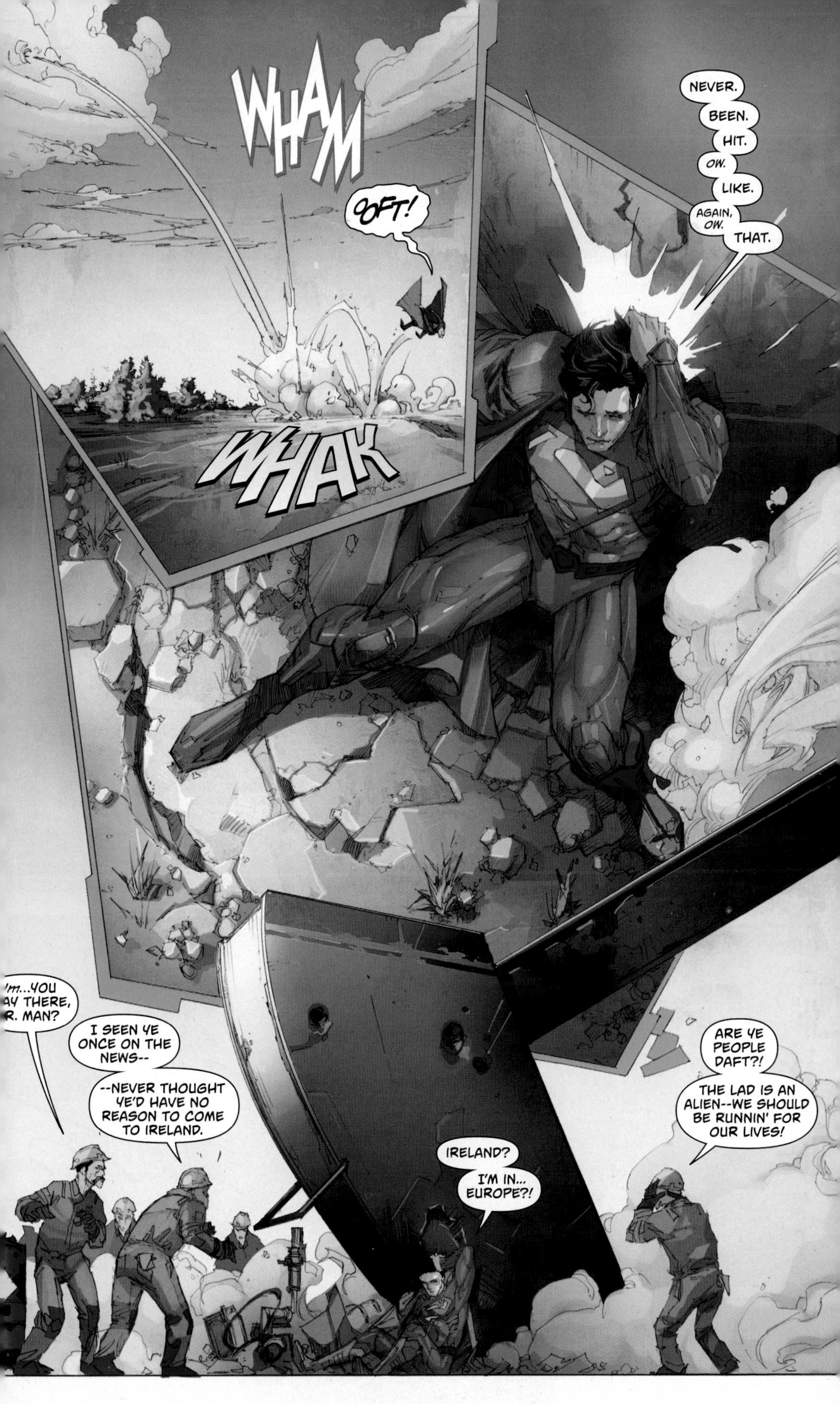
WHAM
OOFT!
WHAK
NEVER.
BEEN.
HIT.
OW.
LIKE.
AGAIN, OW.
THAT.
'M...YOU AY THERE, R. MAN?
I SEEN YE ONCE ON THE NEWS--
--NEVER THOUGHT YE'D HAVE NO REASON TO COME TO IRELAND.
IRELAND?
I'M IN... EUROPE?!
ARE YE PEOPLE DAFT?!
THE LAD IS AN ALIEN--WE SHOULD BE RUNNIN' FOR OUR LIVES!

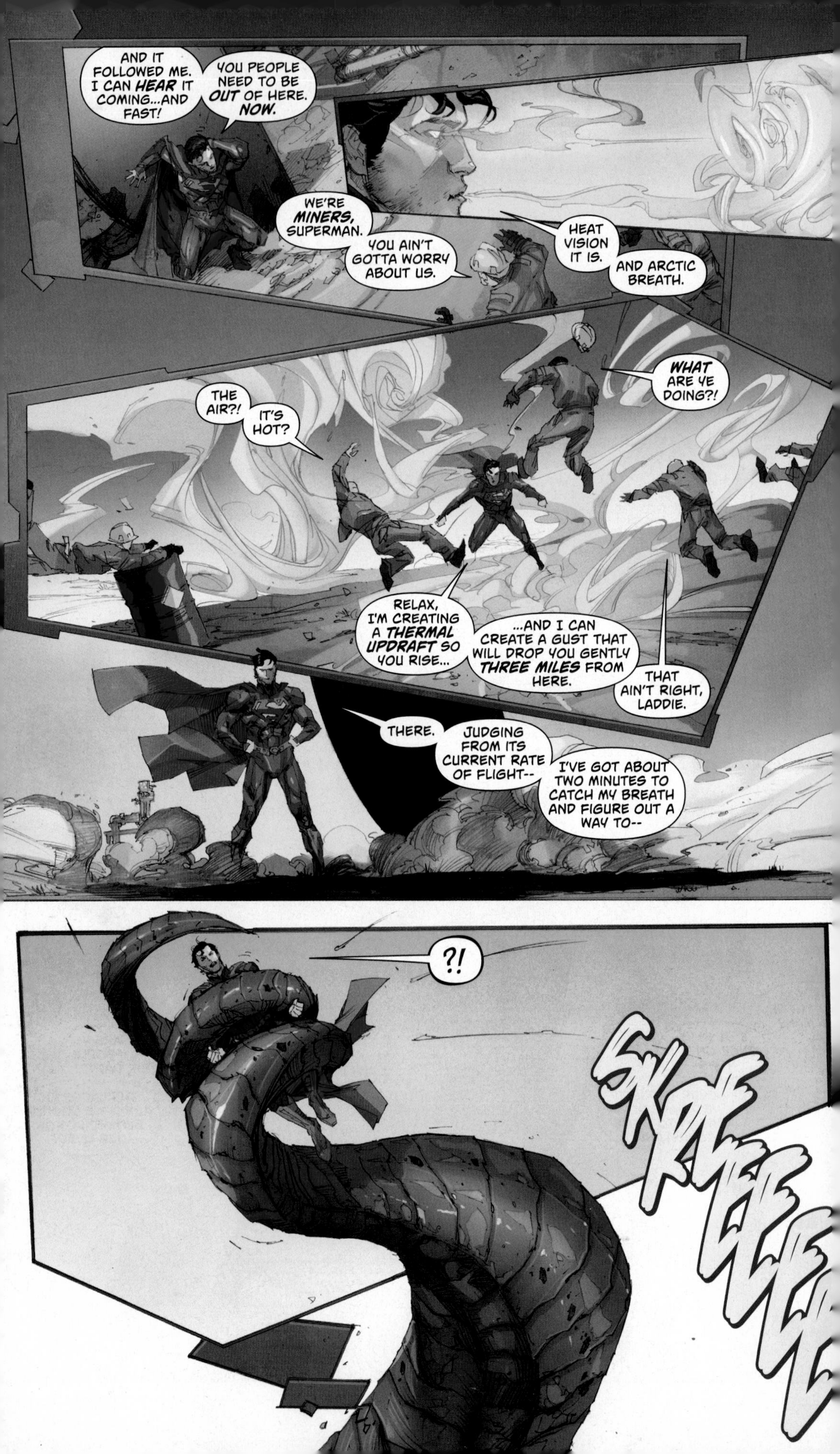

AND IT FOLLOWED ME. I CAN HEAR IT COMING...AND FAST!
YOU PEOPLE NEED TO BE OUT OF HERE. NOW.
WE'RE MINERS, SUPERMAN.
YOU AIN'T GOTTA WORRY ABOUT US.
HEAT VISION IT IS.
AND ARCTIC BREATH.
THE AIR?!
IT'S HOT?
WHAT ARE YE DOING?!
RELAX, I'M CREATING A THERMAL UPDRAFT SO YOU RISE...
...AND I CAN CREATE A GUST THAT WILL DROP YOU GENTLY THREE MILES FROM HERE.
THAT AIN'T RIGHT, LADDIE.
THERE.
JUDGING FROM ITS CURRENT RATE OF FLIGHT--
I'VE GOT ABOUT TWO MINUTES TO CATCH MY BREATH AND FIGURE OUT A WAY TO--
?!
SKREEEEE

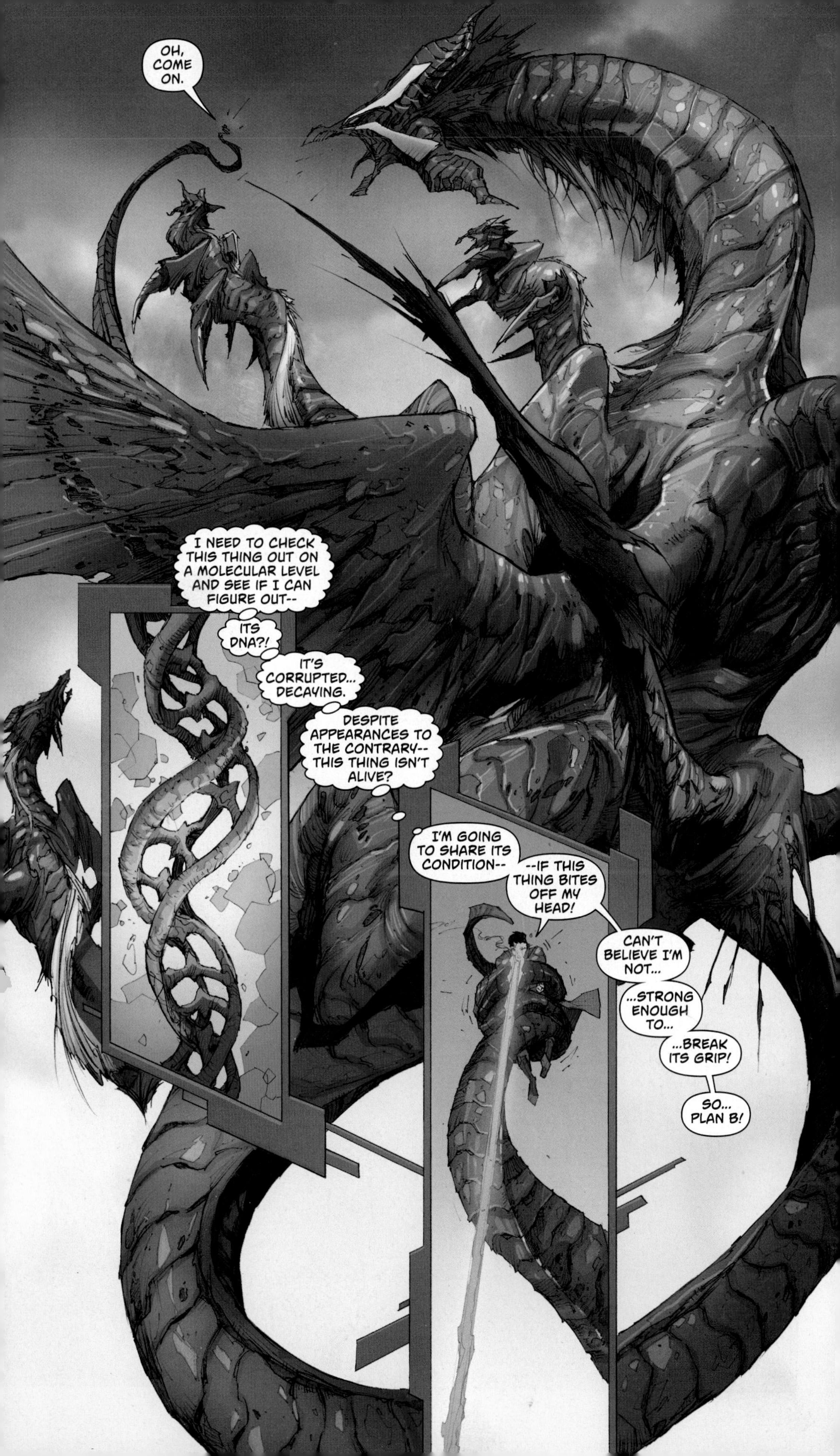
OH, COME ON.
I NEED TO CHECK THIS THING OUT ON A MOLECULAR LEVEL AND SEE IF I CAN FIGURE OUT--
ITS DNA?!
IT'S CORRUPTED... DECAYING.
DESPITE APPEARANCES TO THE CONTRARY-- THIS THING ISN'T ALIVE?
I'M GOING TO SHARE ITS CONDITION--
--IF THIS THING BITES OFF MY HEAD!
CAN'T BELIEVE I'M NOT...
...STRONG ENOUGH TO...
...BREAK ITS GRIP!
SO... PLAN B!

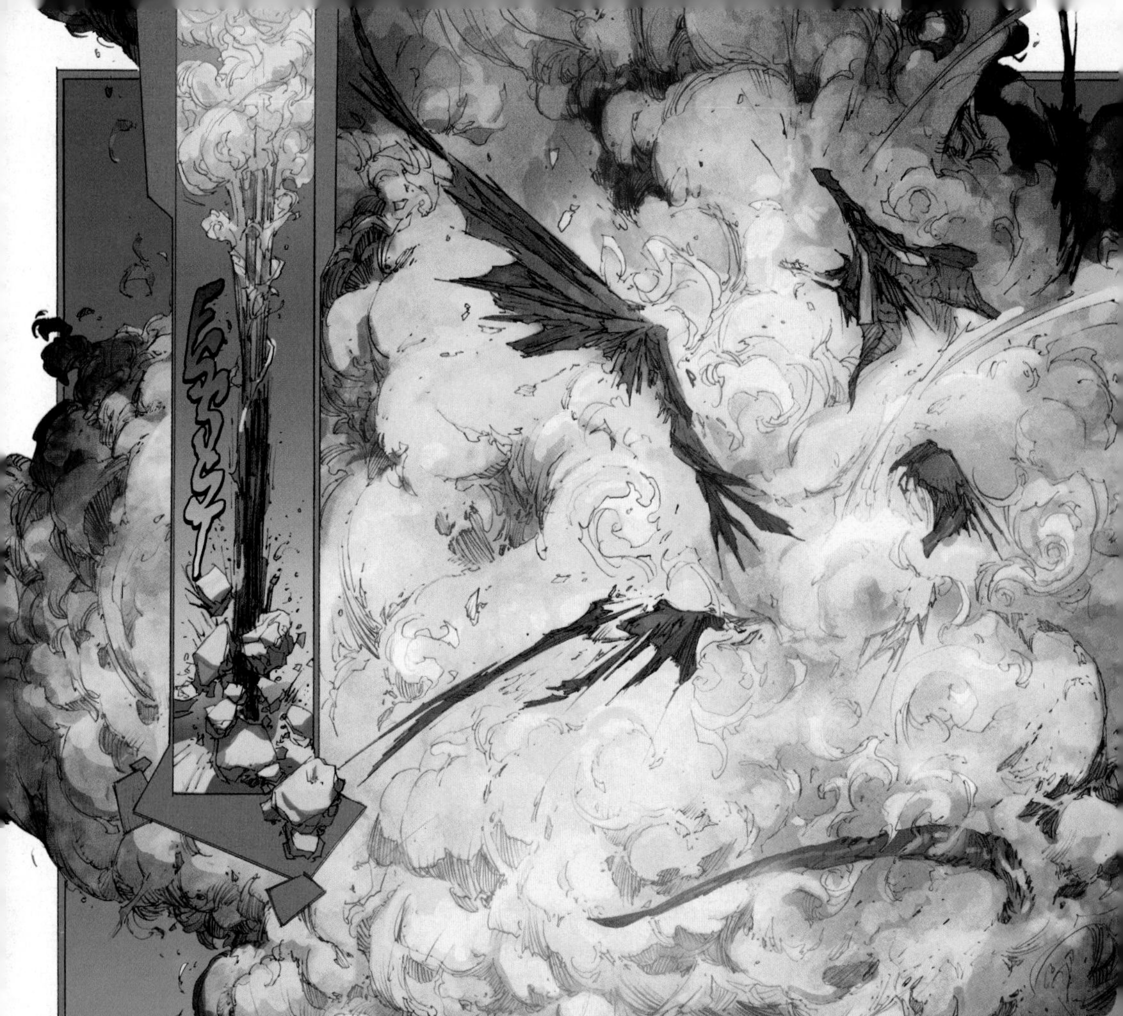
HE USES HIS HEAT VISION TO IGNITE THE OIL BURIED DEEP BENEATH THE EARTH'S SURFACE...
...WITH PREDICTABLE AND CATACLYSMIC RESULTS.
FWABOOM

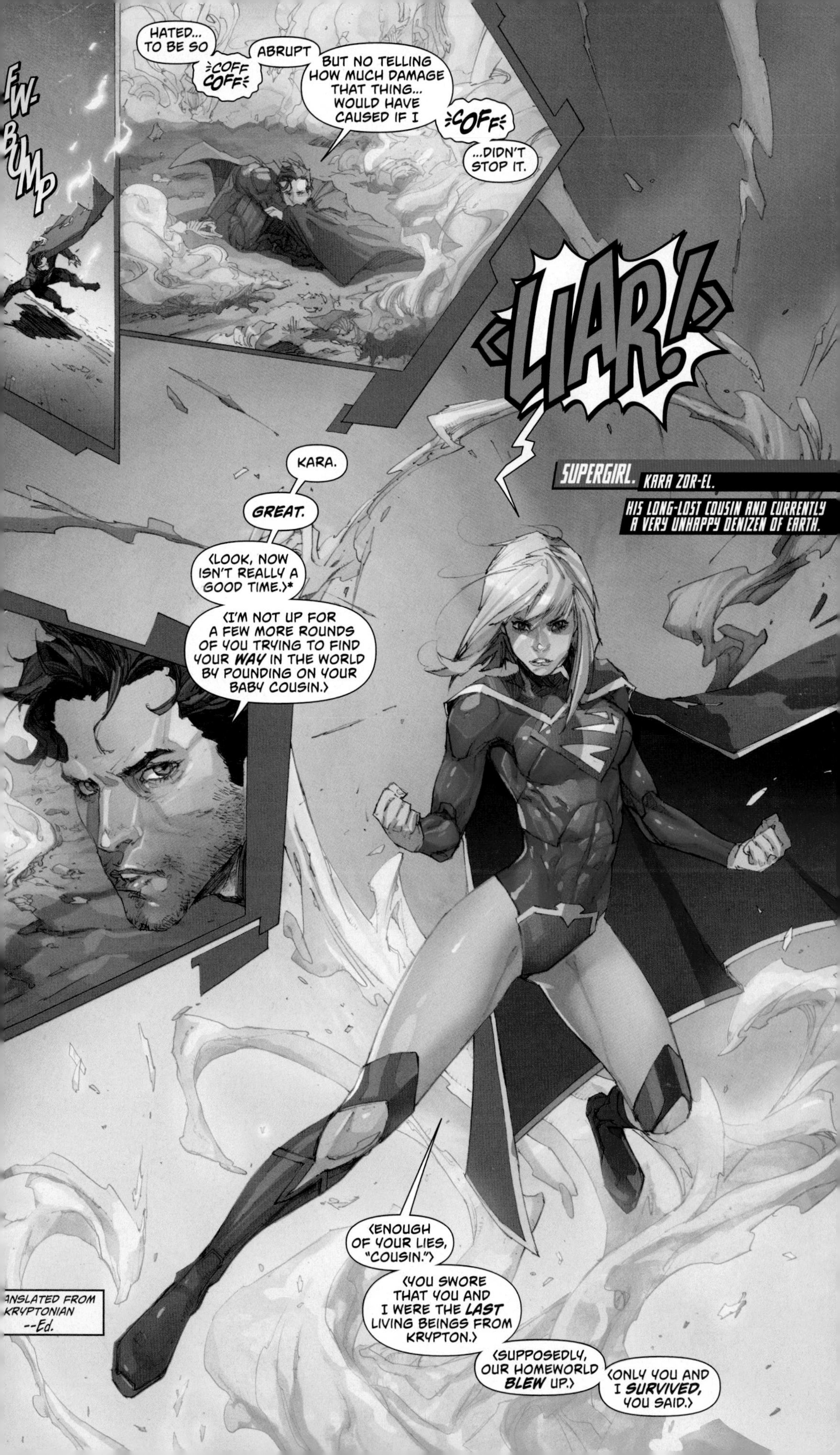

FW-BUMP
HATED... TO BE SO
COFF COFF
ABRUPT
BUT NO TELLING HOW MUCH DAMAGE THAT THING... WOULD HAVE CAUSED IF I
COFF
...DIDN'T STOP IT.
LIAR!
SUPERGIRL. KARA ZOR-EL.
HIS LONG-LOST COUSIN AND CURRENTLY A VERY UNHAPPY DENIZEN OF EARTH.
KARA.
GREAT.
(LOOK, NOW ISN'T REALLY A GOOD TIME.)*
(I'M NOT UP FOR A FEW MORE ROUNDS OF YOU TRYING TO FIND YOUR WAY IN THE WORLD BY POUNDING ON YOUR BABY COUSIN.)
(ENOUGH OF YOUR LIES, "COUSIN.")
(YOU SWORE THAT YOU AND I WERE THE LAST LIVING BEINGS FROM KRYPTON.)
(SUPPOSEDLY, OUR HOMEWORLD BLEW UP.)
(ONLY YOU AND I SURVIVED, YOU SAID.)
ANSLATED FROM KRYPTONIAN --Ed.

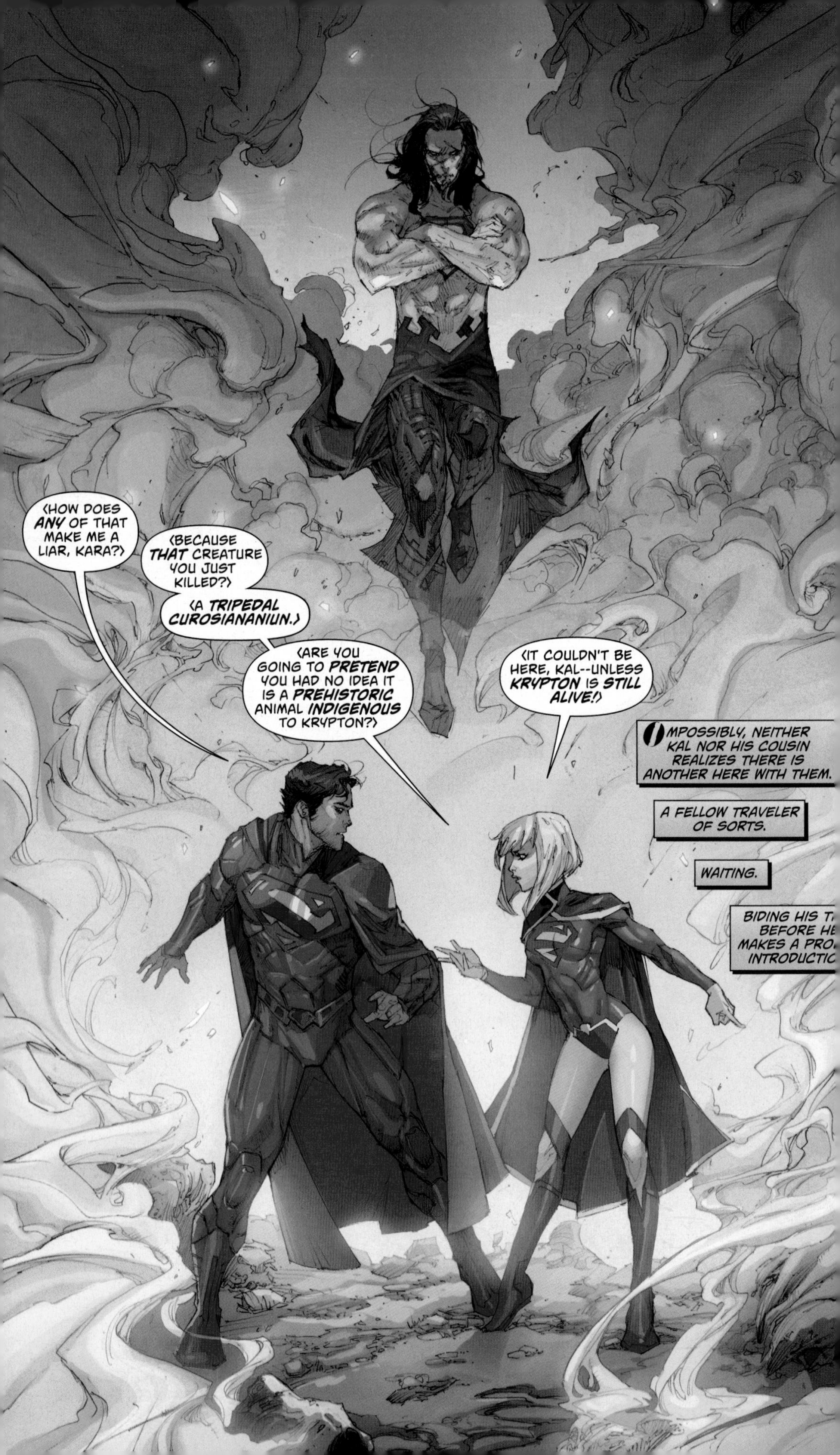

‹HOW DOES ANY OF THAT MAKE ME A LIAR, KARA?›
‹BECAUSE THAT CREATURE YOU JUST KILLED?›
‹A TRIPEDAL CUROSIANANIUN.›
‹ARE YOU GOING TO PRETEND YOU HAD NO IDEA IT IS A PREHISTORIC ANIMAL INDIGENOUS TO KRYPTON?›
‹IT COULDN'T BE HERE, KAL--UNLESS KRYPTON IS STILL ALIVE!›
IMPOSSIBLY, NEITHER KAL NOR HIS COUSIN REALIZES THERE IS ANOTHER HERE WITH THEM.
A FELLOW TRAVELER OF SORTS.
WAITING.

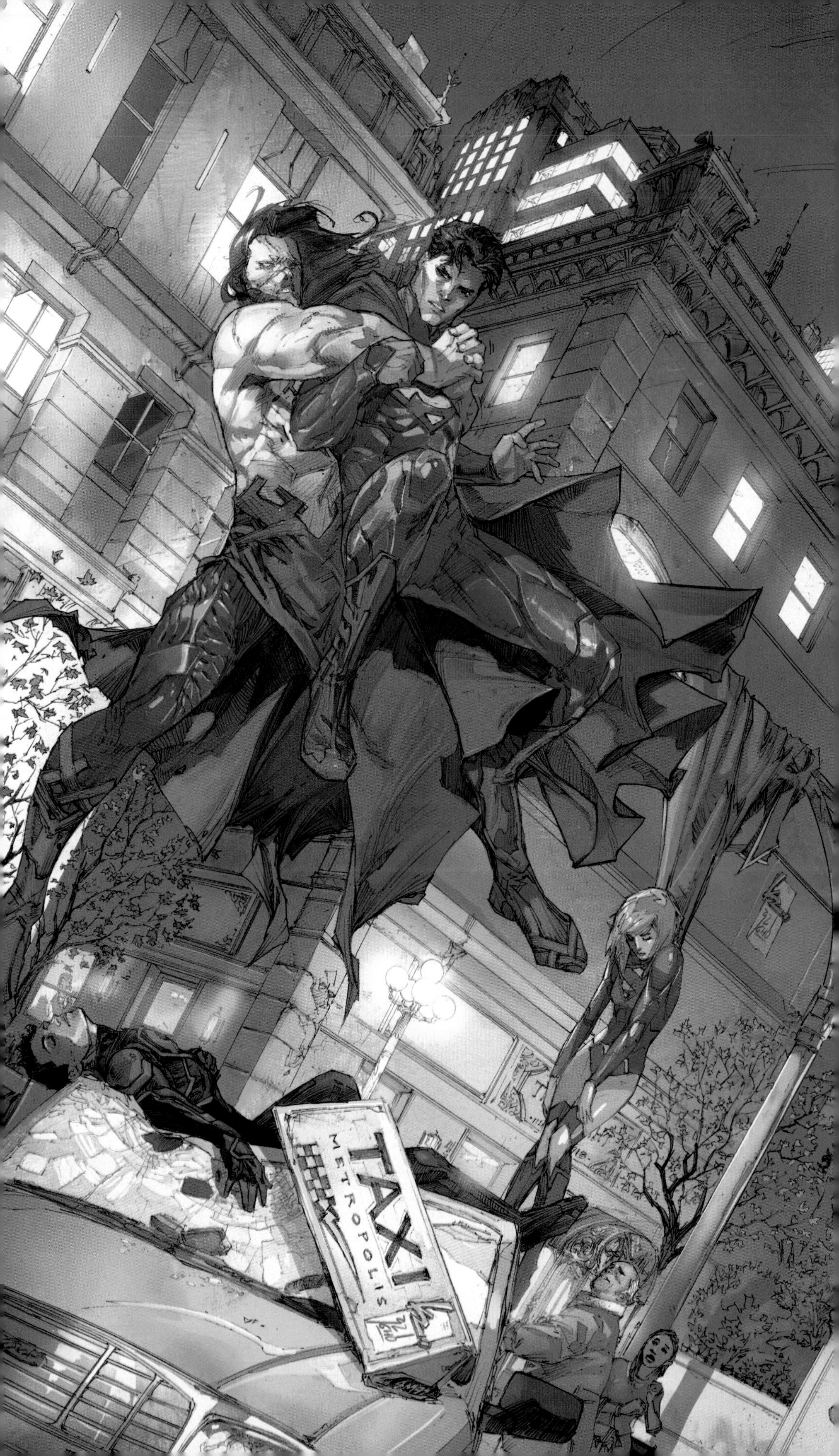
TAXI
METROPOLIS

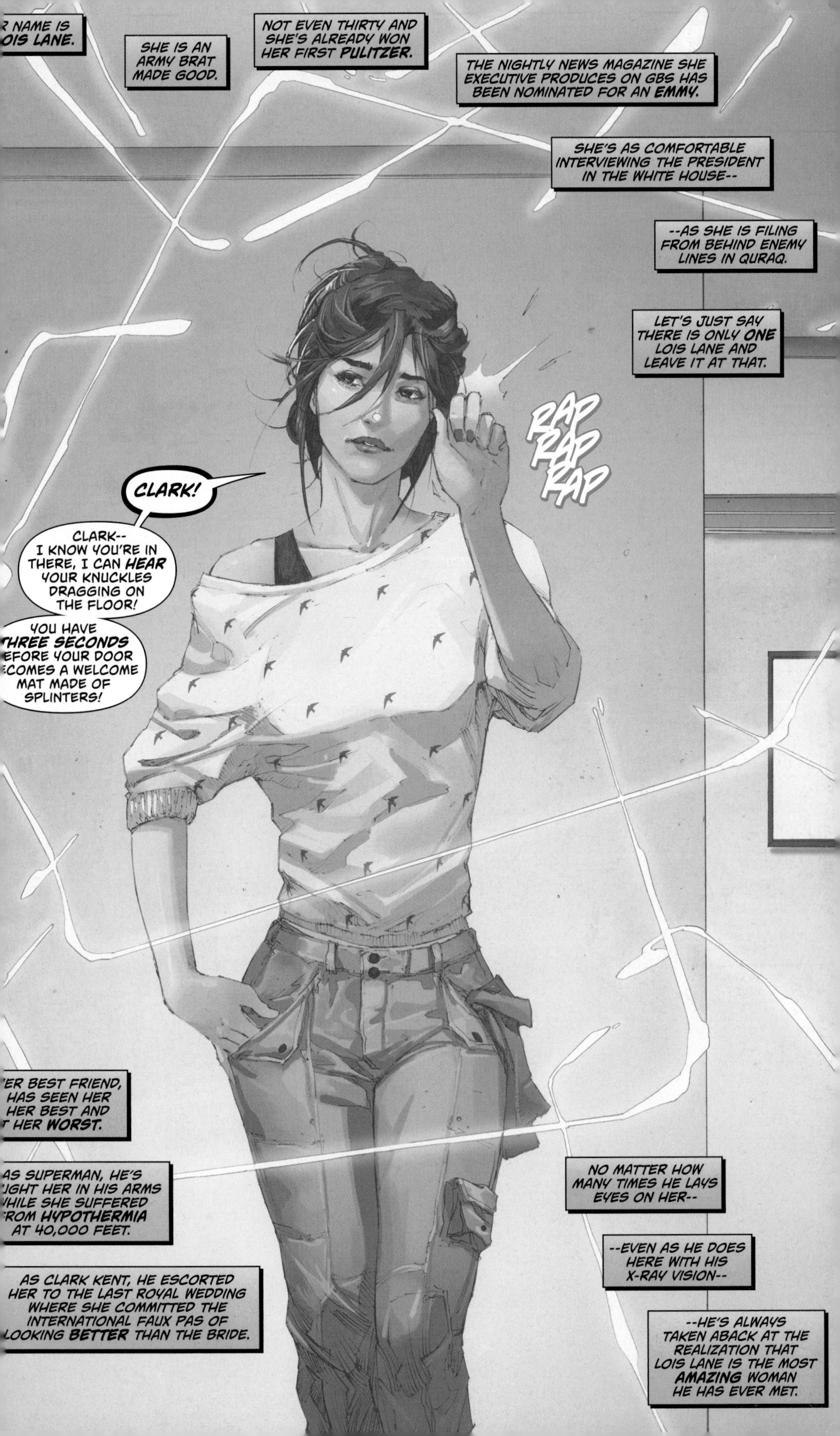
R NAME IS
OIS LANE.
SHE IS AN ARMY BRAT MADE GOOD.
NOT EVEN THIRTY AND SHE'S ALREADY WON HER FIRST PULITZER.
THE NIGHTLY NEWS MAGAZINE SHE EXECUTIVE PRODUCES ON GBS HAS BEEN NOMINATED FOR AN EMMY.
SHE'S AS COMFORTABLE INTERVIEWING THE PRESIDENT IN THE WHITE HOUSE--
--AS SHE IS FILING FROM BEHIND ENEMY LINES IN QURAQ.
LET'S JUST SAY THERE IS ONLY ONE LOIS LANE AND LEAVE IT AT THAT.
RAP RAP RAP
CLARK!
CLARK-- I KNOW YOU'RE IN THERE, I CAN HEAR YOUR KNUCKLES DRAGGING ON THE FLOOR!
YOU HAVE THREE SECONDS EFORE YOUR DOOR ECOMES A WELCOME MAT MADE OF SPLINTERS!
ER BEST FRIEND, HAS SEEN HER HER BEST AND HER WORST.
AS SUPERMAN, HE'S GHT HER IN HIS ARMS HILE SHE SUFFERED ROM HYPOTHERMIA AT 40,000 FEET.
AS CLARK KENT, HE ESCORTED HER TO THE LAST ROYAL WEDDING WHERE SHE COMMITTED THE INTERNATIONAL FAUX PAS OF LOOKING BETTER THAN THE BRIDE.
NO MATTER HOW MANY TIMES HE LAYS EYES ON HER--
--EVEN AS HE DOES HERE WITH HIS X-RAY VISION--
--HE'S ALWAYS TAKEN ABACK AT THE REALIZATION THAT LOIS LANE IS THE MOST AMAZING WOMAN HE HAS EVER MET.

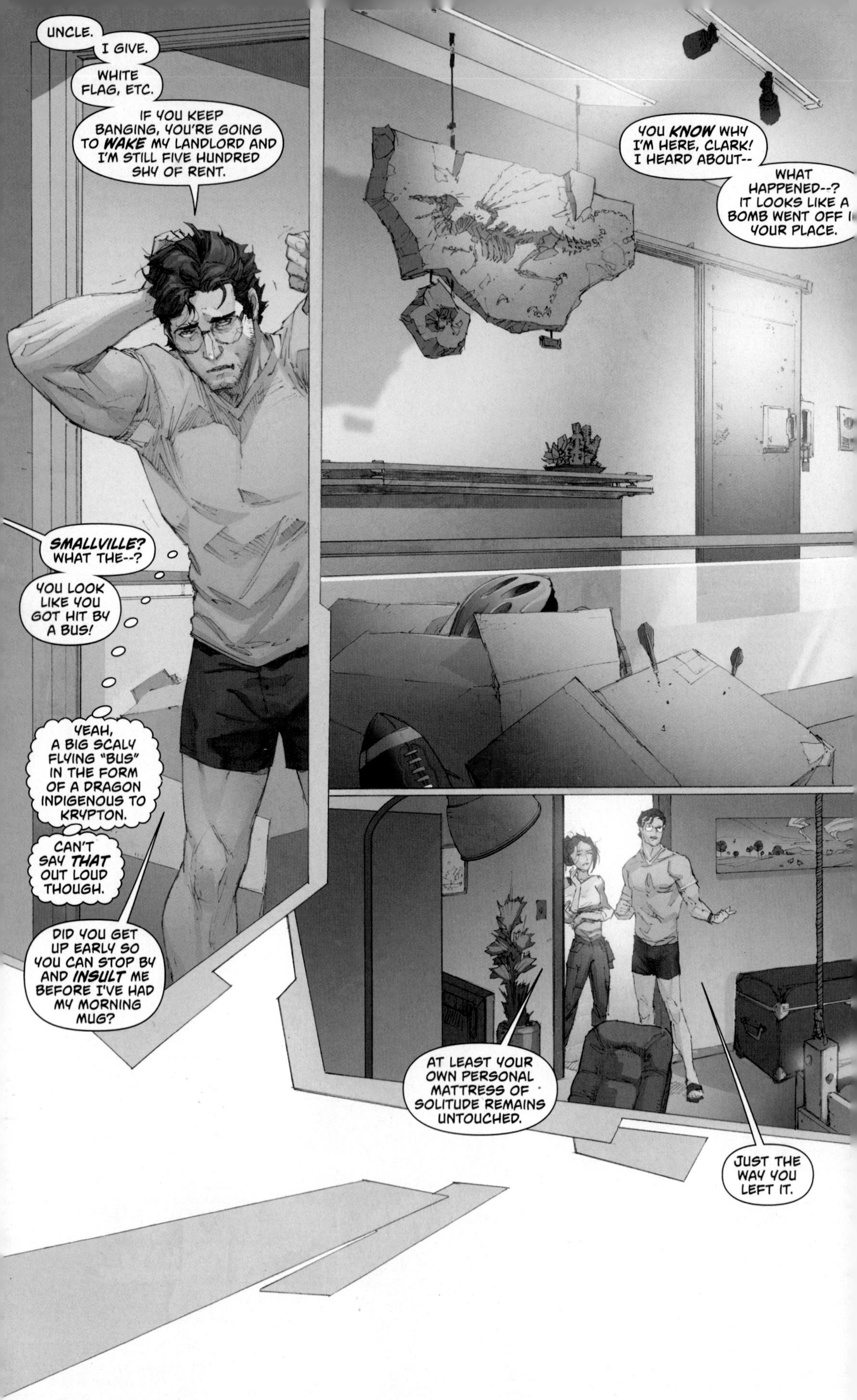
UNCLE.
I GIVE.
WHITE FLAG, ETC.
IF YOU KEEP BANGING, YOU'RE GOING TO WAKE MY LANDLORD AND I'M STILL FIVE HUNDRED SHY OF RENT.
YOU KNOW WHY I'M HERE, CLARK! I HEARD ABOUT--
WHAT HAPPENED--? IT LOOKS LIKE A BOMB WENT OFF I YOUR PLACE.
SMALLVILLE? WHAT THE--?
YOU LOOK LIKE YOU GOT HIT BY A BUS!
YEAH, A BIG SCALY FLYING "BUS" IN THE FORM OF A DRAGON INDIGENOUS TO KRYPTON.
CAN'T SAY THAT OUT LOUD THOUGH.
DID YOU GET UP EARLY SO YOU CAN STOP BY AND INSULT ME BEFORE I'VE HAD MY MORNING MUG?
AT LEAST YOUR OWN PERSONAL MATTRESS OF SOLITUDE REMAINS UNTOUCHED.
JUST THE WAY YOU LEFT IT.

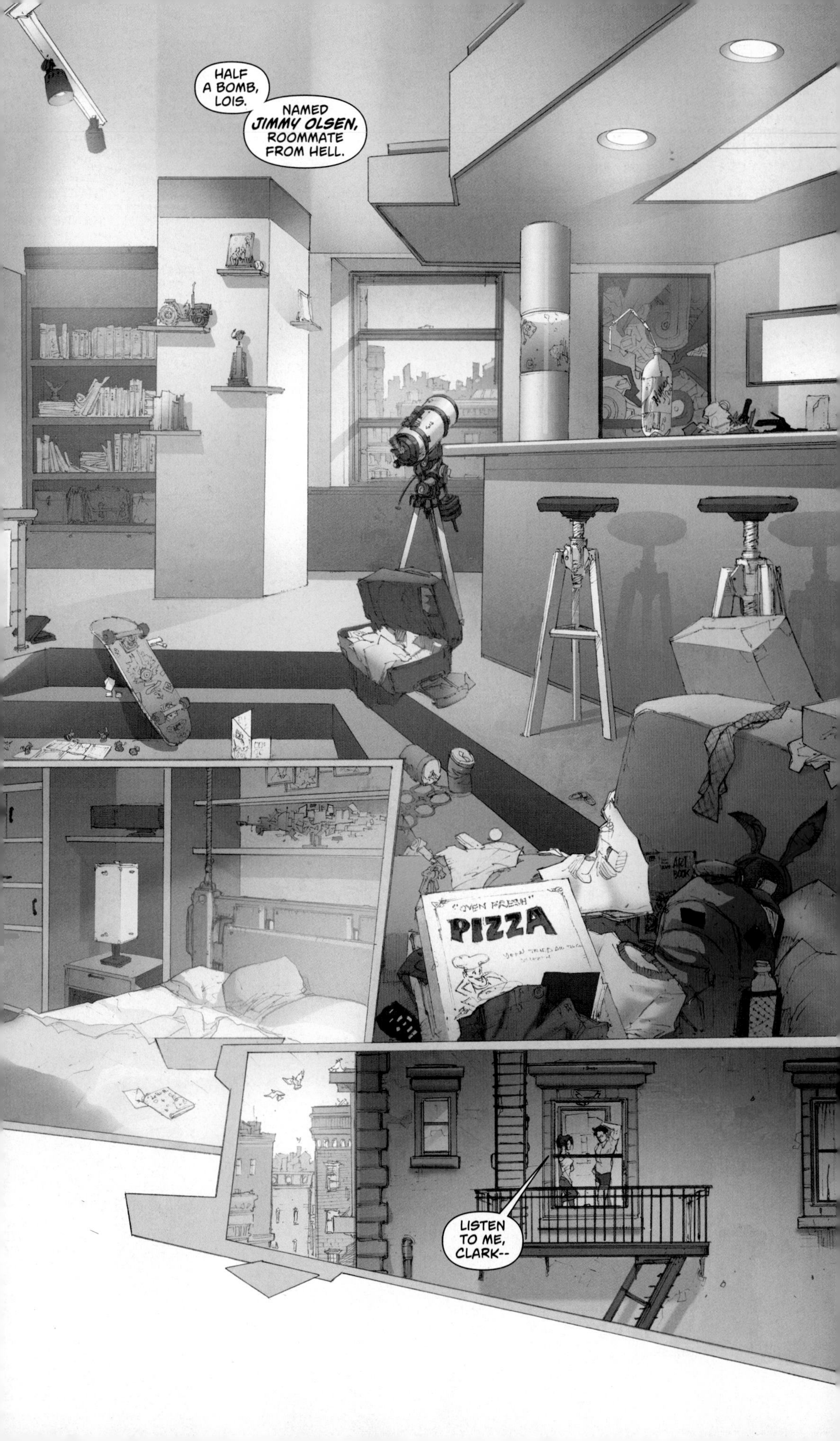
HALF A BOMB, LOIS.
NAMED JIMMY OLSEN, ROOMMATE FROM HELL.
"OVEN FRESH"
PIZZA
ART BOOK
LISTEN TO ME, CLARK--

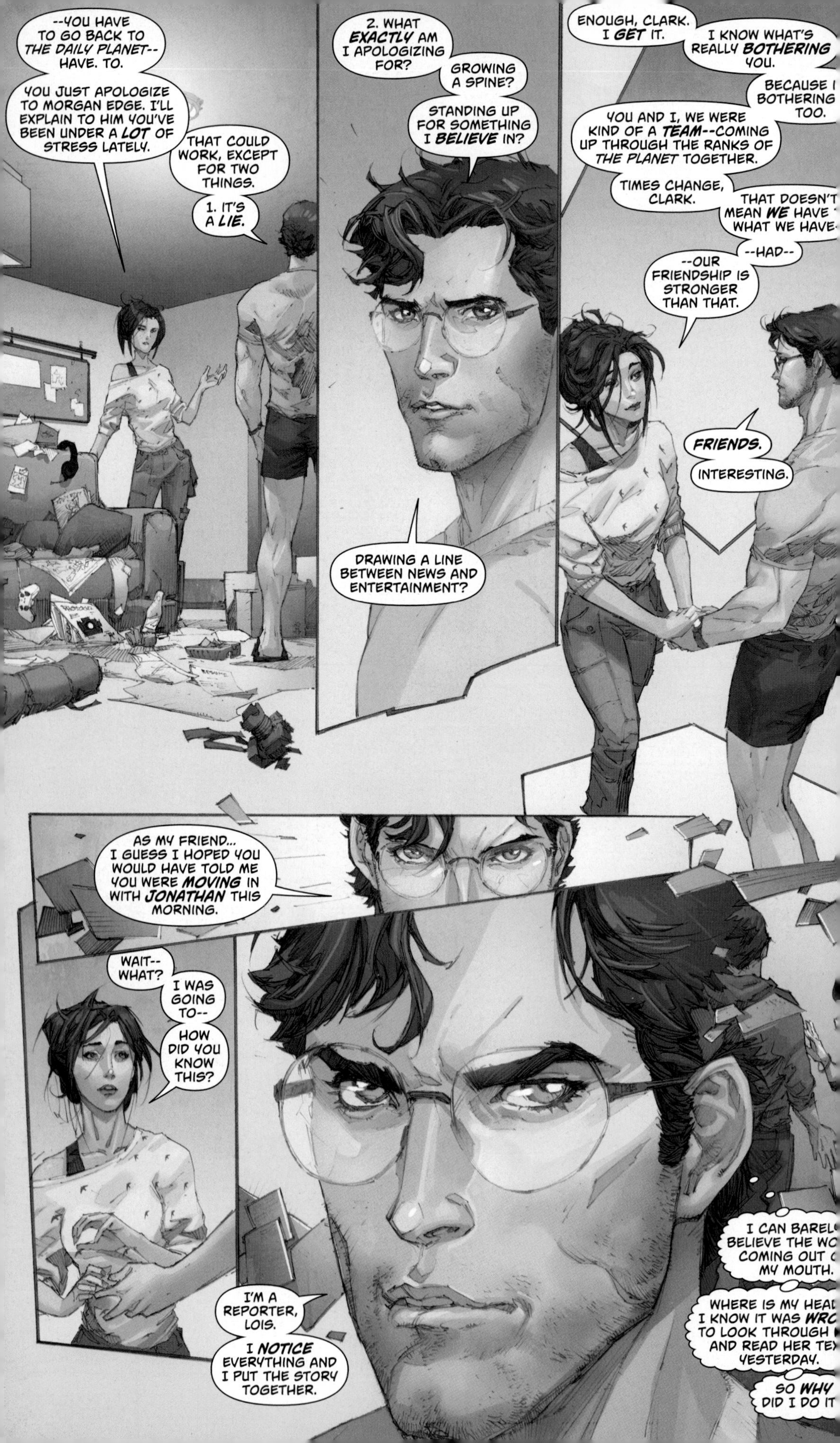
--YOU HAVE TO GO BACK TO THE DAILY PLANET-- HAVE. TO.
YOU JUST APOLOGIZE TO MORGAN EDGE. I'LL EXPLAIN TO HIM YOU'VE BEEN UNDER A LOT OF STRESS LATELY.
THAT COULD WORK, EXCEPT FOR TWO THINGS.
1. IT'S A LIE.
2. WHAT EXACTLY AM I APOLOGIZING FOR?
GROWING A SPINE?
STANDING UP FOR SOMETHING I BELIEVE IN?
DRAWING A LINE BETWEEN NEWS AND ENTERTAINMENT?
ENOUGH, CLARK. I GET IT.
I KNOW WHAT'S REALLY BOTHERING YOU.
BECAUSE I BOTHERING TOO.
YOU AND I, WE WERE KIND OF A TEAM--COMING UP THROUGH THE RANKS OF THE PLANET TOGETHER.
TIMES CHANGE, CLARK.
THAT DOESN'T MEAN WE HAVE T WHAT WE HAVE-
--HAD--
--OUR FRIENDSHIP IS STRONGER THAN THAT.
FRIENDS.
INTERESTING.
AS MY FRIEND... I GUESS I HOPED YOU WOULD HAVE TOLD ME YOU WERE MOVING IN WITH JONATHAN THIS MORNING.
WAIT-- WHAT?
I WAS GOING TO--
HOW DID YOU KNOW THIS?
I'M A REPORTER, LOIS.
I NOTICE EVERYTHING AND I PUT THE STORY TOGETHER.
I CAN BAREL BELIEVE THE WO COMING OUT O MY MOUTH.
WHERE IS MY HEAD I KNOW IT WAS WRO TO LOOK THROUGH AND READ HER TE YESTERDAY.
SO WHY DID I DO IT

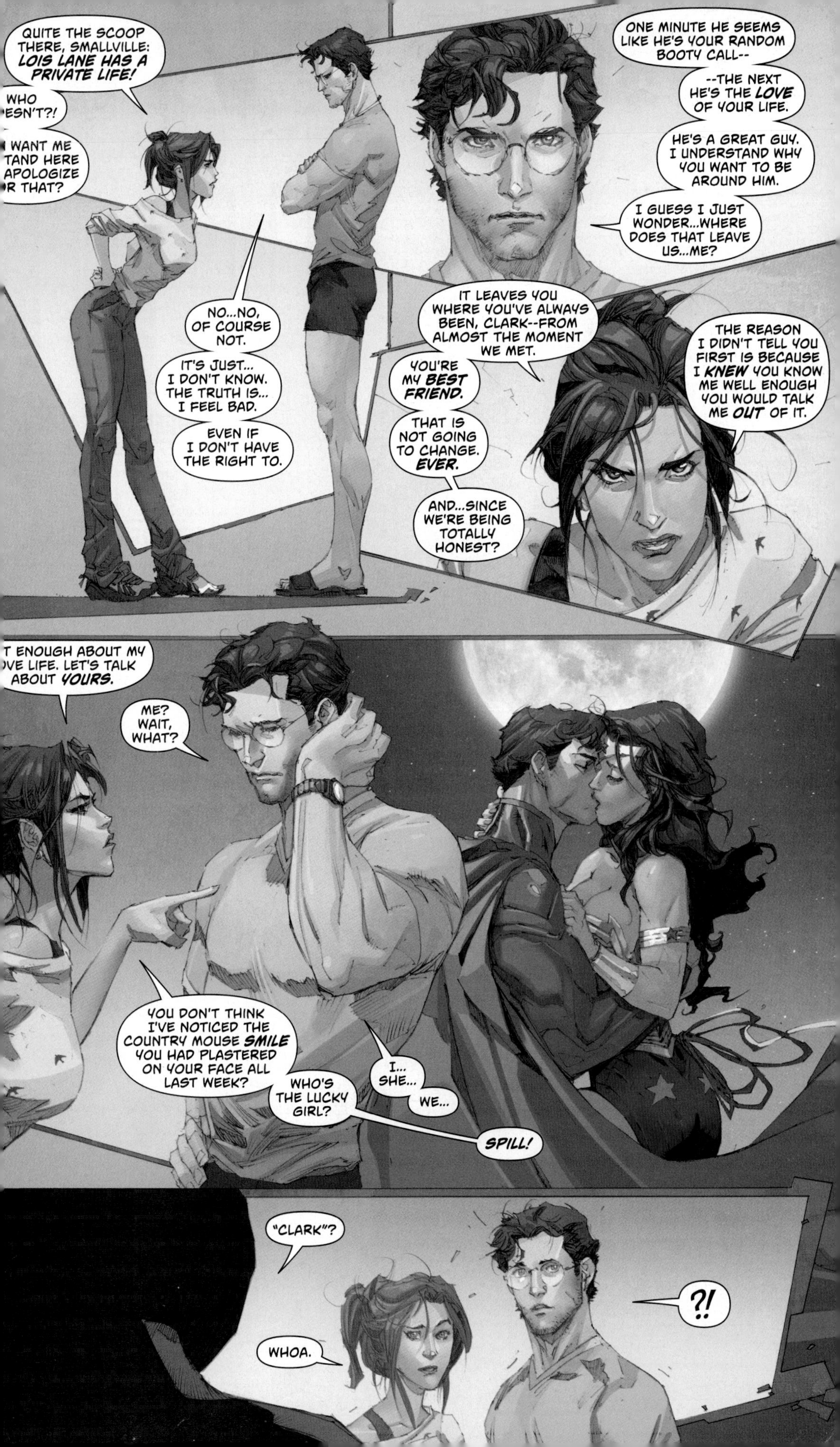
QUITE THE SCOOP THERE, SMALLVILLE: ***LOIS LANE HAS A PRIVATE LIFE!***
WHO ...ESN'T?!
...WANT ME ...TAND HERE ...APOLOGIZE ...R THAT?
ONE MINUTE HE SEEMS LIKE HE'S YOUR RANDOM BOOTY CALL--
--THE NEXT HE'S THE ***LOVE*** OF YOUR LIFE.
HE'S A GREAT GUY. I UNDERSTAND WHY YOU WANT TO BE AROUND HIM.
I GUESS I JUST WONDER...WHERE DOES THAT LEAVE US...ME?
NO...NO, OF COURSE NOT.
IT'S JUST... I DON'T KNOW. THE TRUTH IS... I FEEL BAD.
EVEN IF I DON'T HAVE THE RIGHT TO.
IT LEAVES YOU WHERE YOU'VE ALWAYS BEEN, CLARK--FROM ALMOST THE MOMENT WE MET.
YOU'RE MY ***BEST FRIEND.***
THAT IS NOT GOING TO CHANGE. ***EVER.***
AND...SINCE WE'RE BEING TOTALLY HONEST?
THE REASON I DIDN'T TELL YOU FIRST IS BECAUSE I ***KNEW*** YOU KNOW ME WELL ENOUGH YOU WOULD TALK ME ***OUT*** OF IT.
...T ENOUGH ABOUT MY ...VE LIFE. LET'S TALK ABOUT ***YOURS.***
ME? WAIT, WHAT?
YOU DON'T THINK I'VE NOTICED THE COUNTRY MOUSE ***SMILE*** YOU HAD PLASTERED ON YOUR FACE ALL LAST WEEK?
WHO'S THE LUCKY GIRL?
I... SHE...
WE...
SPILL!
"CLARK"?
?!
WHOA.

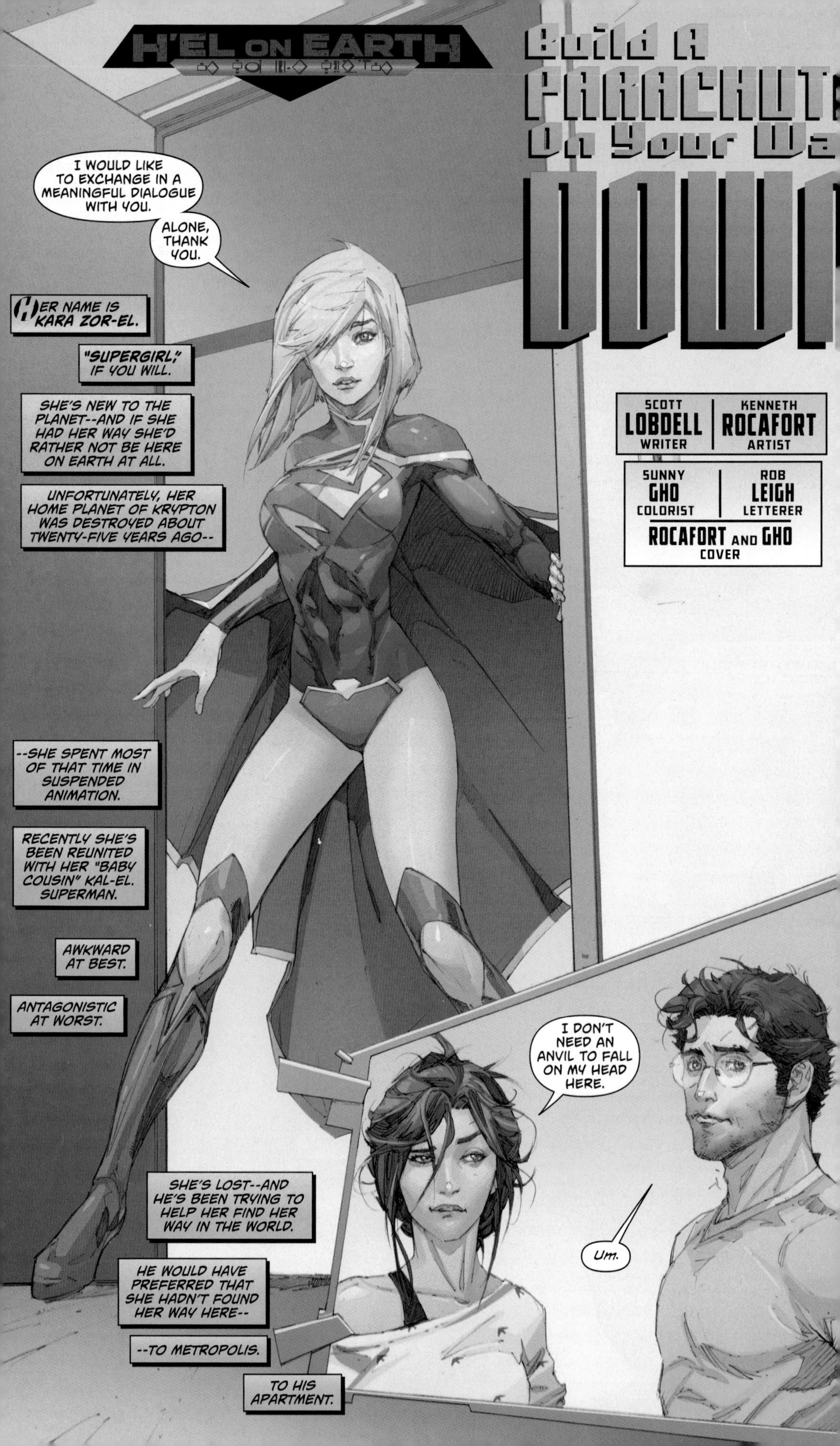
H'EL ON EARTH
Build A PARACHUTE On Your Way DOWN
I WOULD LIKE TO EXCHANGE IN A MEANINGFUL DIALOGUE WITH YOU.
ALONE, THANK YOU.
HER NAME IS KARA ZOR-EL.
"SUPERGIRL," IF YOU WILL.
SHE'S NEW TO THE PLANET--AND IF SHE HAD HER WAY SHE'D RATHER NOT BE HERE ON EARTH AT ALL.
UNFORTUNATELY, HER HOME PLANET OF KRYPTON WAS DESTROYED ABOUT TWENTY-FIVE YEARS AGO--
SCOTT LOBDELL WRITER
KENNETH ROCAFORT ARTIST
SUNNY GHO COLORIST
ROB LEIGH LETTERER
ROCAFORT AND GHO COVER
--SHE SPENT MOST OF THAT TIME IN SUSPENDED ANIMATION.
RECENTLY SHE'S BEEN REUNITED WITH HER "BABY COUSIN" KAL-EL. SUPERMAN.
AWKWARD AT BEST.
ANTAGONISTIC AT WORST.
I DON'T NEED AN ANVIL TO FALL ON MY HEAD HERE.
SHE'S LOST--AND HE'S BEEN TRYING TO HELP HER FIND HER WAY IN THE WORLD.
Um.
HE WOULD HAVE PREFERRED THAT SHE HADN'T FOUND HER WAY HERE--
--TO METROPOLIS.
TO HIS APARTMENT.

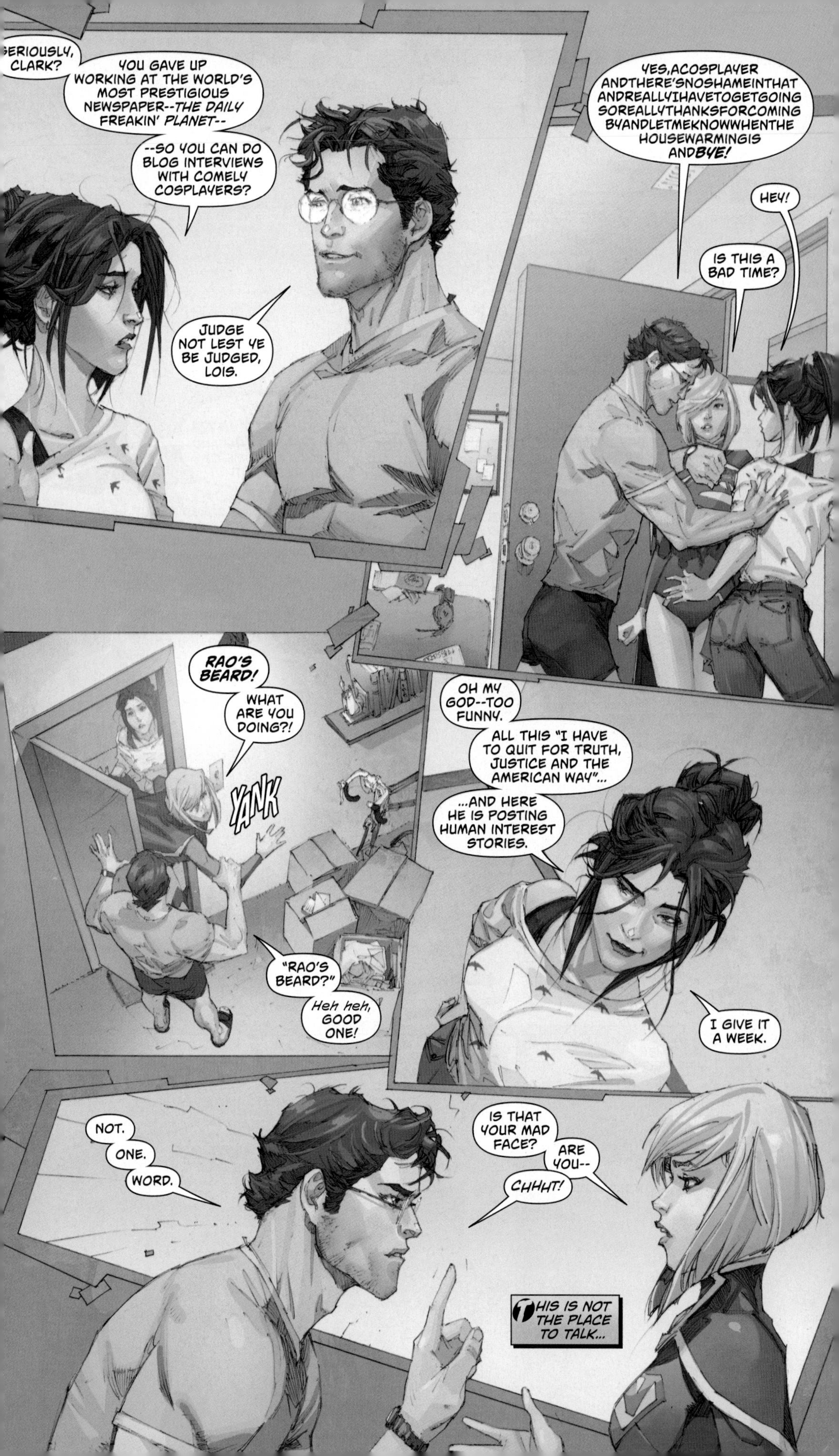

SERIOUSLY, CLARK?
YOU GAVE UP WORKING AT THE WORLD'S MOST PRESTIGIOUS NEWSPAPER--*THE DAILY* FREAKIN' *PLANET*--
--SO YOU CAN DO BLOG INTERVIEWS WITH COMELY COSPLAYERS?
JUDGE NOT LEST YE BE JUDGED, LOIS.
YES,ACOSPLAYER ANDTHERE'SNOSHAMEINTHAT ANDREALLYIHAVETOGETGOING SOREALLYTHANKSFORCOMING BYANDLETMEKNOWWHENTHE HOUSEWARMINGIS AND**BYE!**
HEY!
IS THIS A BAD TIME?
RAO'S BEARD!
WHAT ARE YOU DOING?!
YANK
"RAO'S BEARD?"
Heh heh, GOOD ONE!
OH MY GOD--TOO FUNNY.
ALL THIS "I HAVE TO QUIT FOR TRUTH, JUSTICE AND THE AMERICAN WAY"...
...AND HERE HE IS POSTING HUMAN INTEREST STORIES.
I GIVE IT A WEEK.
NOT.
ONE.
WORD.
IS THAT YOUR MAD FACE?
ARE YOU--
CHHHT!
THIS IS NOT THE PLACE TO TALK...

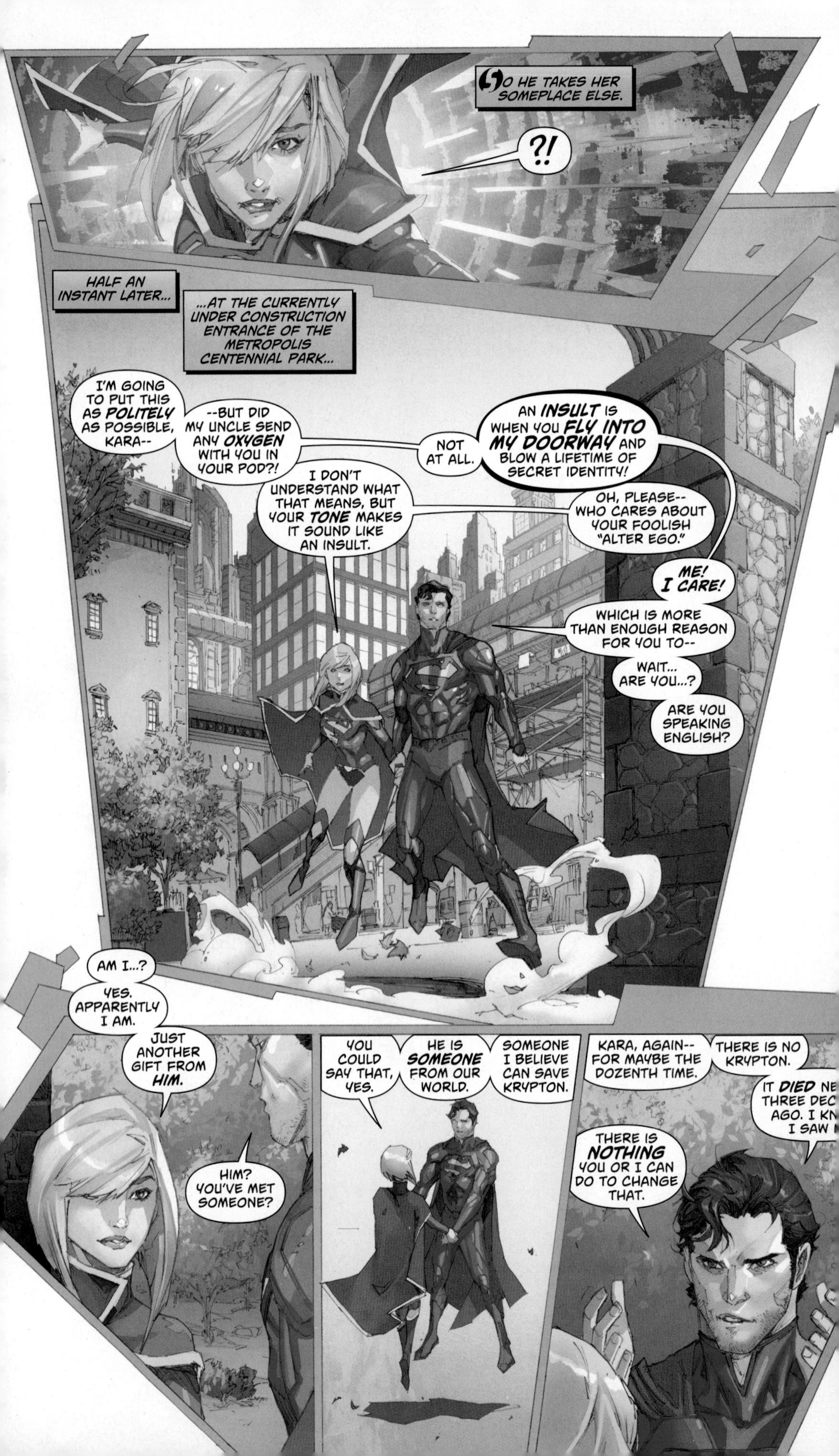

SO HE TAKES HER SOMEPLACE ELSE.
?!
HALF AN INSTANT LATER...
...AT THE CURRENTLY UNDER CONSTRUCTION ENTRANCE OF THE METROPOLIS CENTENNIAL PARK...
I'M GOING TO PUT THIS AS POLITELY AS POSSIBLE, KARA--
--BUT DID MY UNCLE SEND ANY OXYGEN WITH YOU IN YOUR POD?!
I DON'T UNDERSTAND WHAT THAT MEANS, BUT YOUR TONE MAKES IT SOUND LIKE AN INSULT.
NOT AT ALL.
AN INSULT IS WHEN YOU FLY INTO MY DOORWAY AND BLOW A LIFETIME OF SECRET IDENTITY!
OH, PLEASE-- WHO CARES ABOUT YOUR FOOLISH "ALTER EGO."
ME! I CARE!
WHICH IS MORE THAN ENOUGH REASON FOR YOU TO--
WAIT... ARE YOU...?
ARE YOU SPEAKING ENGLISH?
AM I...?
YES. APPARENTLY I AM.
JUST ANOTHER GIFT FROM HIM.
HIM? YOU'VE MET SOMEONE?
YOU COULD SAY THAT, YES.
HE IS SOMEONE FROM OUR WORLD.
SOMEONE I BELIEVE CAN SAVE KRYPTON.
KARA, AGAIN-- FOR MAYBE THE DOZENTH TIME.
THERE IS NO KRYPTON.
THERE IS NOTHING YOU OR I CAN DO TO CHANGE THAT.

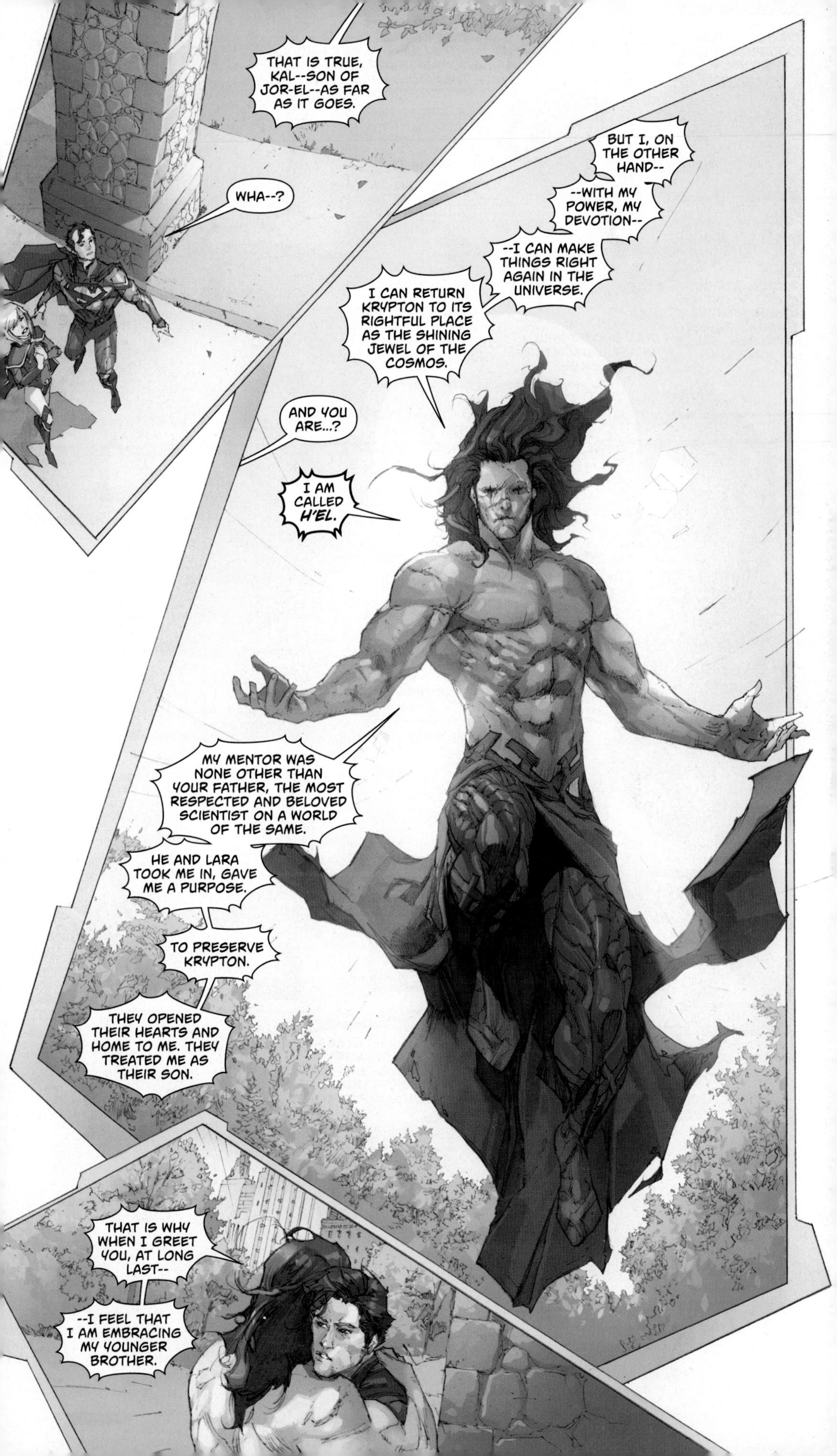
THAT IS TRUE, KAL--SON OF JOR-EL--AS FAR AS IT GOES.
WHA--?
BUT I, ON THE OTHER HAND--
--WITH MY POWER, MY DEVOTION--
--I CAN MAKE THINGS RIGHT AGAIN IN THE UNIVERSE.
I CAN RETURN KRYPTON TO ITS RIGHTFUL PLACE AS THE SHINING JEWEL OF THE COSMOS.
AND YOU ARE...?
I AM CALLED *H'EL.*
MY MENTOR WAS NONE OTHER THAN YOUR FATHER, THE MOST RESPECTED AND BELOVED SCIENTIST ON A WORLD OF THE SAME.
HE AND LARA TOOK ME IN, GAVE ME A PURPOSE.
TO PRESERVE KRYPTON.
THEY OPENED THEIR HEARTS AND HOME TO ME. THEY TREATED ME AS THEIR SON.
THAT IS WHY WHEN I GREET YOU, AT LONG LAST--
--I FEEL THAT I AM EMBRACING MY YOUNGER BROTHER.

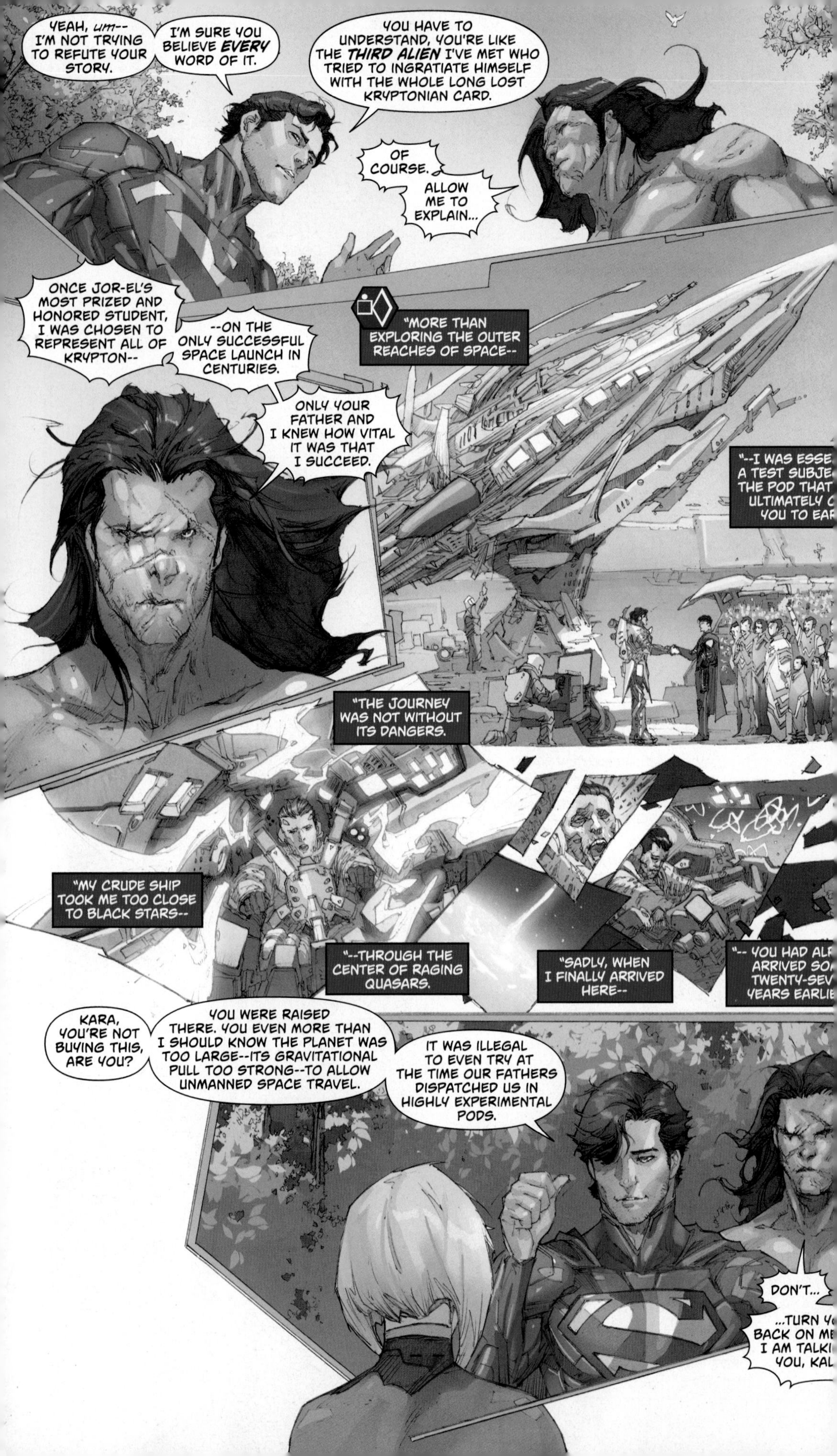
YEAH, um-- I'M NOT TRYING TO REFUTE YOUR STORY.
I'M SURE YOU BELIEVE EVERY WORD OF IT.
YOU HAVE TO UNDERSTAND, YOU'RE LIKE THE THIRD ALIEN I'VE MET WHO TRIED TO INGRATIATE HIMSELF WITH THE WHOLE LONG LOST KRYPTONIAN CARD.
OF COURSE.
ALLOW ME TO EXPLAIN...
ONCE JOR-EL'S MOST PRIZED AND HONORED STUDENT, I WAS CHOSEN TO REPRESENT ALL OF KRYPTON--
--ON THE ONLY SUCCESSFUL SPACE LAUNCH IN CENTURIES.
ONLY YOUR FATHER AND I KNEW HOW VITAL IT WAS THAT I SUCCEED.
"MORE THAN EXPLORING THE OUTER REACHES OF SPACE--
"THE JOURNEY WAS NOT WITHOUT ITS DANGERS.
"MY CRUDE SHIP TOOK ME TOO CLOSE TO BLACK STARS--
"--THROUGH THE CENTER OF RAGING QUASARS.
"SADLY, WHEN I FINALLY ARRIVED HERE--
KARA, YOU'RE NOT BUYING THIS, ARE YOU?
YOU WERE RAISED THERE. YOU EVEN MORE THAN I SHOULD KNOW THE PLANET WAS TOO LARGE--ITS GRAVITATIONAL PULL TOO STRONG--TO ALLOW UNMANNED SPACE TRAVEL.
IT WAS ILLEGAL TO EVEN TRY AT THE TIME OUR FATHERS DISPATCHED US IN HIGHLY EXPERIMENTAL PODS.
DON'T...

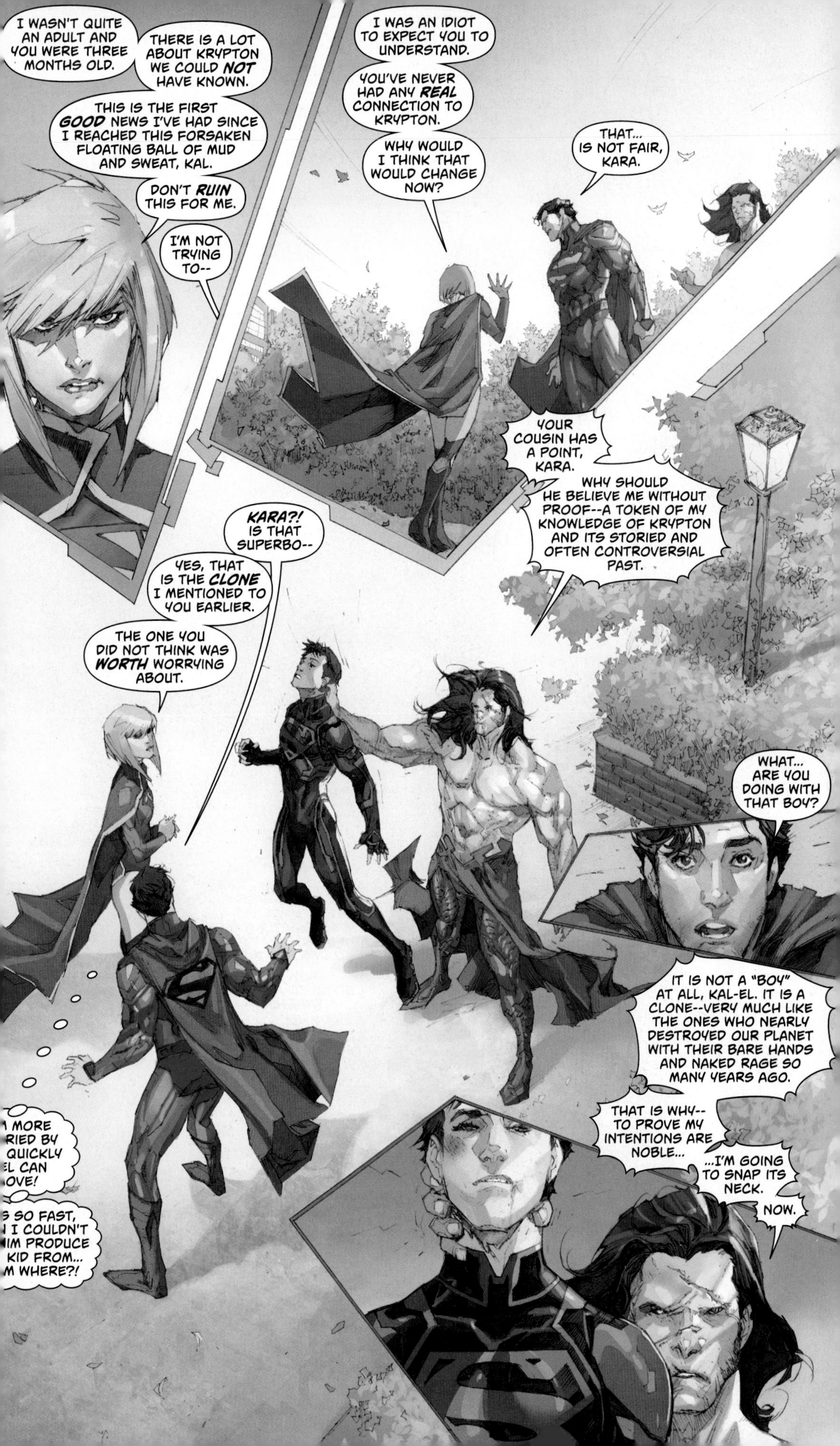
I WASN'T QUITE AN ADULT AND YOU WERE THREE MONTHS OLD.
THERE IS A LOT ABOUT KRYPTON WE COULD NOT HAVE KNOWN.
THIS IS THE FIRST GOOD NEWS I'VE HAD SINCE I REACHED THIS FORSAKEN FLOATING BALL OF MUD AND SWEAT, KAL.
DON'T RUIN THIS FOR ME.
I'M NOT TRYING TO--
I WAS AN IDIOT TO EXPECT YOU TO UNDERSTAND.
YOU'VE NEVER HAD ANY REAL CONNECTION TO KRYPTON.
WHY WOULD I THINK THAT WOULD CHANGE NOW?
THAT... IS NOT FAIR, KARA.
YOUR COUSIN HAS A POINT, KARA.
WHY SHOULD HE BELIEVE ME WITHOUT PROOF--A TOKEN OF MY KNOWLEDGE OF KRYPTON AND ITS STORIED AND OFTEN CONTROVERSIAL PAST.
KARA?! IS THAT SUPERBO--
YES, THAT IS THE CLONE I MENTIONED TO YOU EARLIER.
THE ONE YOU DID NOT THINK WAS WORTH WORRYING ABOUT.
MORE
RIED BY
QUICKLY
EL CAN
OVE!
S SO FAST,
I COULDN'T
IM PRODUCE
KID FROM...
M WHERE?!
WHAT... ARE YOU DOING WITH THAT BOY?
IT IS NOT A "BOY" AT ALL, KAL-EL. IT IS A CLONE--VERY MUCH LIKE THE ONES WHO NEARLY DESTROYED OUR PLANET WITH THEIR BARE HANDS AND NAKED RAGE SO MANY YEARS AGO.
THAT IS WHY-- TO PROVE MY INTENTIONS ARE NOBLE...
...I'M GOING TO SNAP ITS NECK.
NOW.

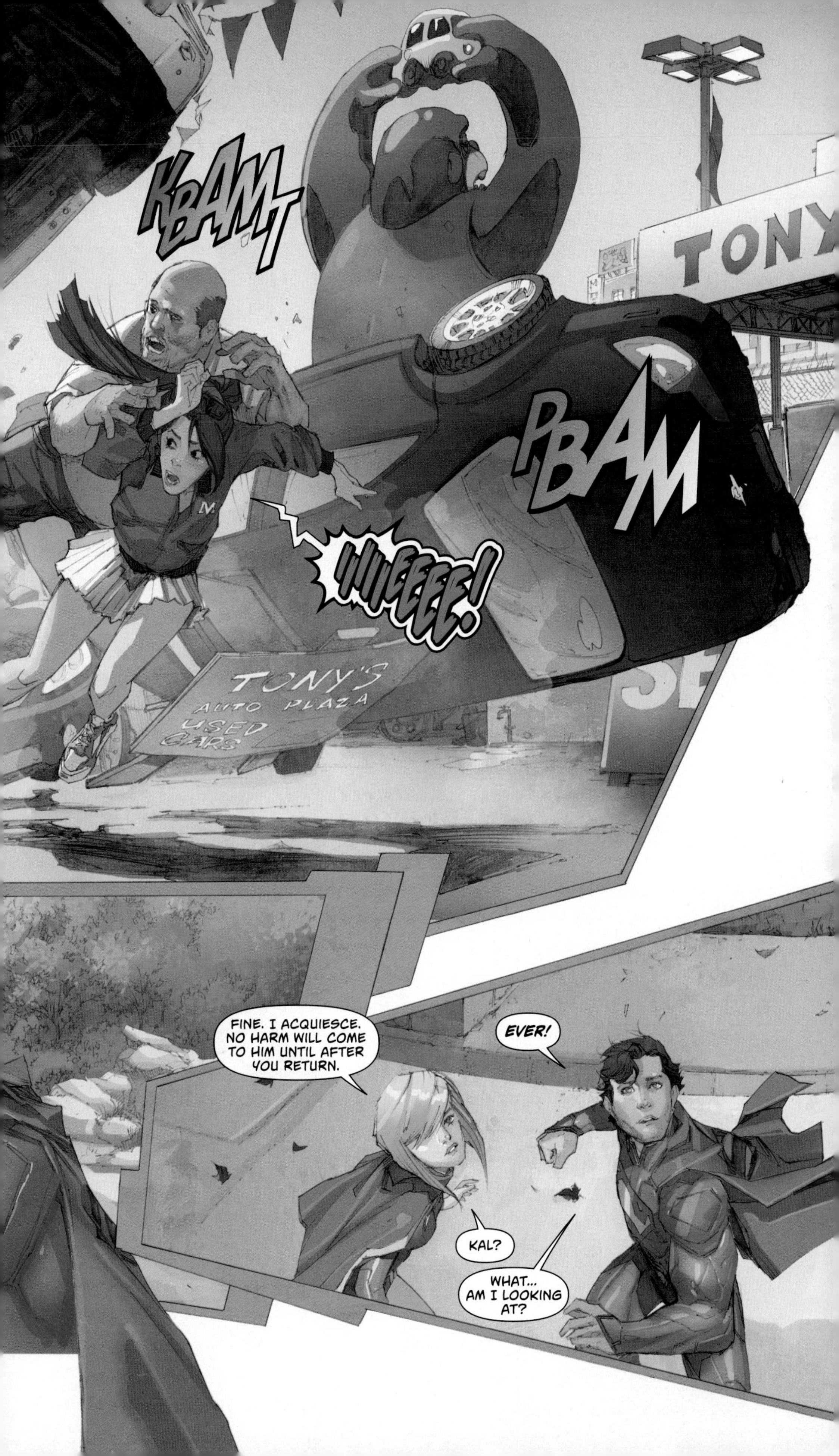
KBAM
PBAM
WWEEEE!
TONY
TONY'S
AUTO PLAZA
USED
CARS
FINE. I ACQUIESCE. NO HARM WILL COME TO HIM UNTIL AFTER YOU RETURN.
EVER!
KAL?
WHAT... AM I LOOKING AT?

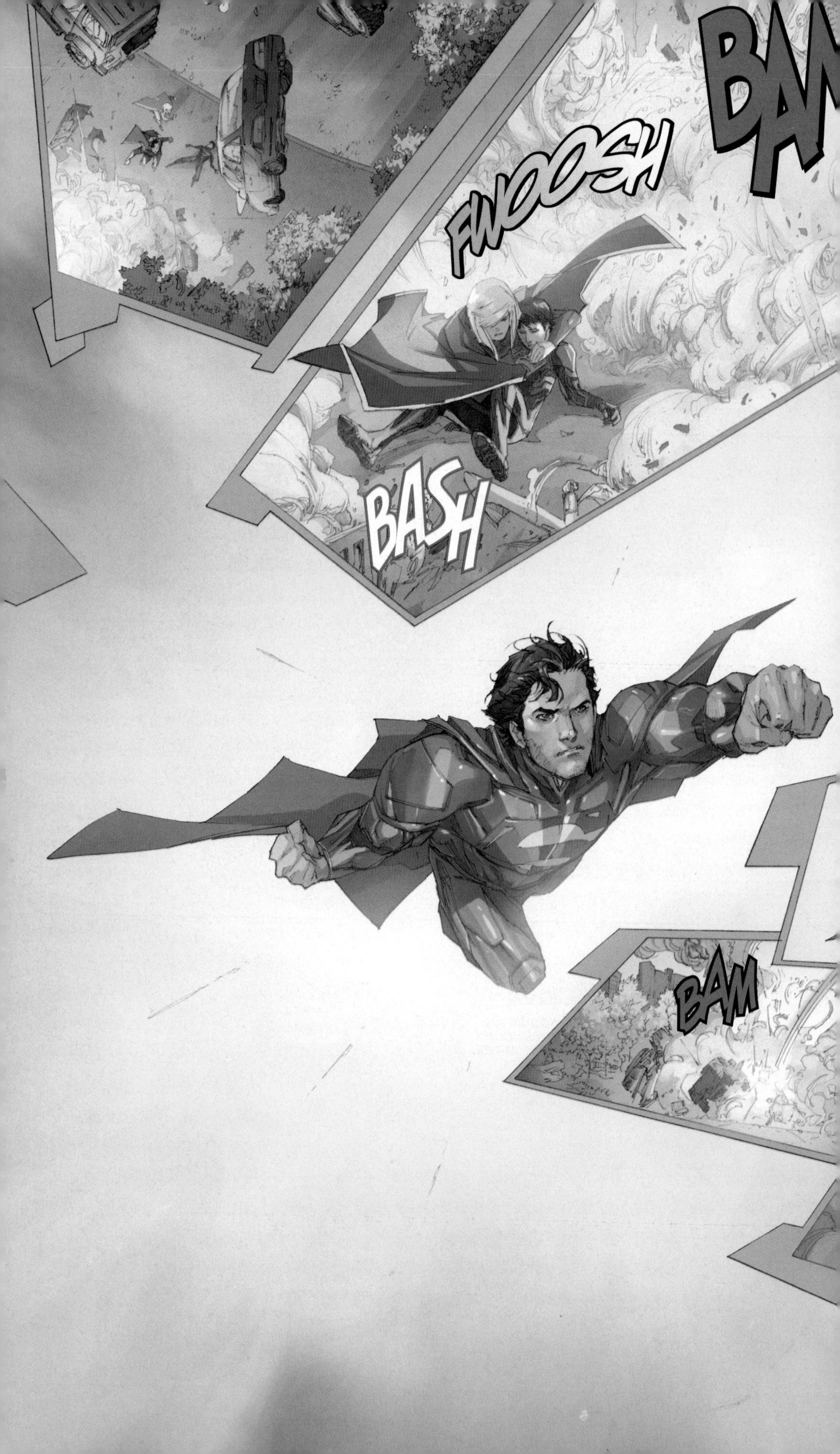
FWOOSH
BASH
BAM

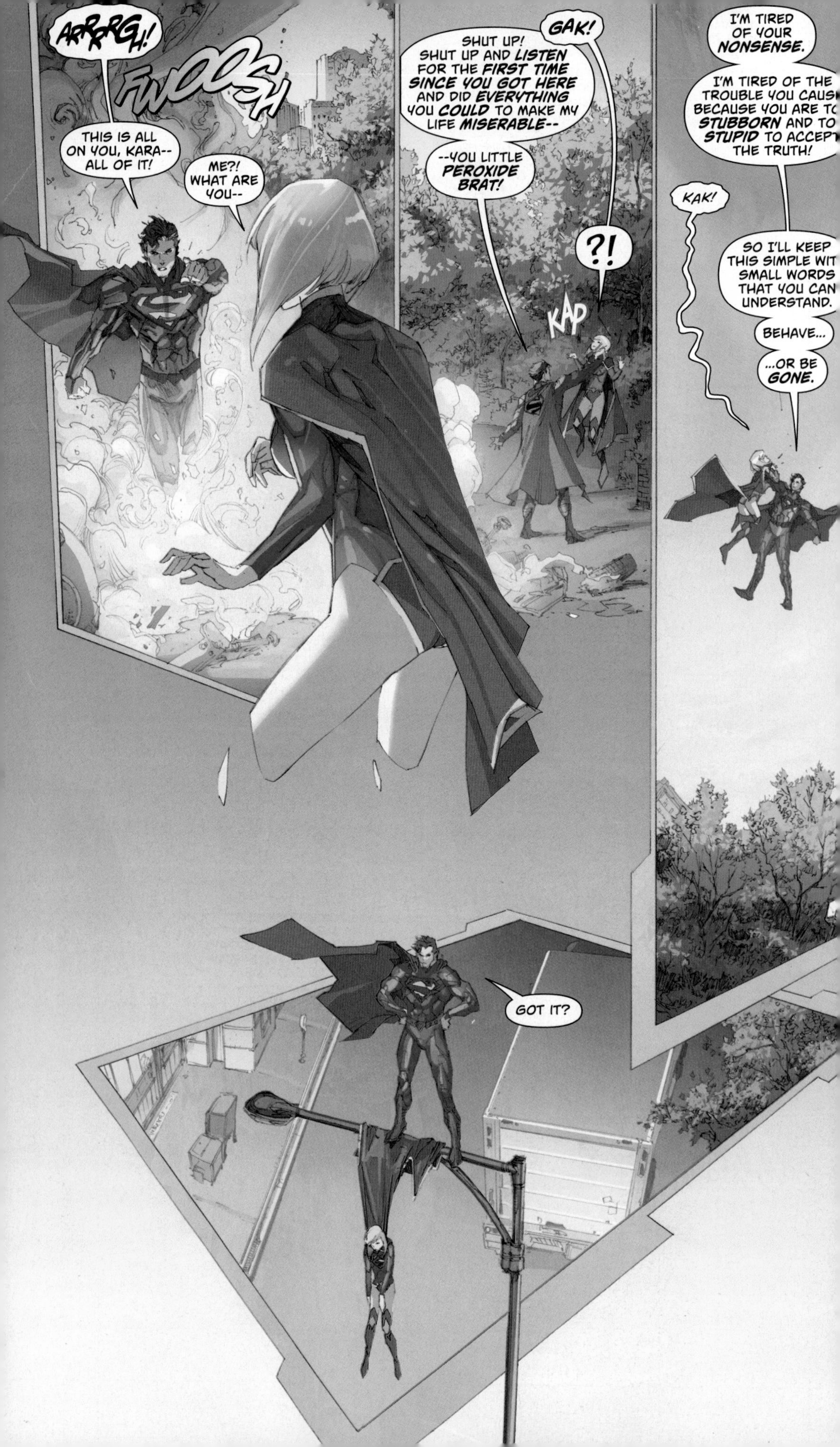

ARRRRGH!
FWOOSH
THIS IS ALL ON YOU, KARA-- ALL OF IT!
ME?! WHAT ARE YOU--
GAK!
SHUT UP! SHUT UP AND LISTEN FOR THE FIRST TIME SINCE YOU GOT HERE AND DID EVERYTHING YOU COULD TO MAKE MY LIFE MISERABLE--
--YOU LITTLE PEROXIDE BRAT!
?!
KAP
I'M TIRED OF YOUR NONSENSE.
I'M TIRED OF THE TROUBLE YOU CAUS BECAUSE YOU ARE TO STUBBORN AND TO STUPID TO ACCEPT THE TRUTH!
KAK!
SO I'LL KEEP THIS SIMPLE WIT SMALL WORDS THAT YOU CAN UNDERSTAND.
BEHAVE...
...OR BE GONE.
GOT IT?

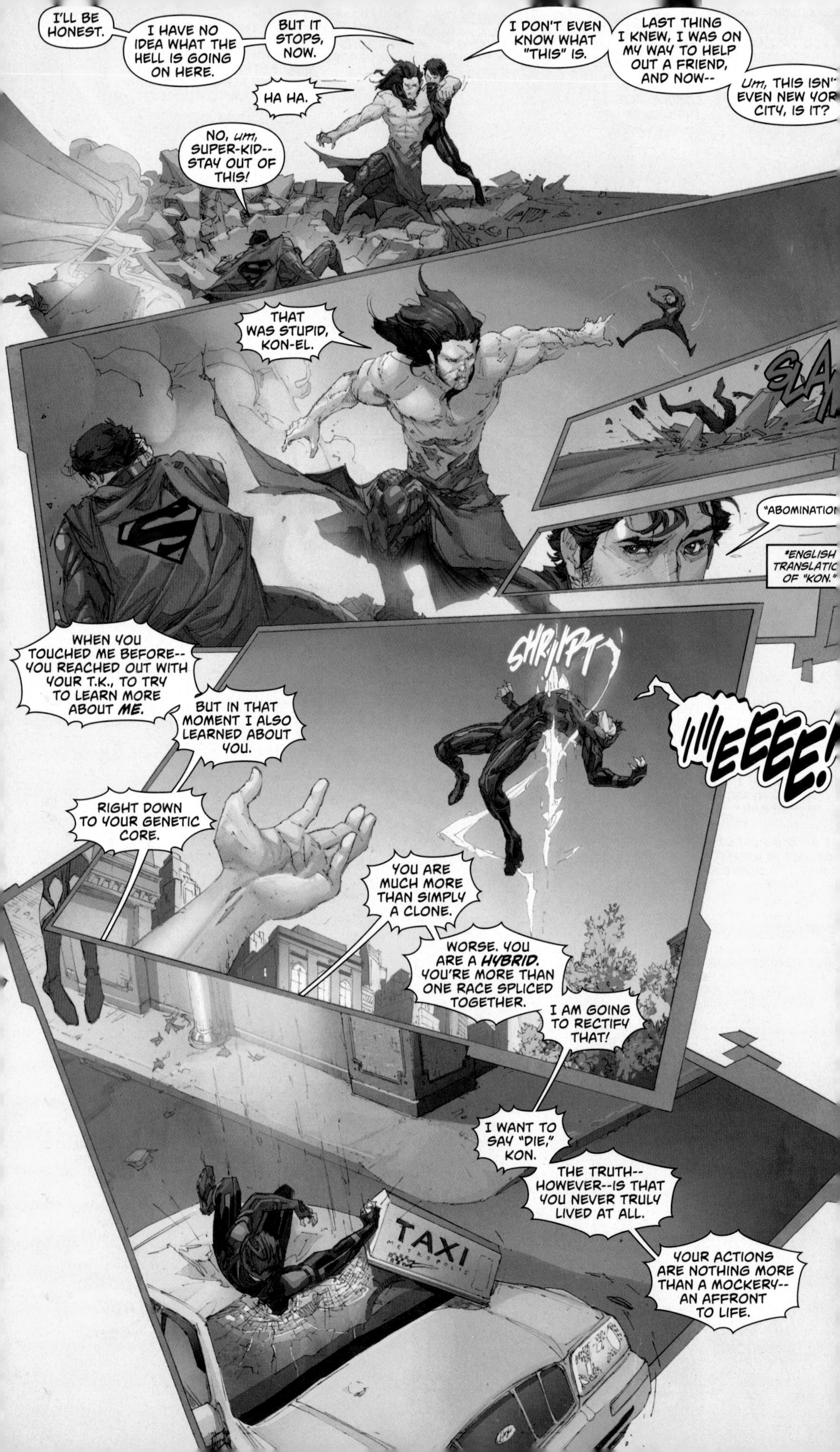
I'LL BE HONEST.
I HAVE NO IDEA WHAT THE HELL IS GOING ON HERE.
BUT IT STOPS, NOW.
HA HA.
NO, *um*, SUPER-KID-- STAY OUT OF THIS!
I DON'T EVEN KNOW WHAT "THIS" IS.
LAST THING I KNEW, I WAS ON MY WAY TO HELP OUT A FRIEND, AND NOW--
Um, THIS ISN' EVEN NEW YOR CITY, IS IT?
THAT WAS STUPID, KON-EL.
SLA
"ABOMINATION
*ENGLISH TRANSLATIC OF "KON."
WHEN YOU TOUCHED ME BEFORE-- YOU REACHED OUT WITH YOUR T.K., TO TRY TO LEARN MORE ABOUT *ME*.
BUT IN THAT MOMENT I ALSO LEARNED ABOUT YOU.
SHRIIPT
EEEE!
RIGHT DOWN TO YOUR GENETIC CORE.
YOU ARE MUCH MORE THAN SIMPLY A CLONE.
WORSE. YOU ARE A *HYBRID*. YOU'RE MORE THAN ONE RACE SPLICED TOGETHER.
I AM GOING TO RECTIFY THAT!
I WANT TO SAY "DIE," KON.
THE TRUTH-- HOWEVER--IS THAT YOU NEVER TRULY LIVED AT ALL.
TAXI
YOUR ACTIONS ARE NOTHING MORE THAN A MOCKERY-- AN AFFRONT TO LIFE.

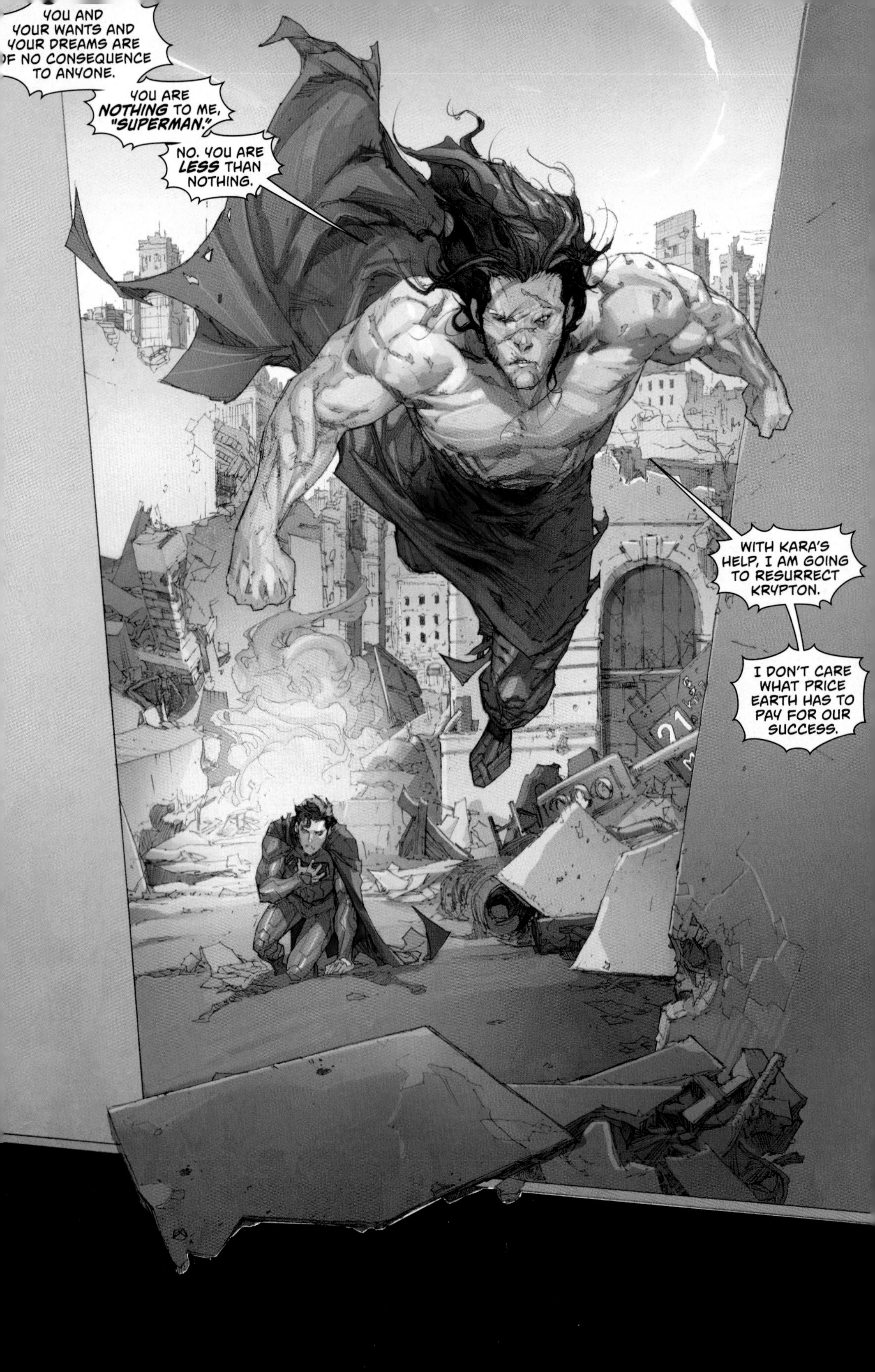

YOU AND YOUR WANTS AND YOUR DREAMS ARE OF NO CONSEQUENCE TO ANYONE.
YOU ARE NOTHING TO ME, "SUPERMAN."
NO. YOU ARE LESS THAN NOTHING.
WITH KARA'S HELP, I AM GOING TO RESURRECT KRYPTON.
I DON'T CARE WHAT PRICE EARTH HAS TO PAY FOR OUR SUCCESS.

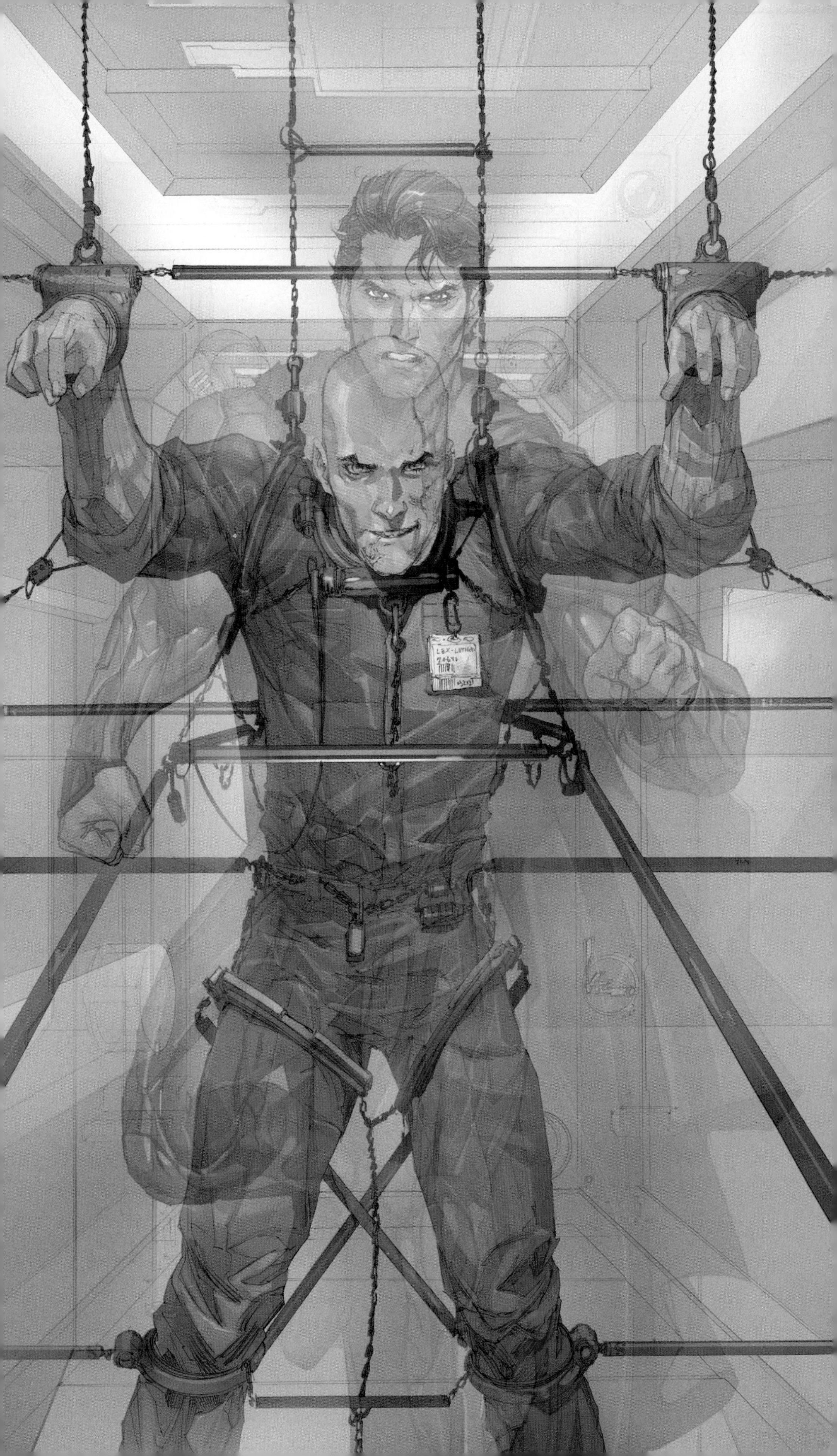

LEX-LUTHOR

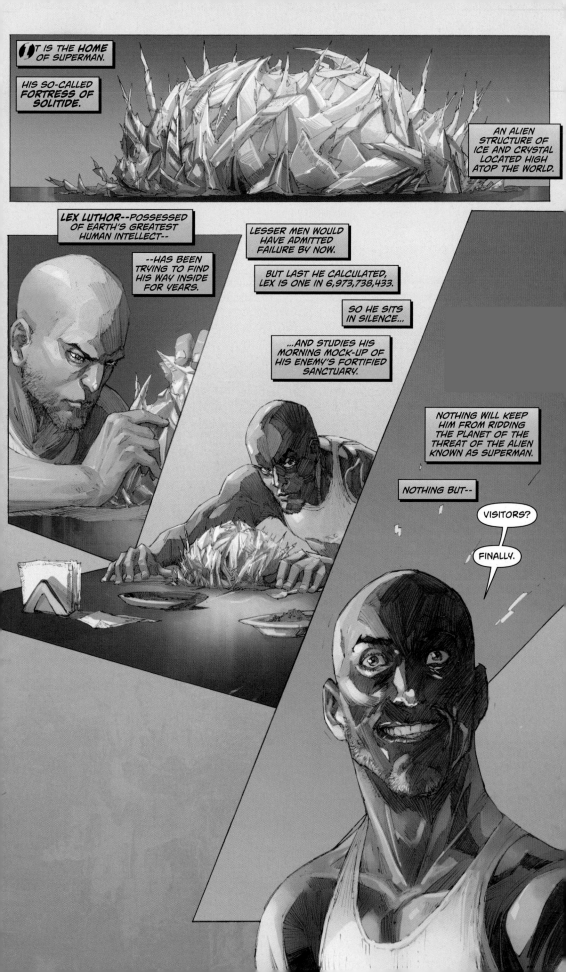

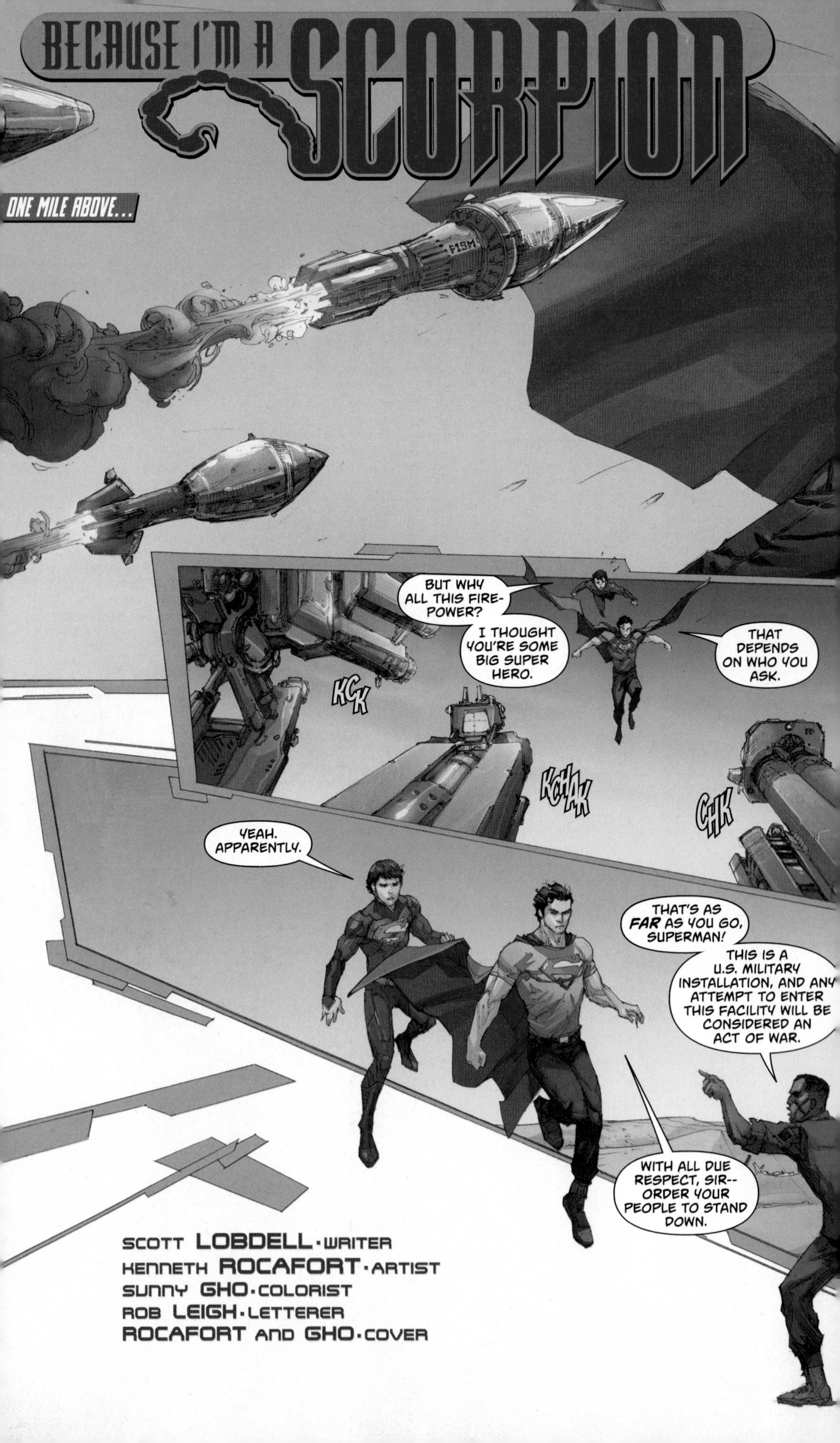
BECAUSE I'M A SCORPION
ONE MILE ABOVE...
BUT WHY ALL THIS FIRE-POWER?
I THOUGHT YOU'RE SOME BIG SUPER HERO.
THAT DEPENDS ON WHO YOU ASK.
KCK
KCHAK
CHK
YEAH. APPARENTLY.
THAT'S AS FAR AS YOU GO, SUPERMAN!
THIS IS A U.S. MILITARY INSTALLATION, AND ANY ATTEMPT TO ENTER THIS FACILITY WILL BE CONSIDERED AN ACT OF WAR.
WITH ALL DUE RESPECT, SIR-- ORDER YOUR PEOPLE TO STAND DOWN.
SCOTT LOBDELL · WRITER
KENNETH ROCAFORT · ARTIST
SUNNY GHO · COLORIST
ROB LEIGH · LETTERER
ROCAFORT AND GHO · COVER

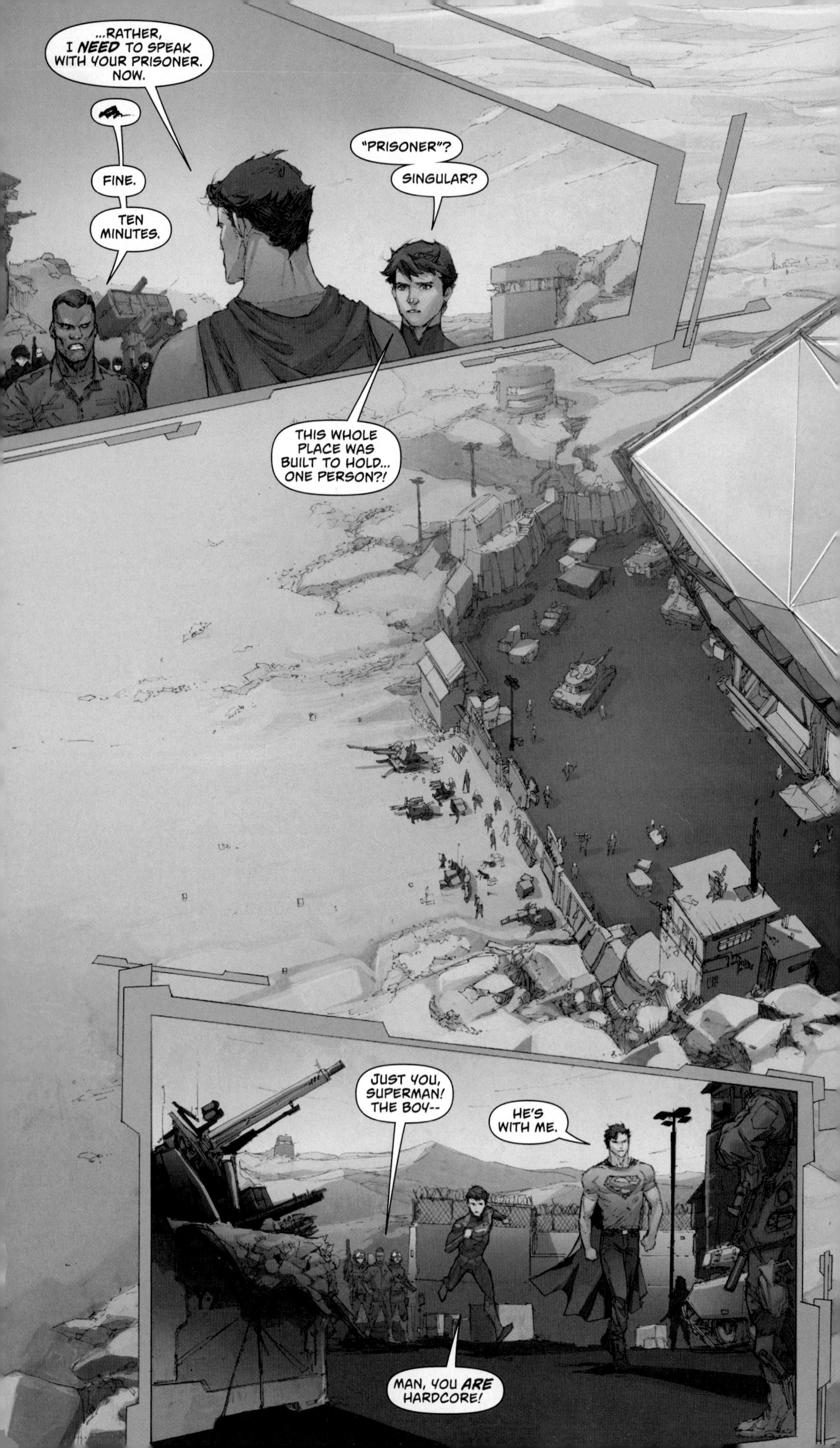

...RATHER, I NEED TO SPEAK WITH YOUR PRISONER. NOW.
FINE.
TEN MINUTES.
"PRISONER"?
SINGULAR?
THIS WHOLE PLACE WAS BUILT TO HOLD... ONE PERSON?!
JUST YOU, SUPERMAN! THE BOY--
HE'S WITH ME.
MAN, YOU ARE HARDCORE!

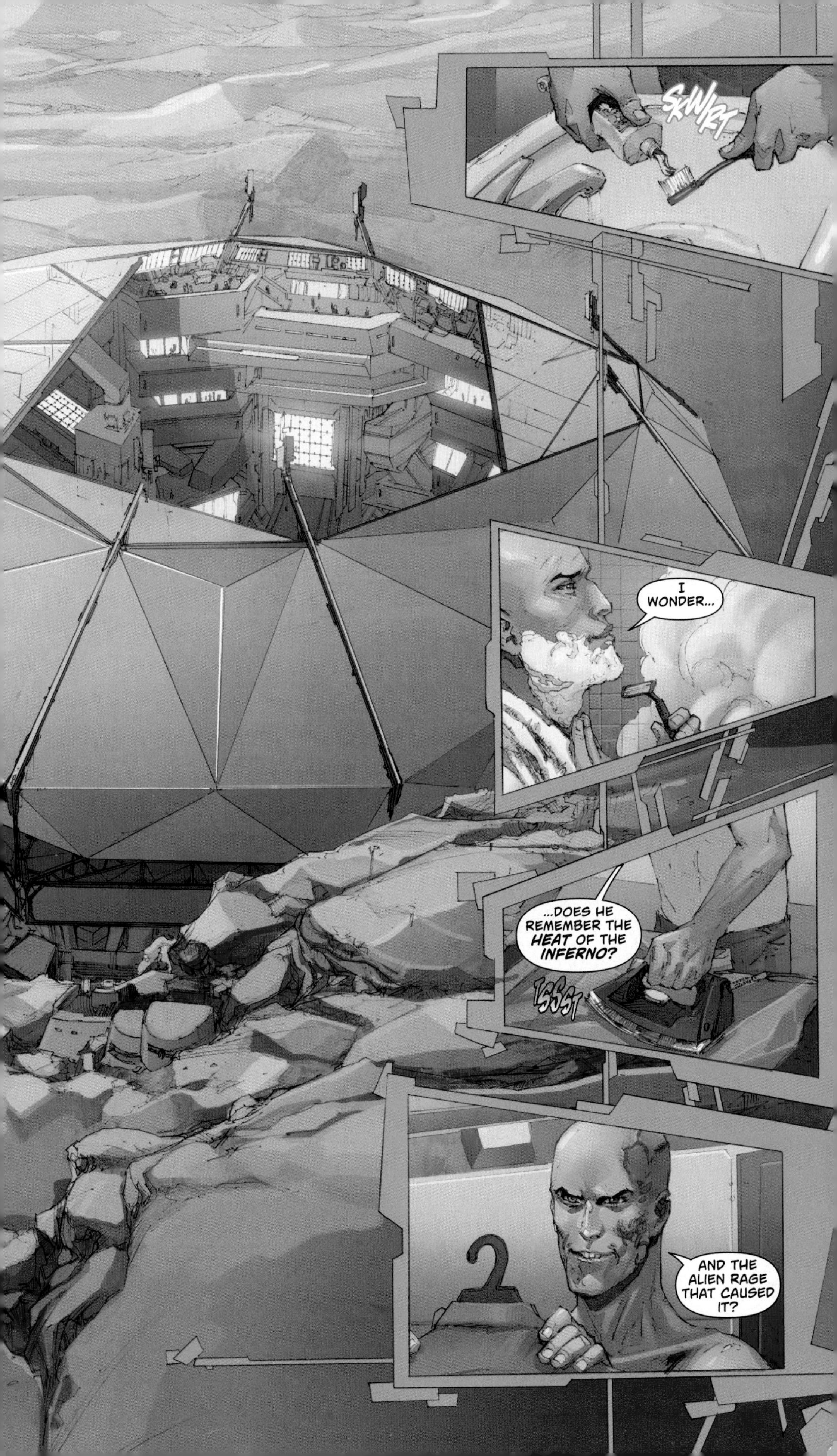
SKWIRT
I WONDER...
...DOES HE REMEMBER THE HEAT OF THE INFERNO?
TSSST
AND THE ALIEN RAGE THAT CAUSED IT?

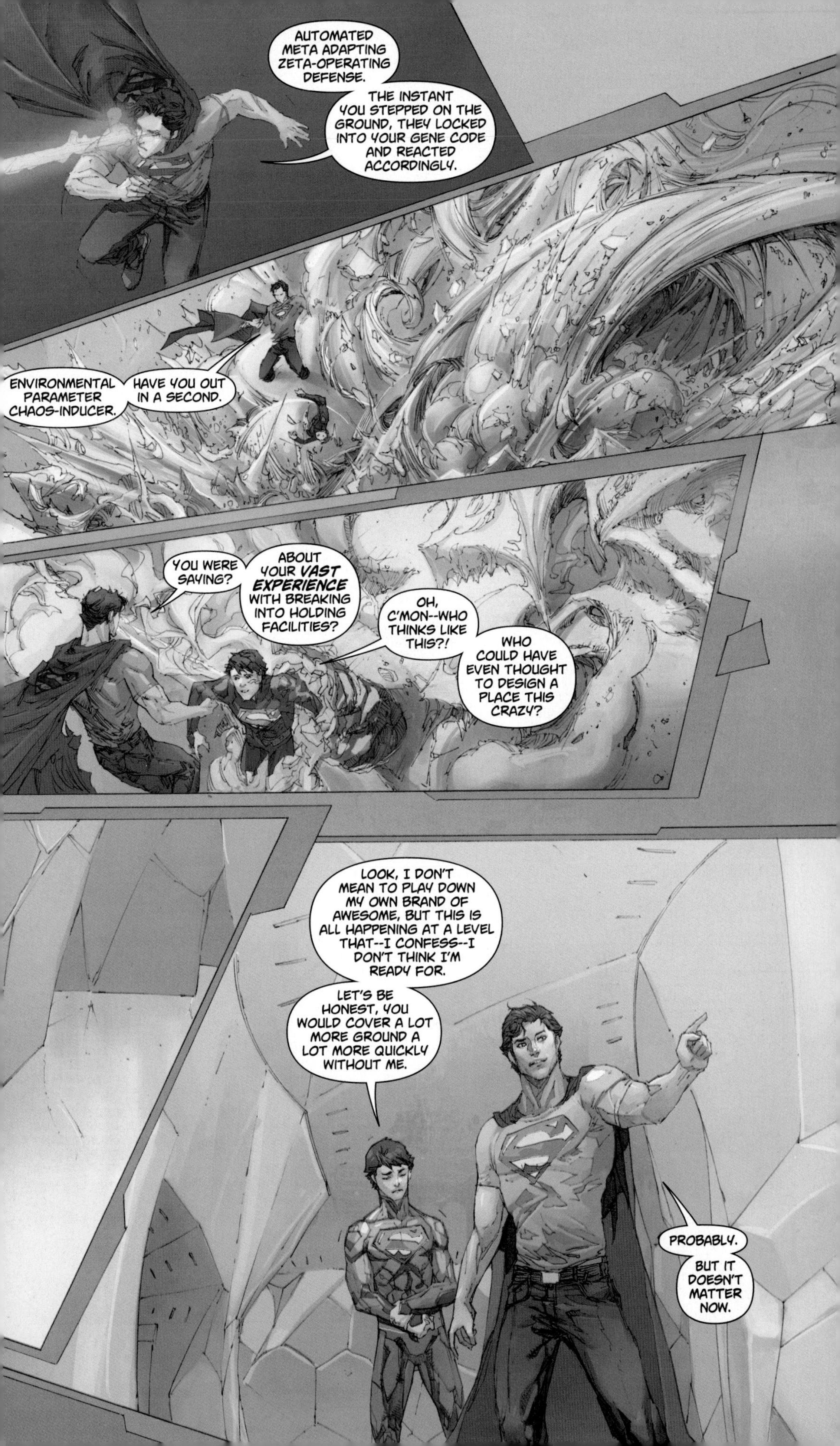
AUTOMATED META ADAPTING ZETA-OPERATING DEFENSE.
THE INSTANT YOU STEPPED ON THE GROUND, THEY LOCKED INTO YOUR GENE CODE AND REACTED ACCORDINGLY.
ENVIRONMENTAL PARAMETER CHAOS-INDUCER.
HAVE YOU OUT IN A SECOND.
YOU WERE SAYING?
ABOUT YOUR ***VAST EXPERIENCE*** WITH BREAKING INTO HOLDING FACILITIES?
OH, C'MON--WHO THINKS LIKE THIS?!
WHO COULD HAVE EVEN THOUGHT TO DESIGN A PLACE THIS CRAZY?
LOOK, I DON'T MEAN TO PLAY DOWN MY OWN BRAND OF AWESOME, BUT THIS IS ALL HAPPENING AT A LEVEL THAT--I CONFESS--I DON'T THINK I'M READY FOR.
LET'S BE HONEST, YOU WOULD COVER A LOT MORE GROUND A LOT MORE QUICKLY WITHOUT ME.
PROBABLY.
BUT IT DOESN'T MATTER NOW.

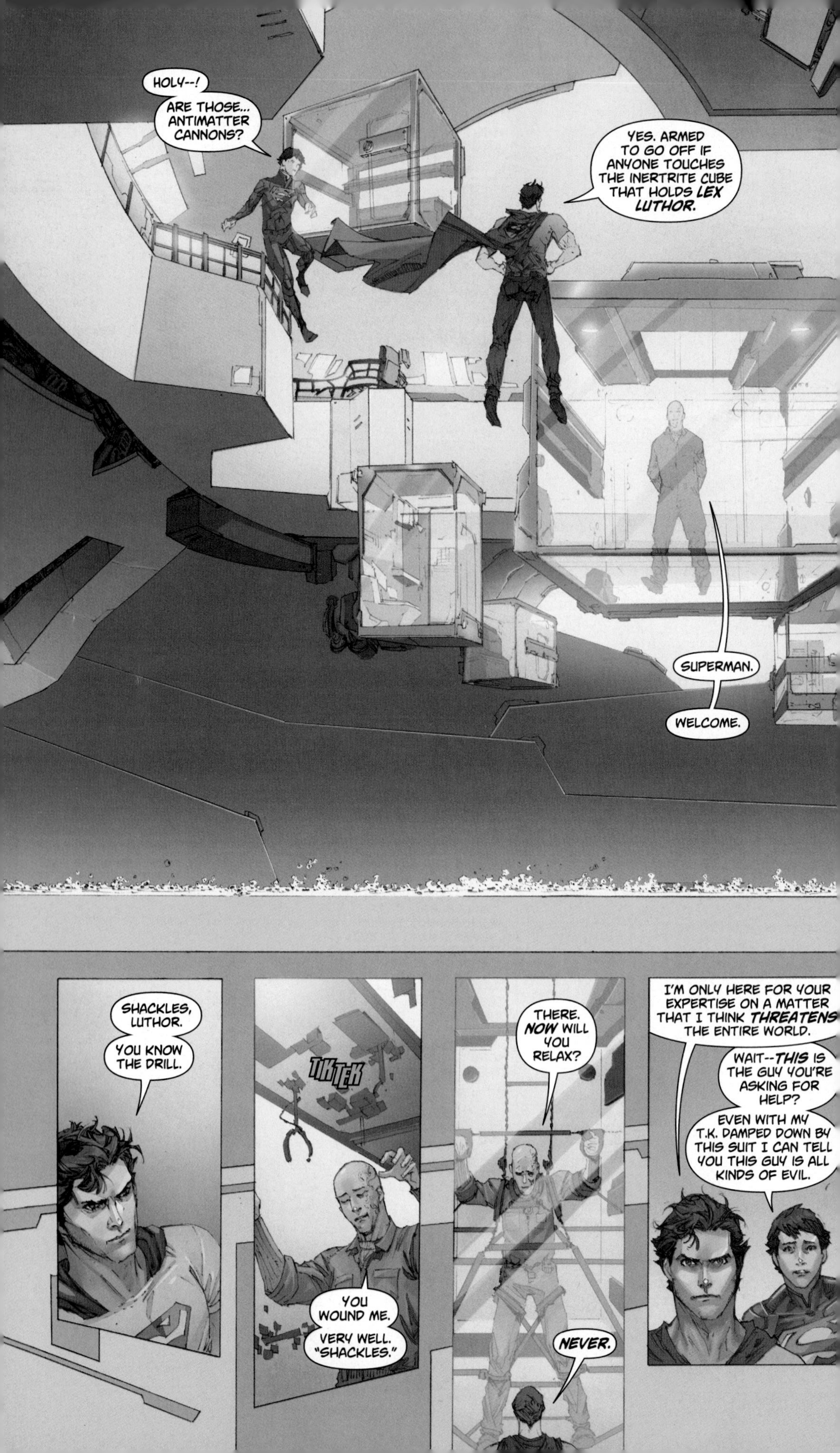
HOLY--!
ARE THOSE... ANTIMATTER CANNONS?
YES. ARMED TO GO OFF IF ANYONE TOUCHES THE INERTRITE CUBE THAT HOLDS *LEX LUTHOR.*
SUPERMAN.
WELCOME.
SHACKLES, LUTHOR.
YOU KNOW THE DRILL.
TIKTEK
YOU WOUND ME.
VERY WELL. "SHACKLES."
THERE. *NOW* WILL YOU RELAX?
NEVER.
I'M ONLY HERE FOR YOUR EXPERTISE ON A MATTER THAT I THINK *THREATENS* THE ENTIRE WORLD.
WAIT--*THIS* IS THE GUY YOU'RE ASKING FOR HELP?
EVEN WITH MY T.K. DAMPED DOWN BY THIS SUIT I CAN TELL YOU THIS GUY IS ALL KINDS OF EVIL.

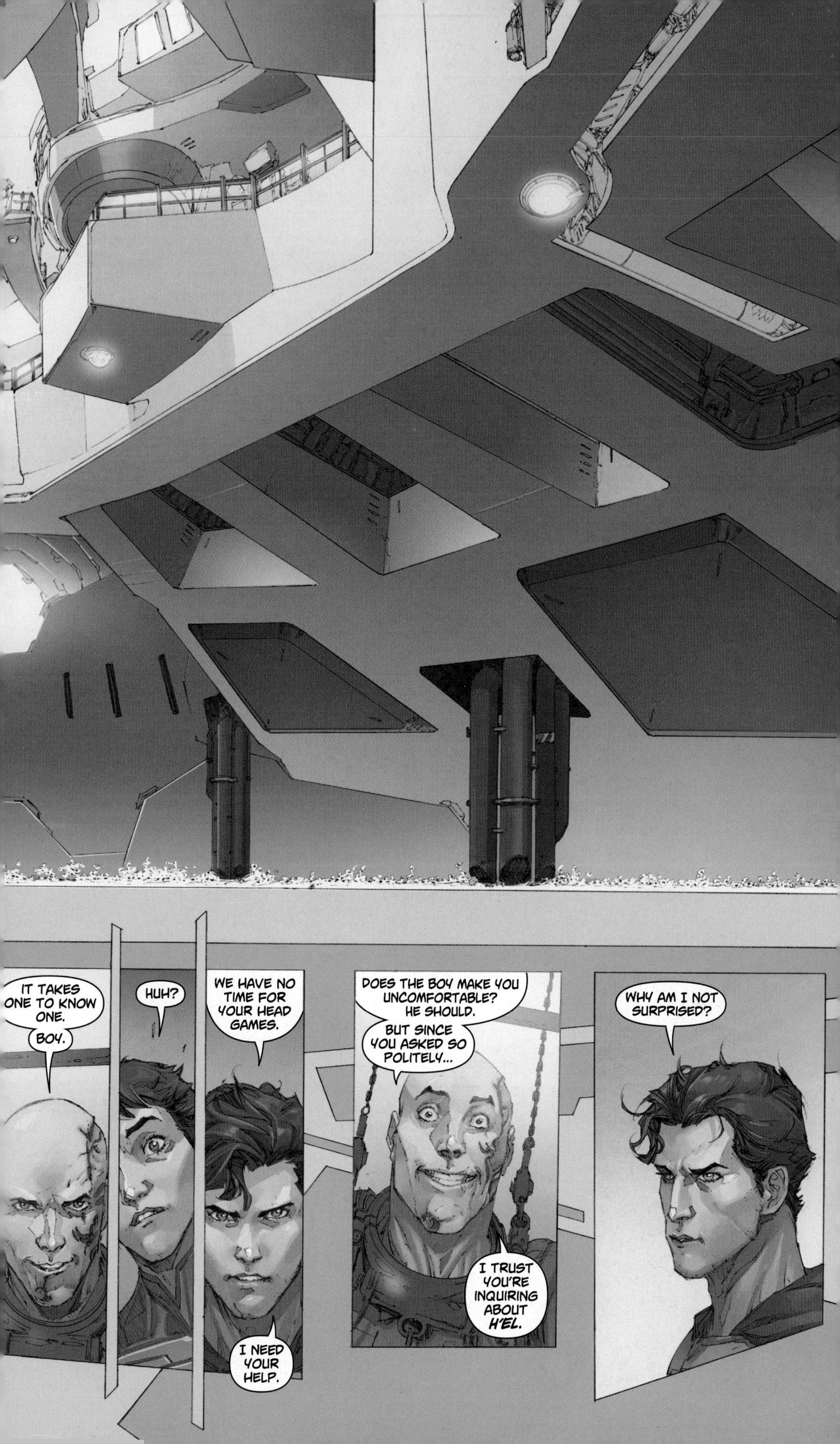

IT TAKES ONE TO KNOW ONE.
BOY.
HUH?
WE HAVE NO TIME FOR YOUR HEAD GAMES.
I NEED YOUR HELP.
DOES THE BOY MAKE YOU UNCOMFORTABLE? HE SHOULD.
BUT SINCE YOU ASKED SO POLITELY...
I TRUST YOU'RE INQUIRING ABOUT H'EL.
WHY AM I NOT SURPRISED?

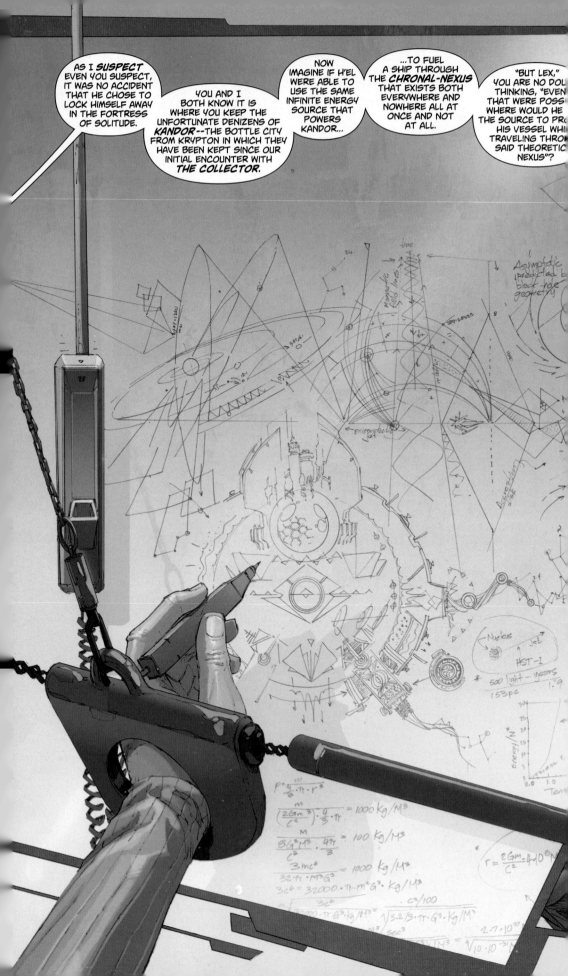

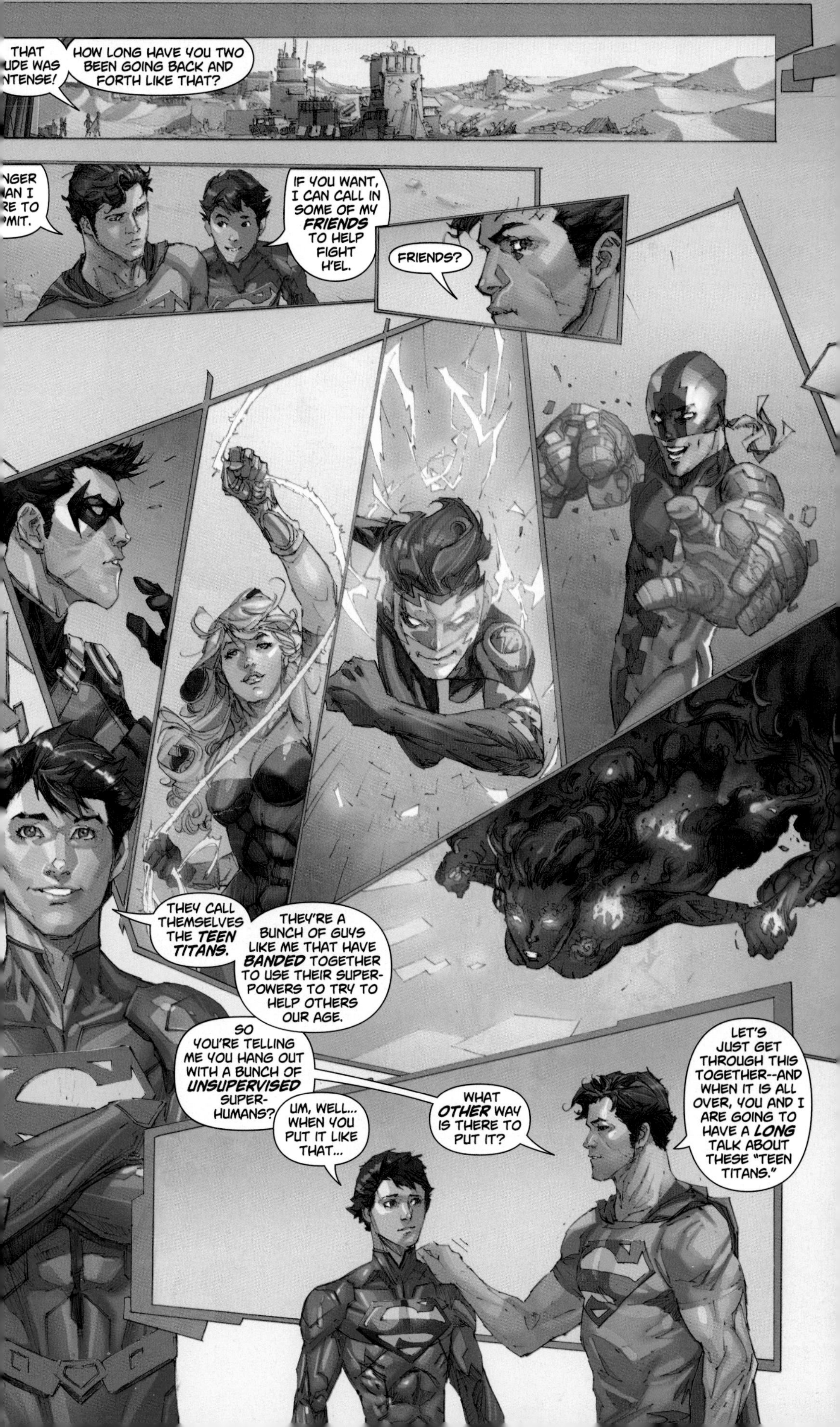
THAT ...UDE WAS ...NTENSE!
HOW LONG HAVE YOU TWO BEEN GOING BACK AND FORTH LIKE THAT?
...NGER ...AN I ...RE TO ...MIT.
IF YOU WANT, I CAN CALL IN SOME OF MY FRIENDS TO HELP FIGHT H'EL.
FRIENDS?
THEY CALL THEMSELVES THE TEEN TITANS.
THEY'RE A BUNCH OF GUYS LIKE ME THAT HAVE BANDED TOGETHER TO USE THEIR SUPER-POWERS TO TRY TO HELP OTHERS OUR AGE.
SO YOU'RE TELLING ME YOU HANG OUT WITH A BUNCH OF UNSUPERVISED SUPER-HUMANS?
UM, WELL... WHEN YOU PUT IT LIKE THAT...
WHAT OTHER WAY IS THERE TO PUT IT?
LET'S JUST GET THROUGH THIS TOGETHER--AND WHEN IT IS ALL OVER, YOU AND I ARE GOING TO HAVE A LONG TALK ABOUT THESE "TEEN TITANS."

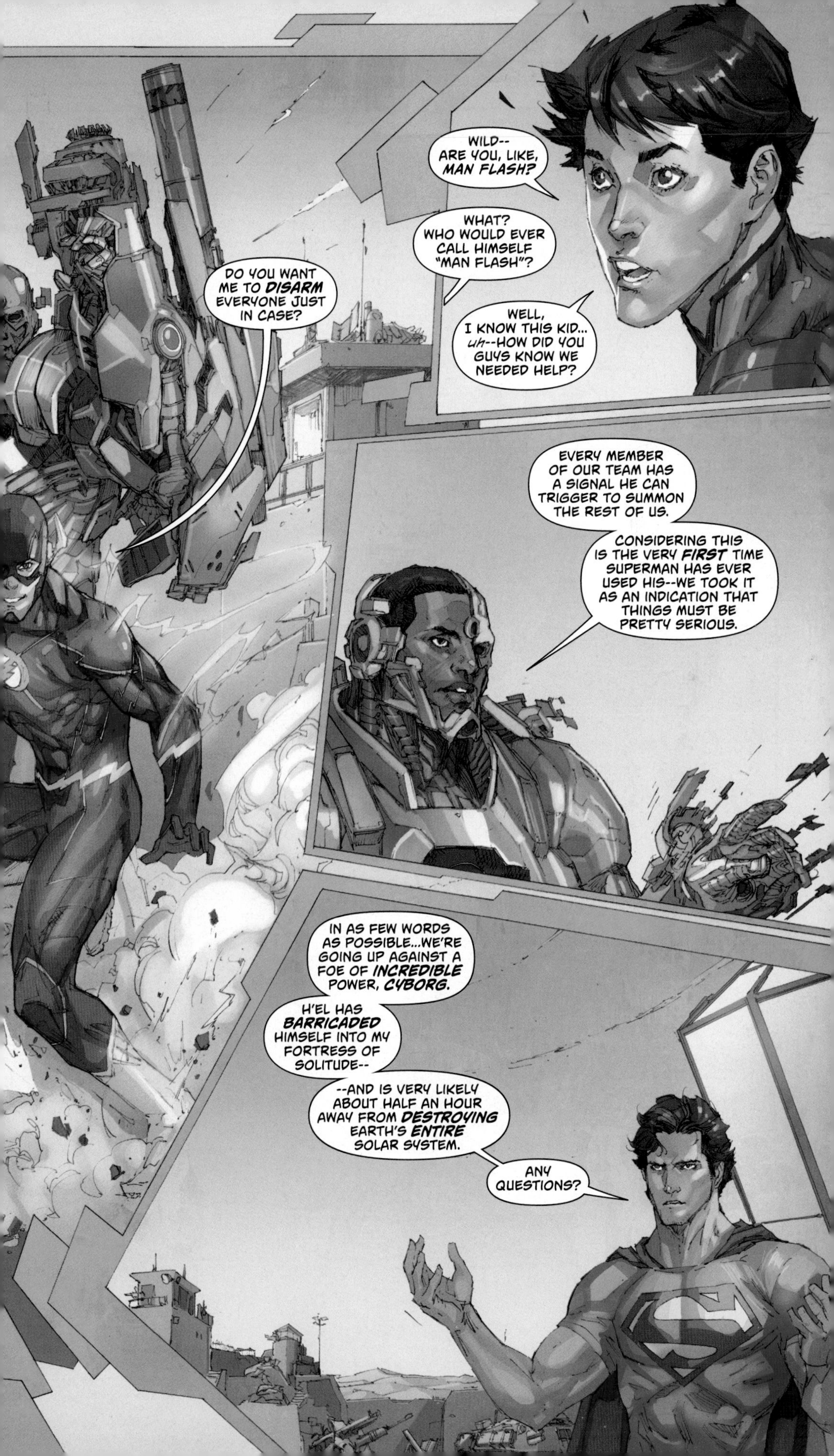
WILD-- ARE YOU, LIKE, MAN FLASH?
WHAT? WHO WOULD EVER CALL HIMSELF "MAN FLASH"?
WELL, I KNOW THIS KID... uh--HOW DID YOU GUYS KNOW WE NEEDED HELP?
DO YOU WANT ME TO DISARM EVERYONE JUST IN CASE?
EVERY MEMBER OF OUR TEAM HAS A SIGNAL HE CAN TRIGGER TO SUMMON THE REST OF US.
CONSIDERING THIS IS THE VERY FIRST TIME SUPERMAN HAS EVER USED HIS--WE TOOK IT AS AN INDICATION THAT THINGS MUST BE PRETTY SERIOUS.
IN AS FEW WORDS AS POSSIBLE...WE'RE GOING UP AGAINST A FOE OF INCREDIBLE POWER, CYBORG.
H'EL HAS BARRICADED HIMSELF INTO MY FORTRESS OF SOLITUDE--
--AND IS VERY LIKELY ABOUT HALF AN HOUR AWAY FROM DESTROYING EARTH'S ENTIRE SOLAR SYSTEM.
ANY QUESTIONS?

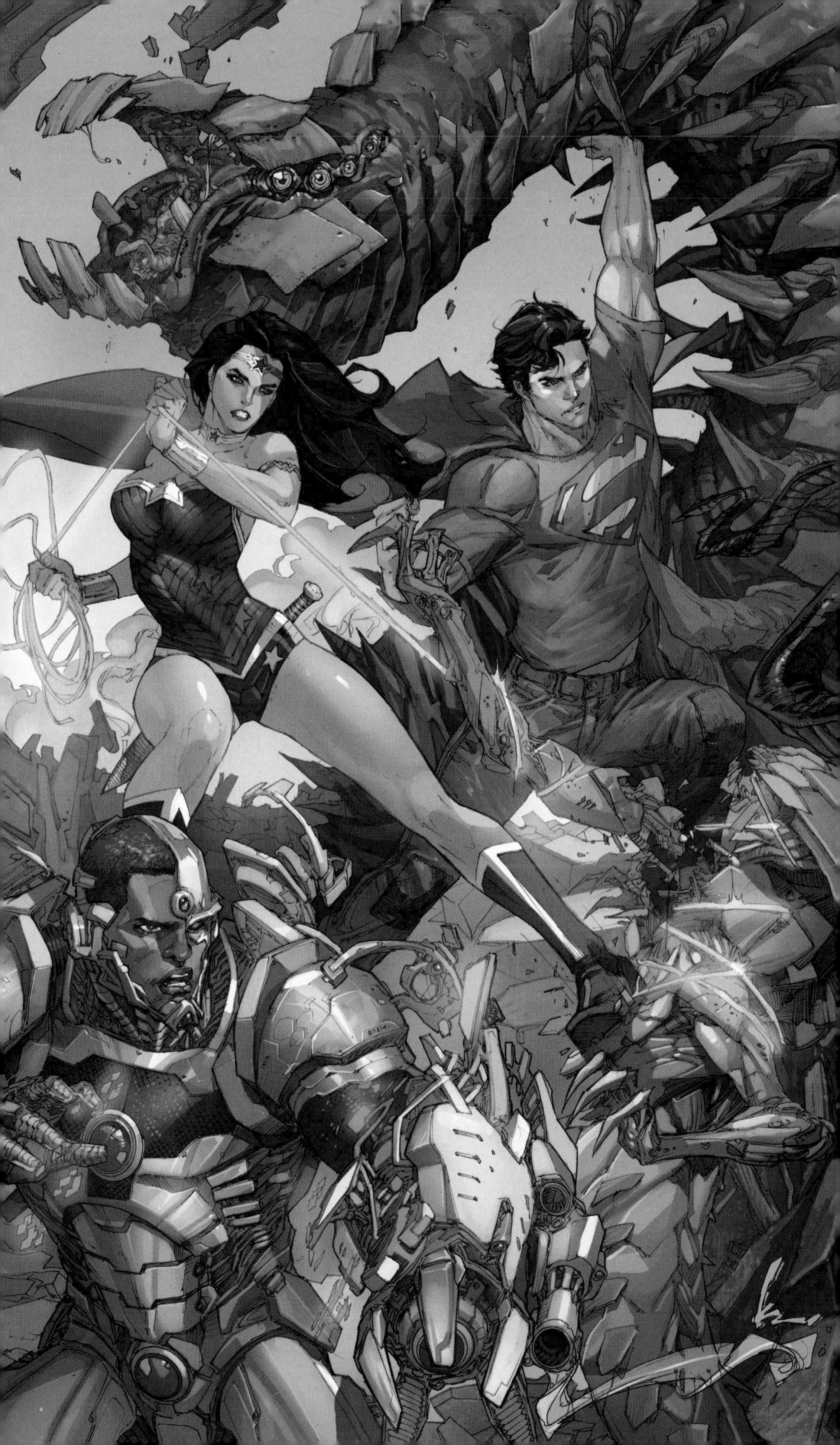

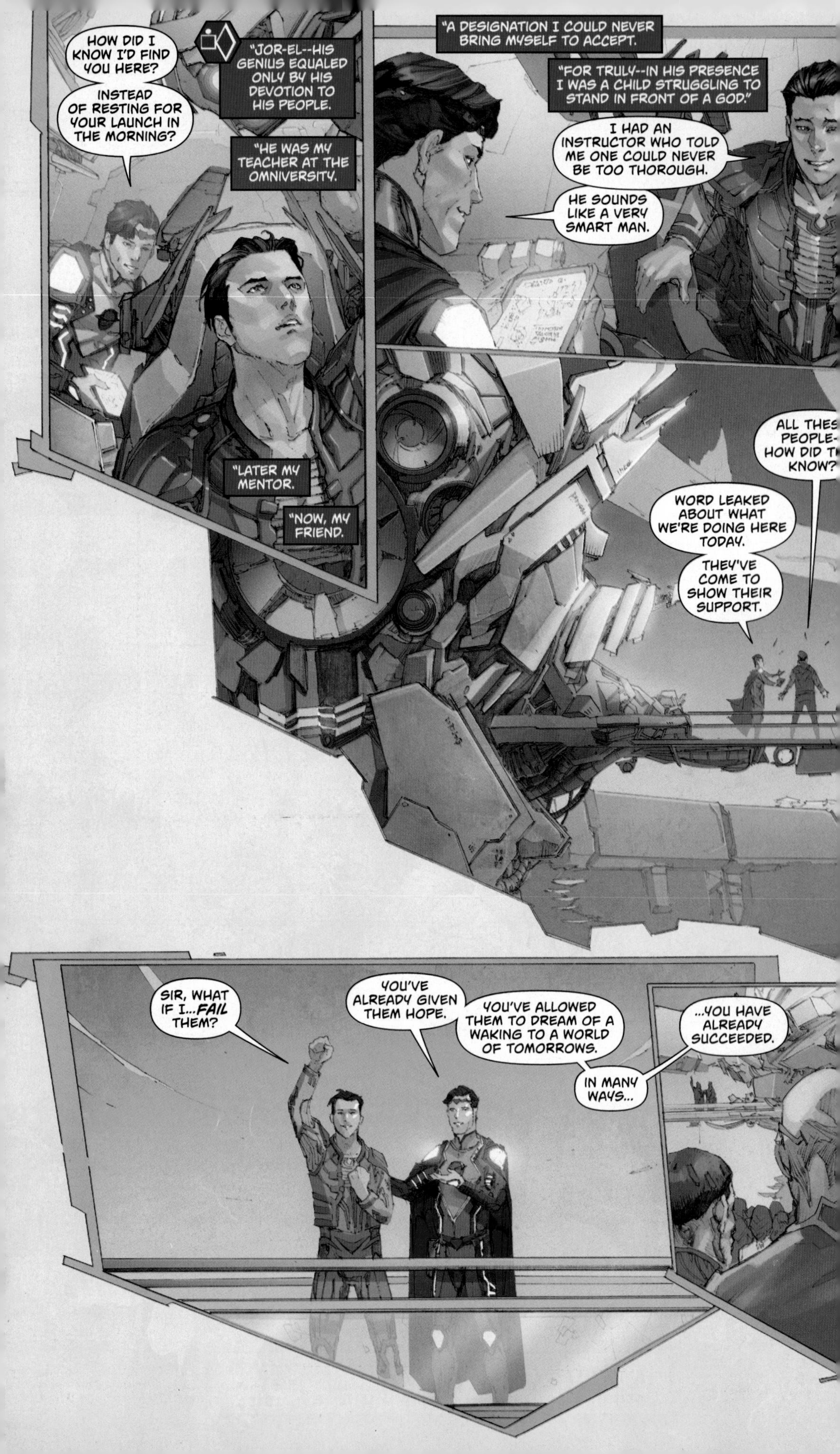
HOW DID I KNOW I'D FIND YOU HERE?
INSTEAD OF RESTING FOR YOUR LAUNCH IN THE MORNING?
"JOR-EL--HIS GENIUS EQUALED ONLY BY HIS DEVOTION TO HIS PEOPLE.
"HE WAS MY TEACHER AT THE OMNIVERSITY.
"LATER MY MENTOR.
"NOW, MY FRIEND.
"A DESIGNATION I COULD NEVER BRING MYSELF TO ACCEPT.
"FOR TRULY--IN HIS PRESENCE I WAS A CHILD STRUGGLING TO STAND IN FRONT OF A GOD."
I HAD AN INSTRUCTOR WHO TOLD ME ONE COULD NEVER BE TOO THOROUGH.
HE SOUNDS LIKE A VERY SMART MAN.
ALL THES PEOPLE- HOW DID T KNOW?
WORD LEAKED ABOUT WHAT WE'RE DOING HERE TODAY.
THEY'VE COME TO SHOW THEIR SUPPORT.
SIR, WHAT IF I...FAIL THEM?
YOU'VE ALREADY GIVEN THEM HOPE.
YOU'VE ALLOWED THEM TO DREAM OF A WAKING TO A WORLD OF TOMORROWS.
IN MANY WAYS...
...YOU HAVE ALREADY SUCCEEDED.

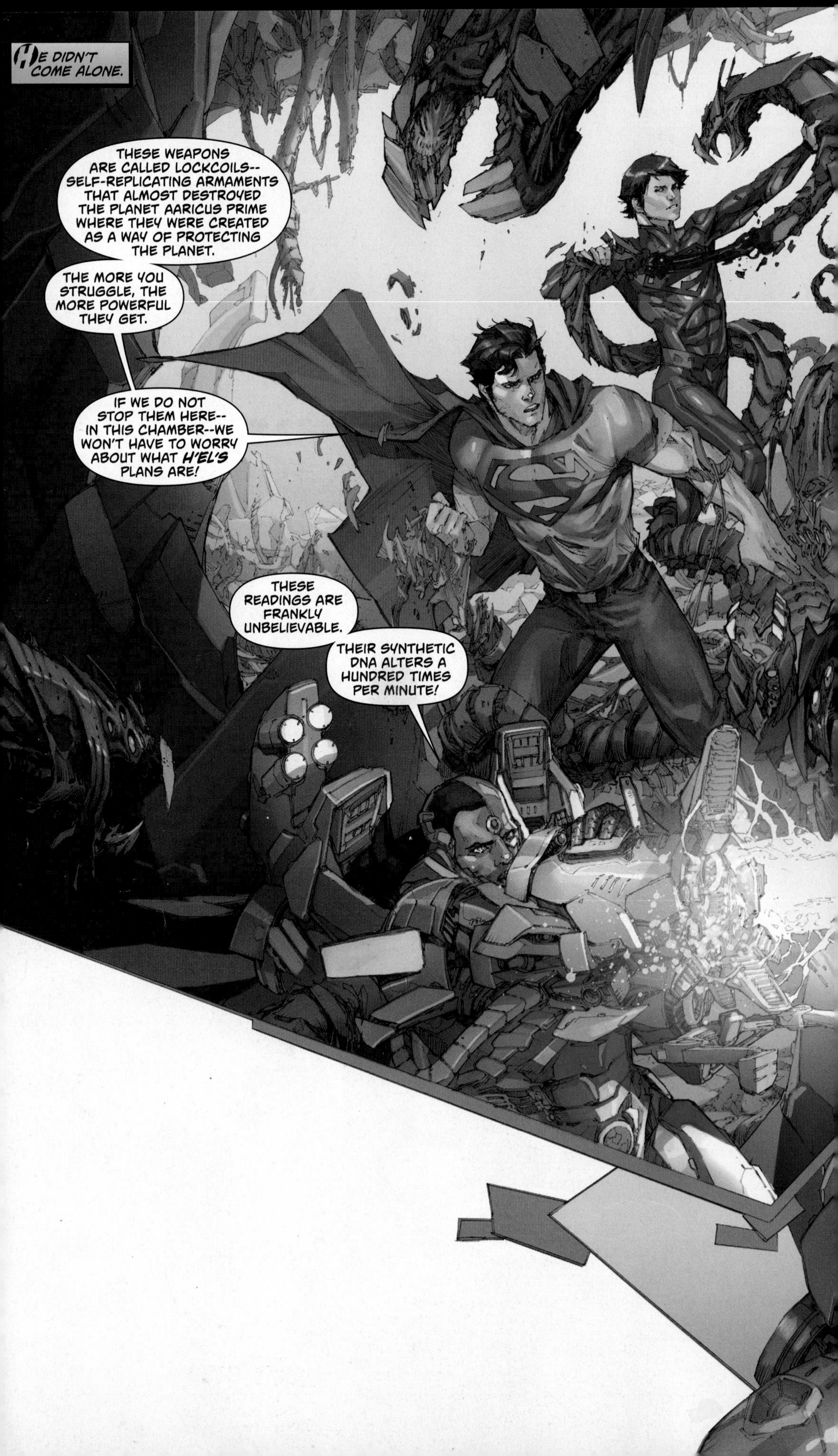
HE DIDN'T COME ALONE.
THESE WEAPONS ARE CALLED LOCKCOILS-- SELF-REPLICATING ARMAMENTS THAT ALMOST DESTROYED THE PLANET AARICUS PRIME WHERE THEY WERE CREATED AS A WAY OF PROTECTING THE PLANET.
THE MORE YOU STRUGGLE, THE MORE POWERFUL THEY GET.
IF WE DO NOT STOP THEM HERE-- IN THIS CHAMBER--WE WON'T HAVE TO WORRY ABOUT WHAT *H'EL'S* PLANS ARE!
THESE READINGS ARE FRANKLY UNBELIEVABLE.
THEIR SYNTHETIC DNA ALTERS A HUNDRED TIMES PER MINUTE!

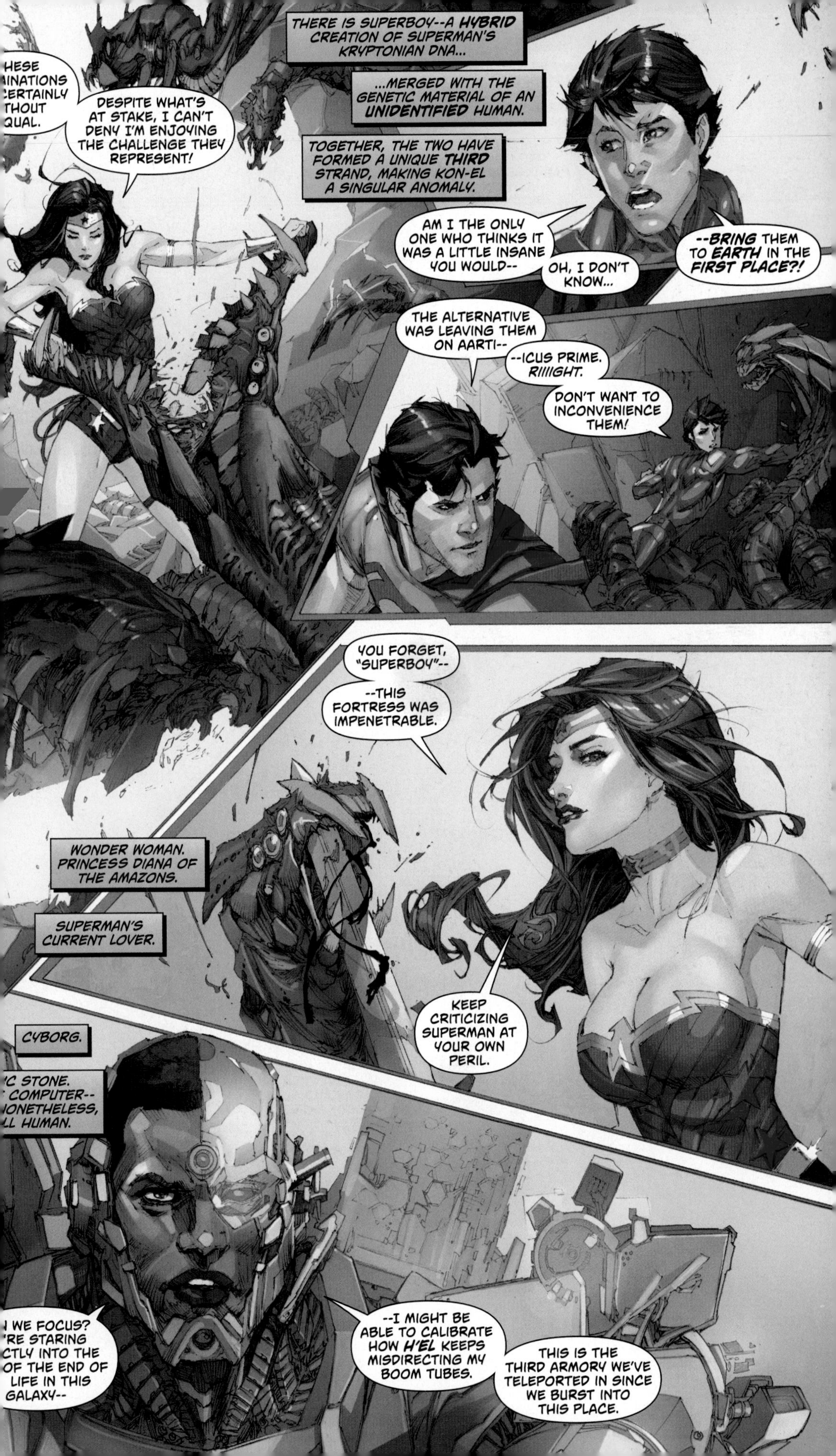
HESE
INATIONS
ERTAINLY
THOUT
QUAL.
DESPITE WHAT'S AT STAKE, I CAN'T DENY I'M ENJOYING THE CHALLENGE THEY REPRESENT!
THERE IS SUPERBOY--A HYBRID CREATION OF SUPERMAN'S KRYPTONIAN DNA...
...MERGED WITH THE GENETIC MATERIAL OF AN UNIDENTIFIED HUMAN.
TOGETHER, THE TWO HAVE FORMED A UNIQUE THIRD STRAND, MAKING KON-EL A SINGULAR ANOMALY.
AM I THE ONLY ONE WHO THINKS IT WAS A LITTLE INSANE YOU WOULD--
OH, I DON'T KNOW...
--BRING THEM TO EARTH IN THE FIRST PLACE?!
THE ALTERNATIVE WAS LEAVING THEM ON AARTI--
--ICUS PRIME. RIIIIGHT.
DON'T WANT TO INCONVENIENCE THEM!
YOU FORGET, "SUPERBOY"--
--THIS FORTRESS WAS IMPENETRABLE.
WONDER WOMAN. PRINCESS DIANA OF THE AMAZONS.
SUPERMAN'S CURRENT LOVER.
KEEP CRITICIZING SUPERMAN AT YOUR OWN PERIL.
CYBORG.
C STONE.
COMPUTER--
NONETHELESS,
LL HUMAN.
WE FOCUS?
RE STARING
CTLY INTO THE
OF THE END OF
LIFE IN THIS
GALAXY--
--I MIGHT BE ABLE TO CALIBRATE HOW H'EL KEEPS MISDIRECTING MY BOOM TUBES.
THIS IS THE THIRD ARMORY WE'VE TELEPORTED IN SINCE WE BURST INTO THIS PLACE.

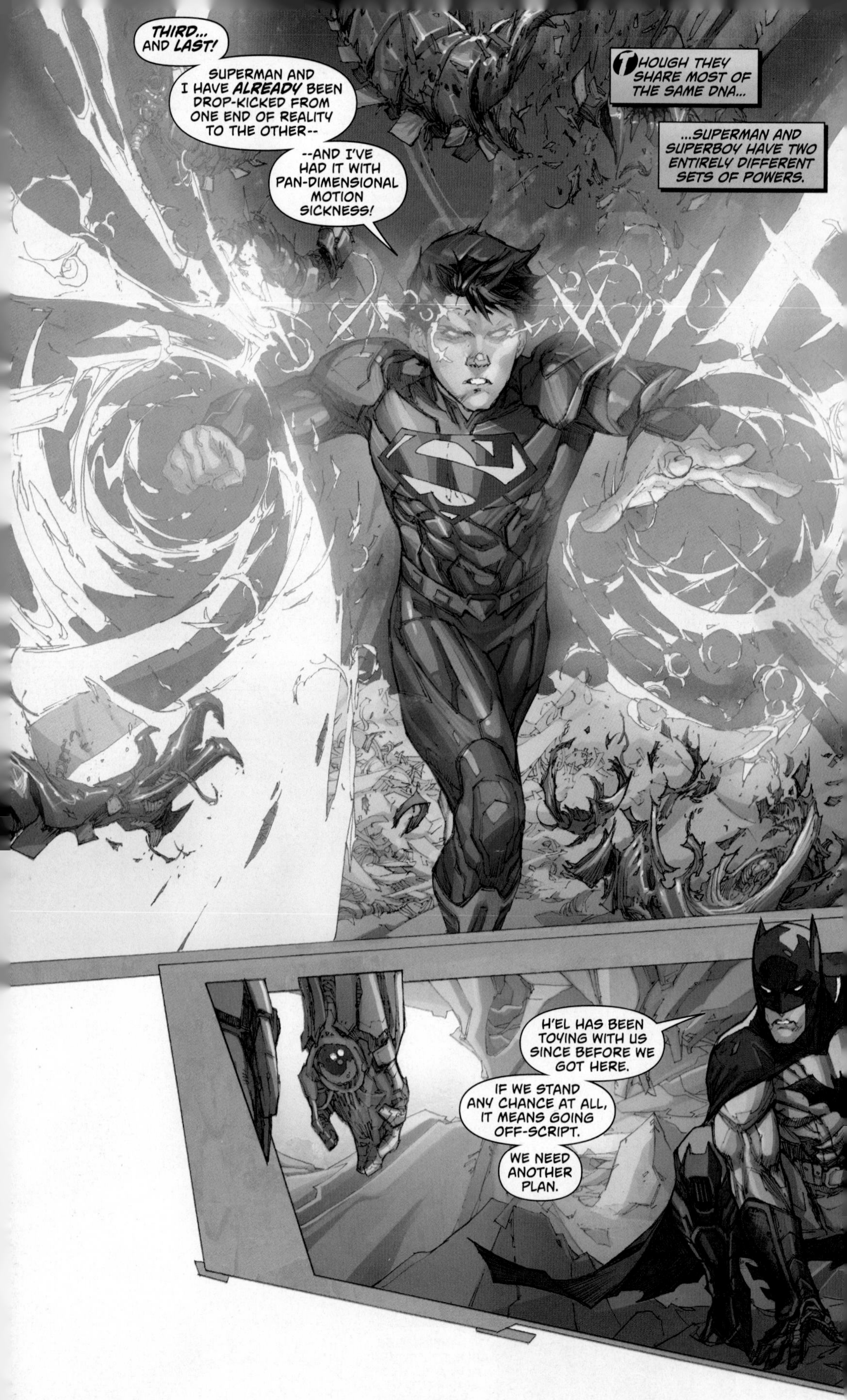
THIRD... AND LAST!
SUPERMAN AND I HAVE ALREADY BEEN DROP-KICKED FROM ONE END OF REALITY TO THE OTHER--
THOUGH THEY SHARE MOST OF THE SAME DNA...
...SUPERMAN AND SUPERBOY HAVE TWO ENTIRELY DIFFERENT SETS OF POWERS.
--AND I'VE HAD IT WITH PAN-DIMENSIONAL MOTION SICKNESS!
H'EL HAS BEEN TOYING WITH US SINCE BEFORE WE GOT HERE.
IF WE STAND ANY CHANCE AT ALL, IT MEANS GOING OFF-SCRIPT.
WE NEED ANOTHER PLAN.

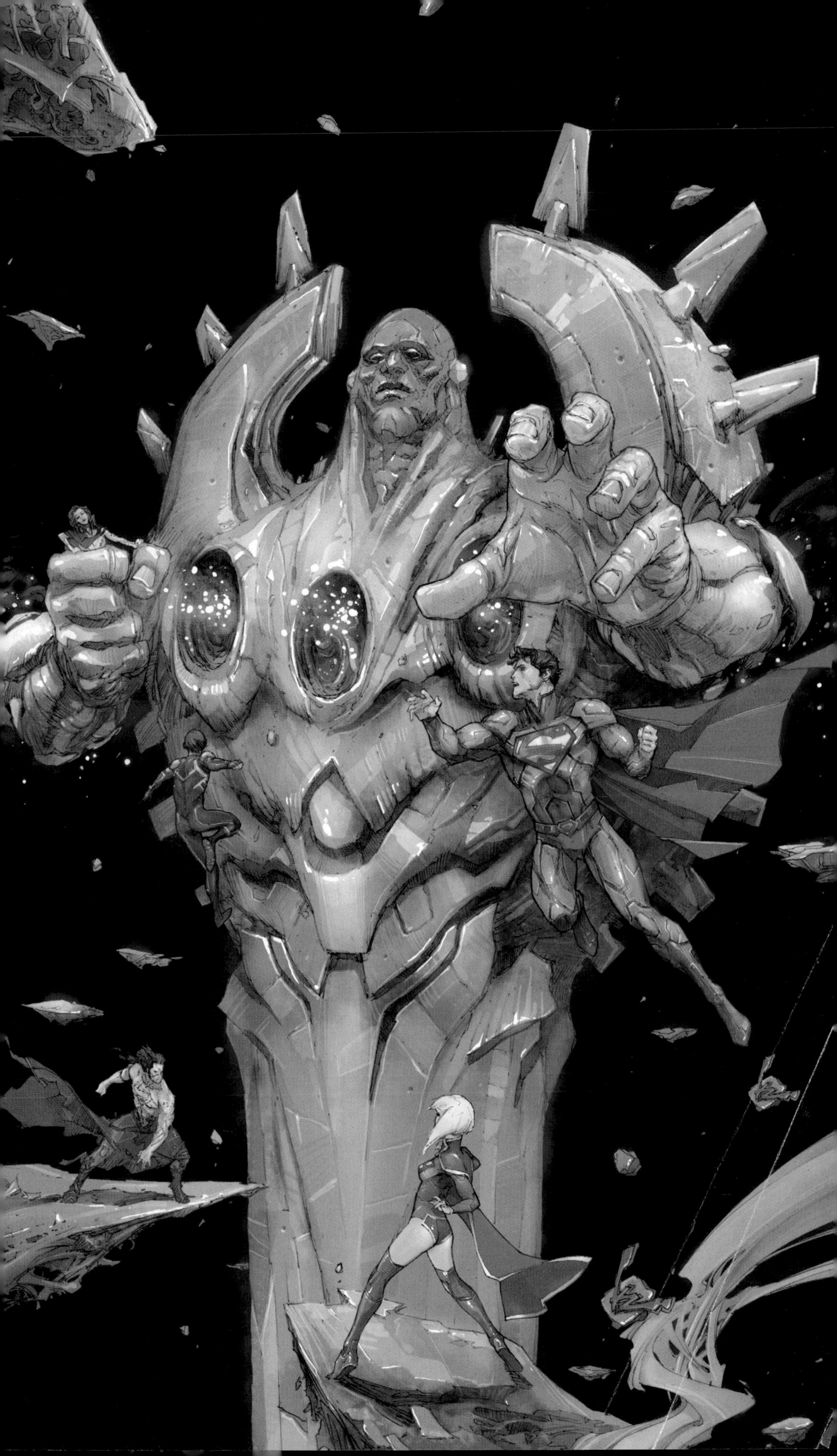

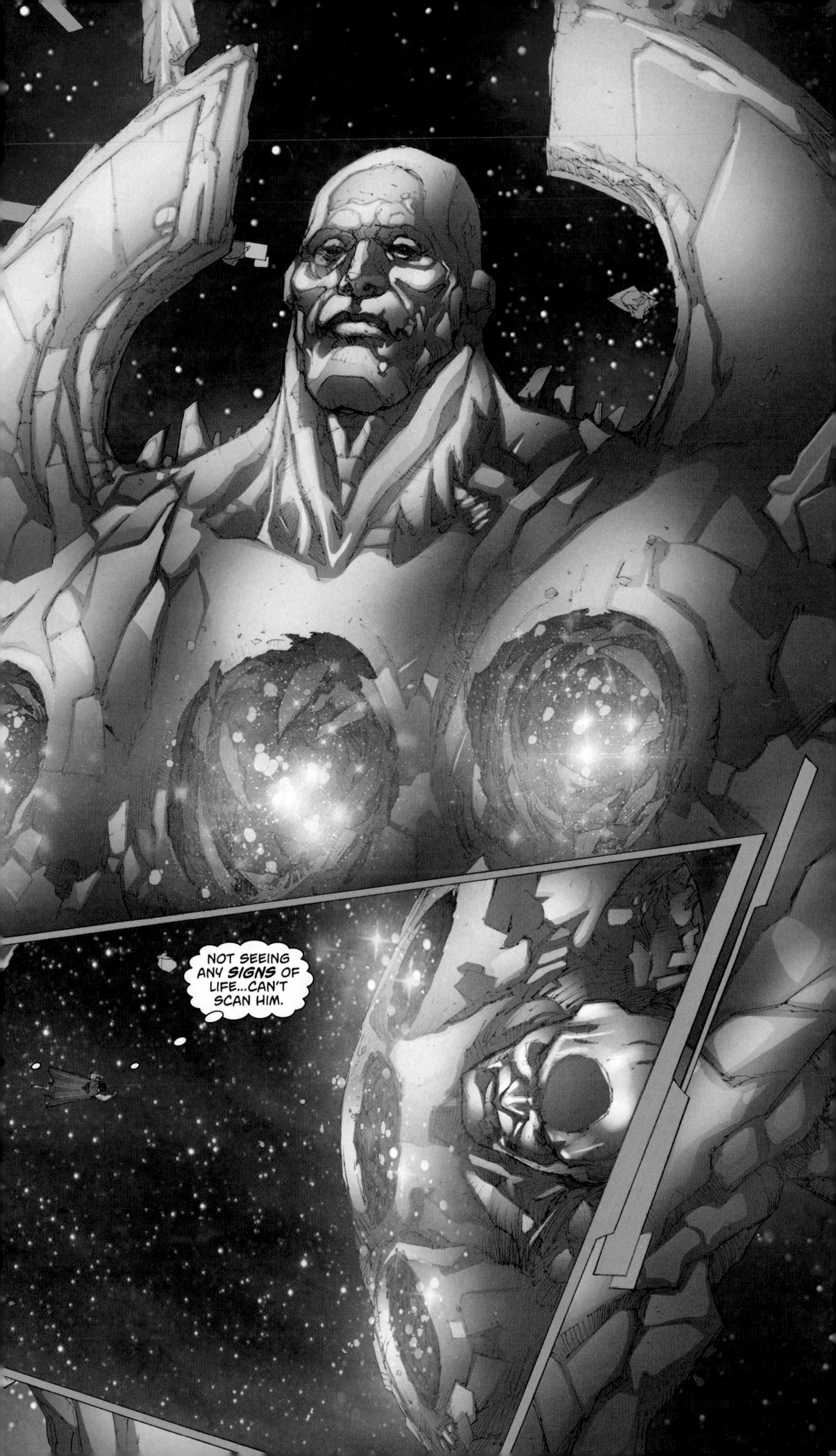
NOT SEEING ANY SIGNS OF LIFE...CAN'T SCAN HIM.

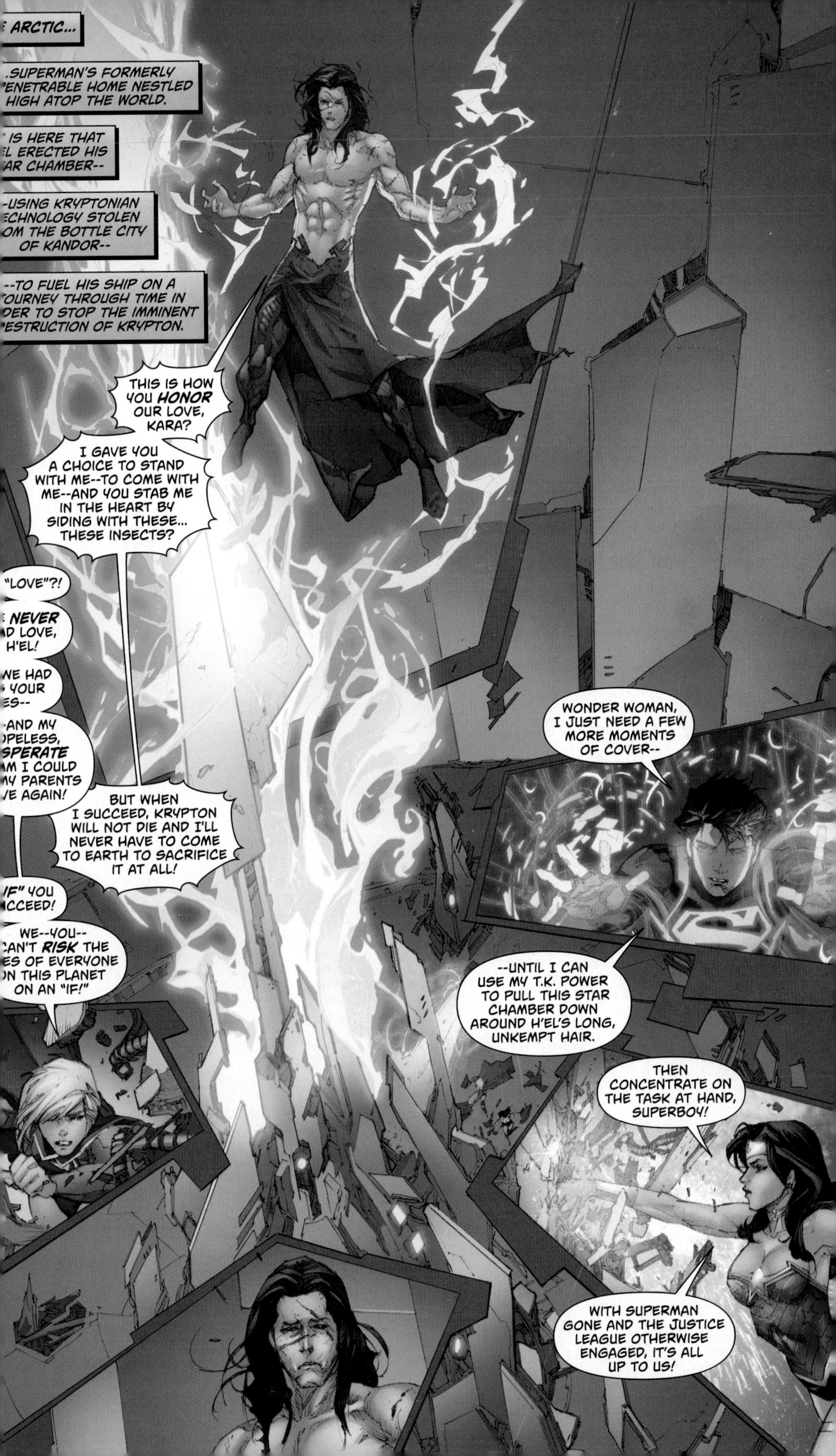
ARCTIC...
SUPERMAN'S FORMERLY PENETRABLE HOME NESTLED HIGH ATOP THE WORLD.
IS HERE THAT EL ERECTED HIS AR CHAMBER--
-USING KRYPTONIAN ECHNOLOGY STOLEN OM THE BOTTLE CITY OF KANDOR--
--TO FUEL HIS SHIP ON A JOURNEY THROUGH TIME IN DER TO STOP THE IMMINENT DESTRUCTION OF KRYPTON.
THIS IS HOW YOU HONOR OUR LOVE, KARA?
I GAVE YOU A CHOICE TO STAND WITH ME--TO COME WITH ME--AND YOU STAB ME IN THE HEART BY SIDING WITH THESE... THESE INSECTS?
"LOVE"?!
NEVER D LOVE, H'EL!
WE HAD YOUR ES--
-AND MY OPELESS, SPERATE M I COULD MY PARENTS E AGAIN!
BUT WHEN I SUCCEED, KRYPTON WILL NOT DIE AND I'LL NEVER HAVE TO COME TO EARTH TO SACRIFICE IT AT ALL!
IF" YOU CCEED!
WE--YOU-- CAN'T RISK THE ES OF EVERYONE N THIS PLANET ON AN "IF!"
WONDER WOMAN, I JUST NEED A FEW MORE MOMENTS OF COVER--
--UNTIL I CAN USE MY T.K. POWER TO PULL THIS STAR CHAMBER DOWN AROUND H'EL'S LONG, UNKEMPT HAIR.
THEN CONCENTRATE ON THE TASK AT HAND, SUPERBOY!
WITH SUPERMAN GONE AND THE JUSTICE LEAGUE OTHERWISE ENGAGED, IT'S ALL UP TO US!

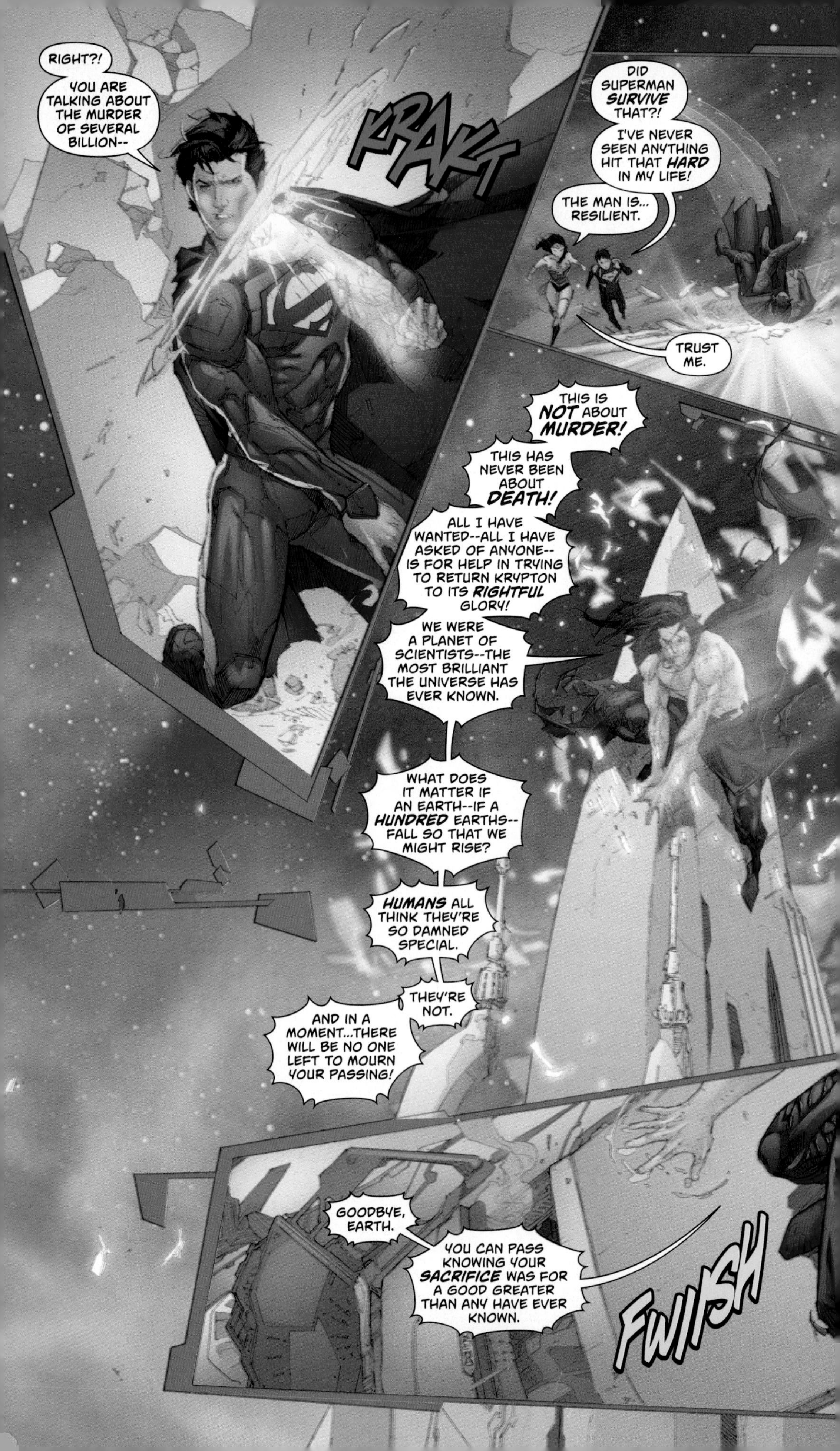
RIGHT?!
YOU ARE TALKING ABOUT THE MURDER OF SEVERAL BILLION--
KRAKT
DID SUPERMAN SURVIVE THAT?!
I'VE NEVER SEEN ANYTHING HIT THAT HARD IN MY LIFE!
THE MAN IS... RESILIENT.
TRUST ME.
THIS IS NOT ABOUT MURDER!
THIS HAS NEVER BEEN ABOUT DEATH!
ALL I HAVE WANTED--ALL I HAVE ASKED OF ANYONE-- IS FOR HELP IN TRYING TO RETURN KRYPTON TO ITS RIGHTFUL GLORY!
WE WERE A PLANET OF SCIENTISTS--THE MOST BRILLIANT THE UNIVERSE HAS EVER KNOWN.
WHAT DOES IT MATTER IF AN EARTH--IF A HUNDRED EARTHS-- FALL SO THAT WE MIGHT RISE?
HUMANS ALL THINK THEY'RE SO DAMNED SPECIAL.
THEY'RE NOT.
AND IN A MOMENT...THERE WILL BE NO ONE LEFT TO MOURN YOUR PASSING!
GOODBYE, EARTH.
YOU CAN PASS KNOWING YOUR SACRIFICE WAS FOR A GOOD GREATER THAN ANY HAVE EVER KNOWN.
FWISH

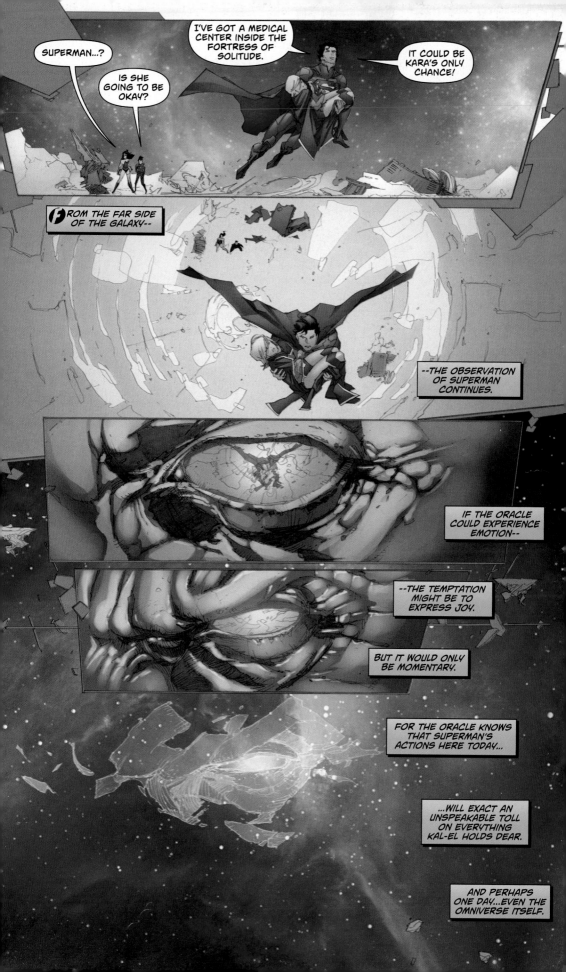

m issue #0

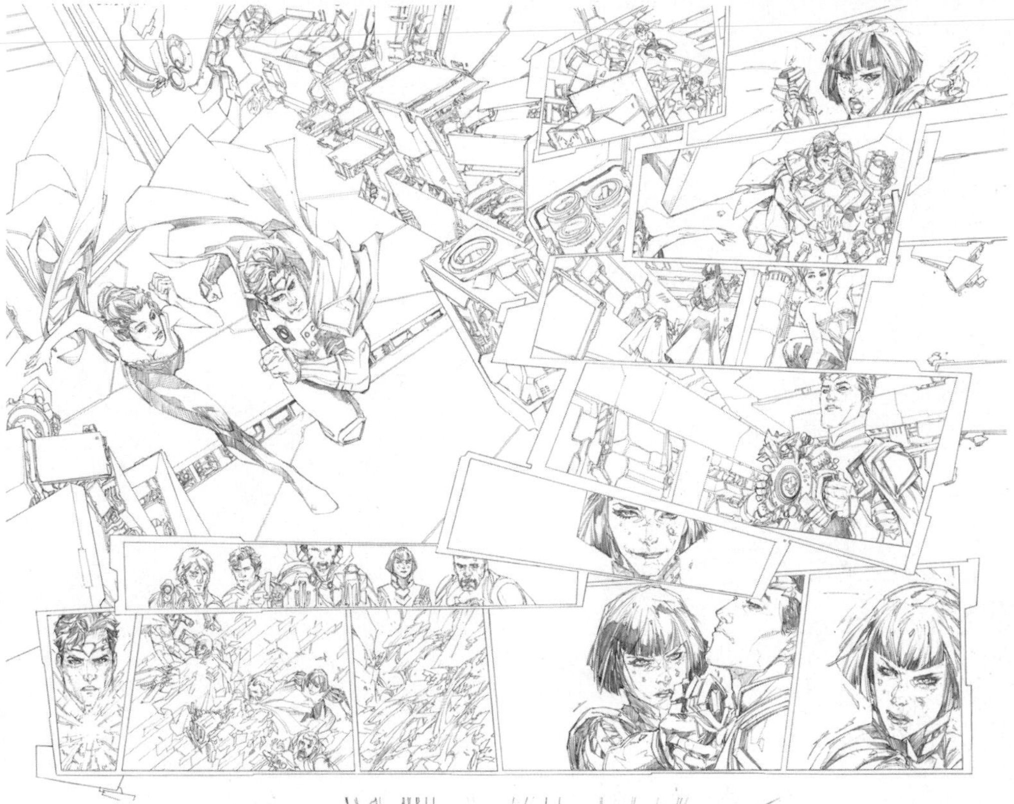

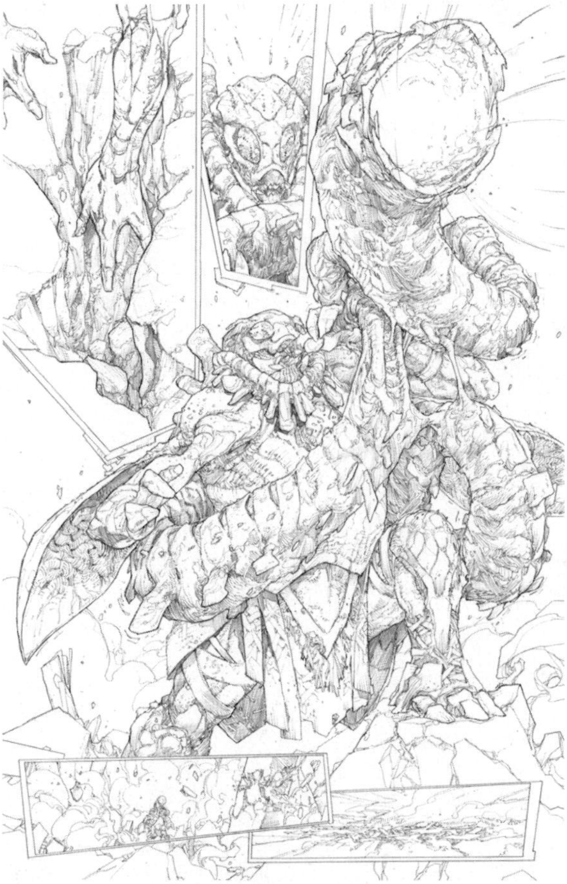

From issue #13

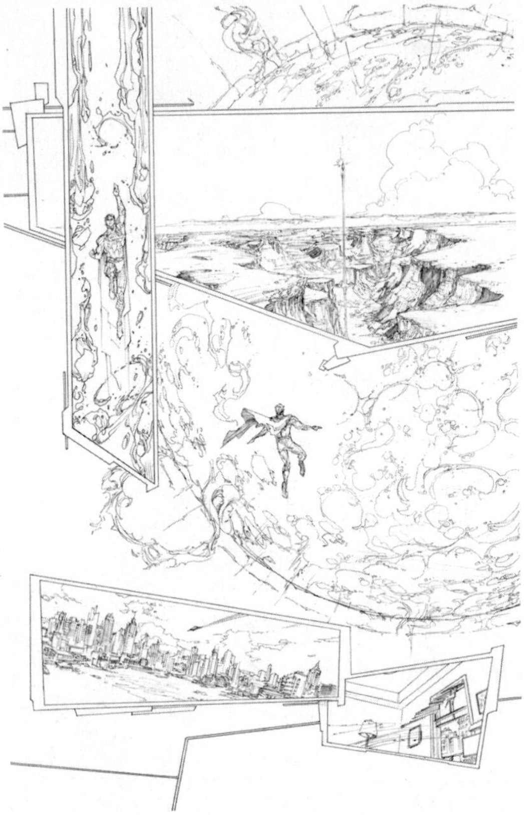

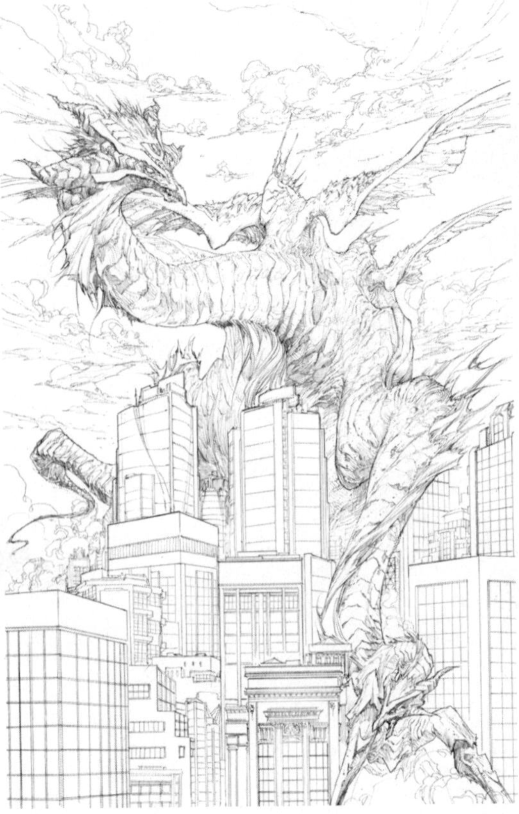

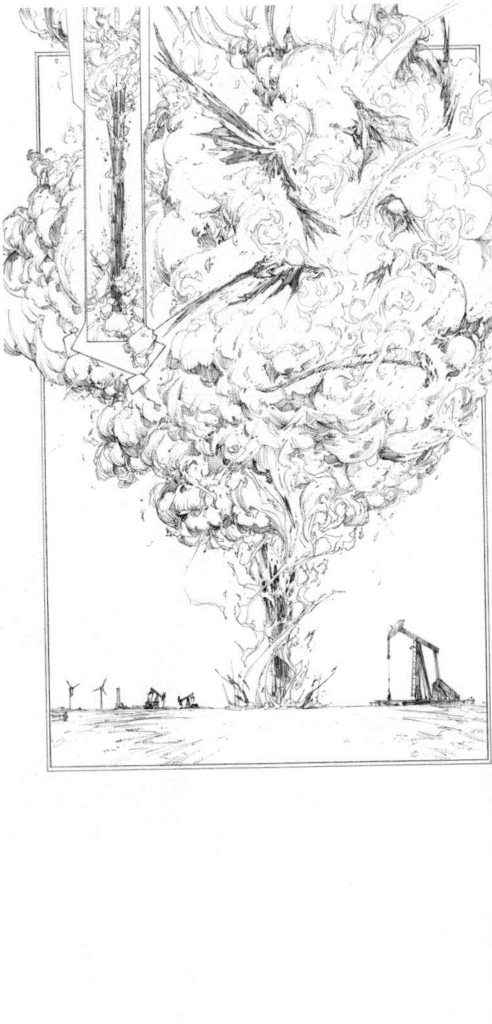

From issue #15

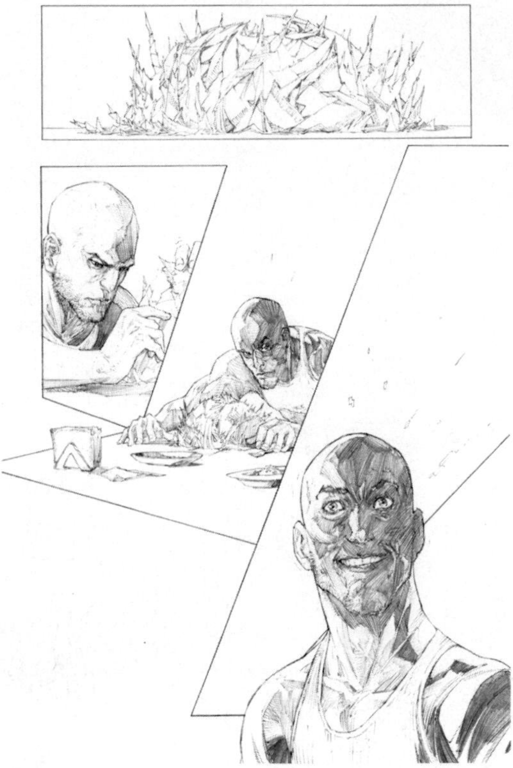

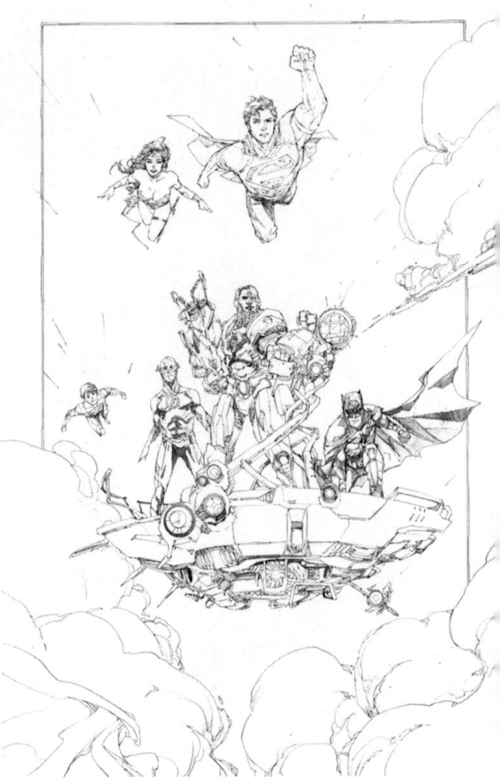

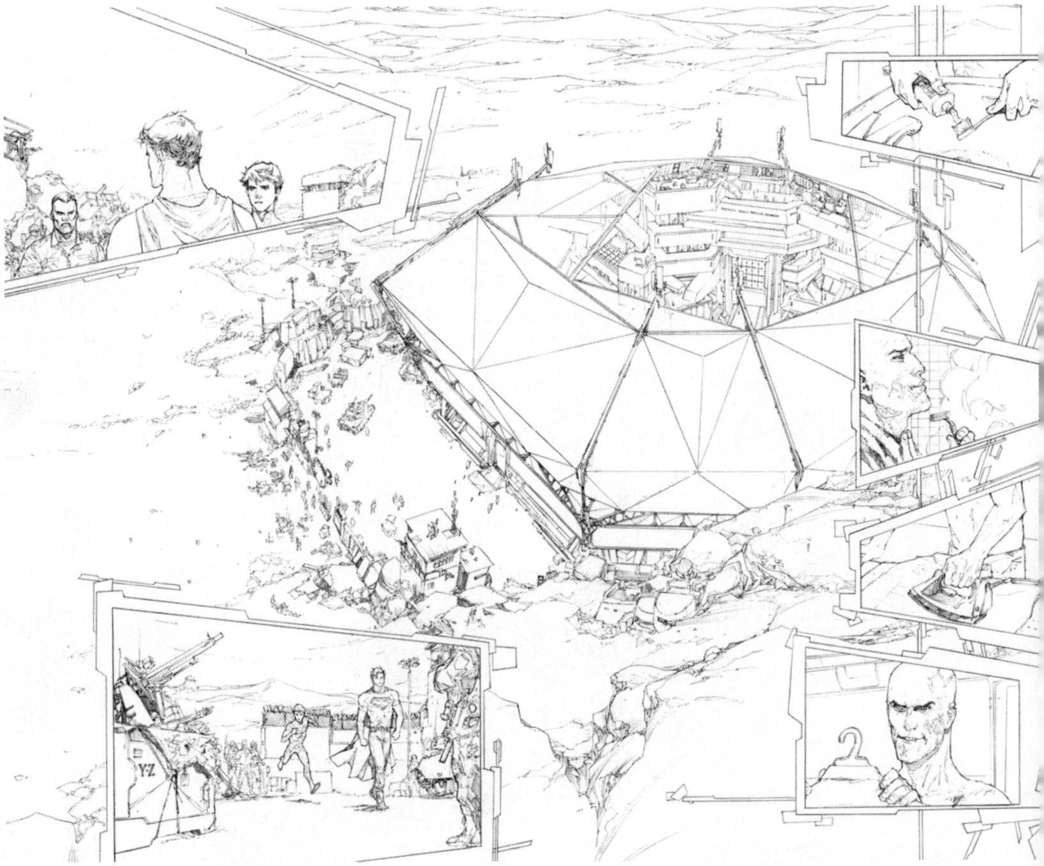

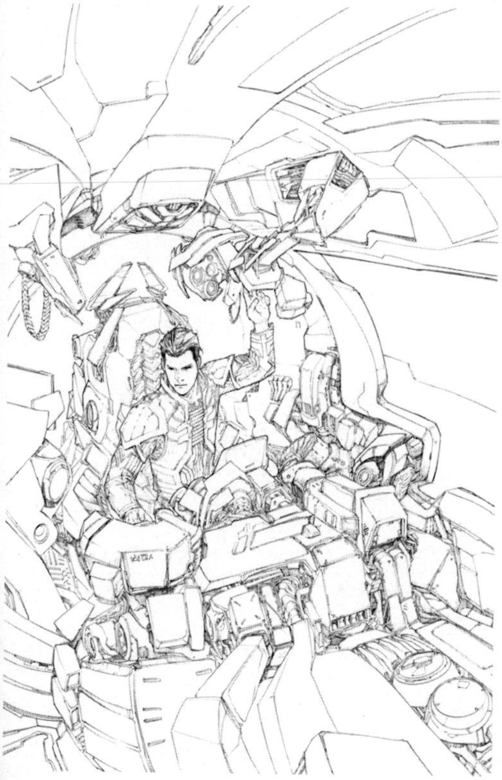

From issue #16

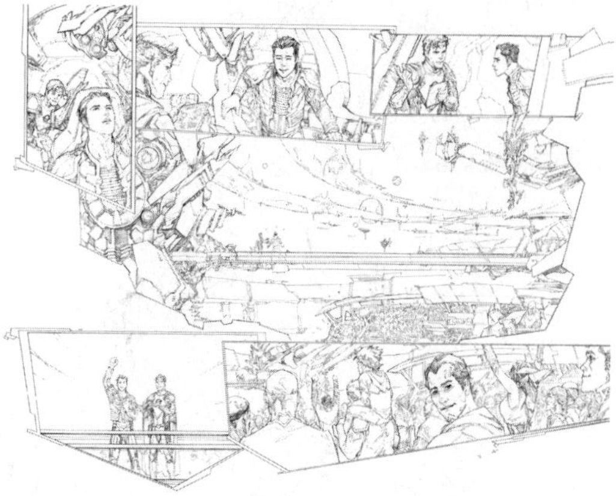

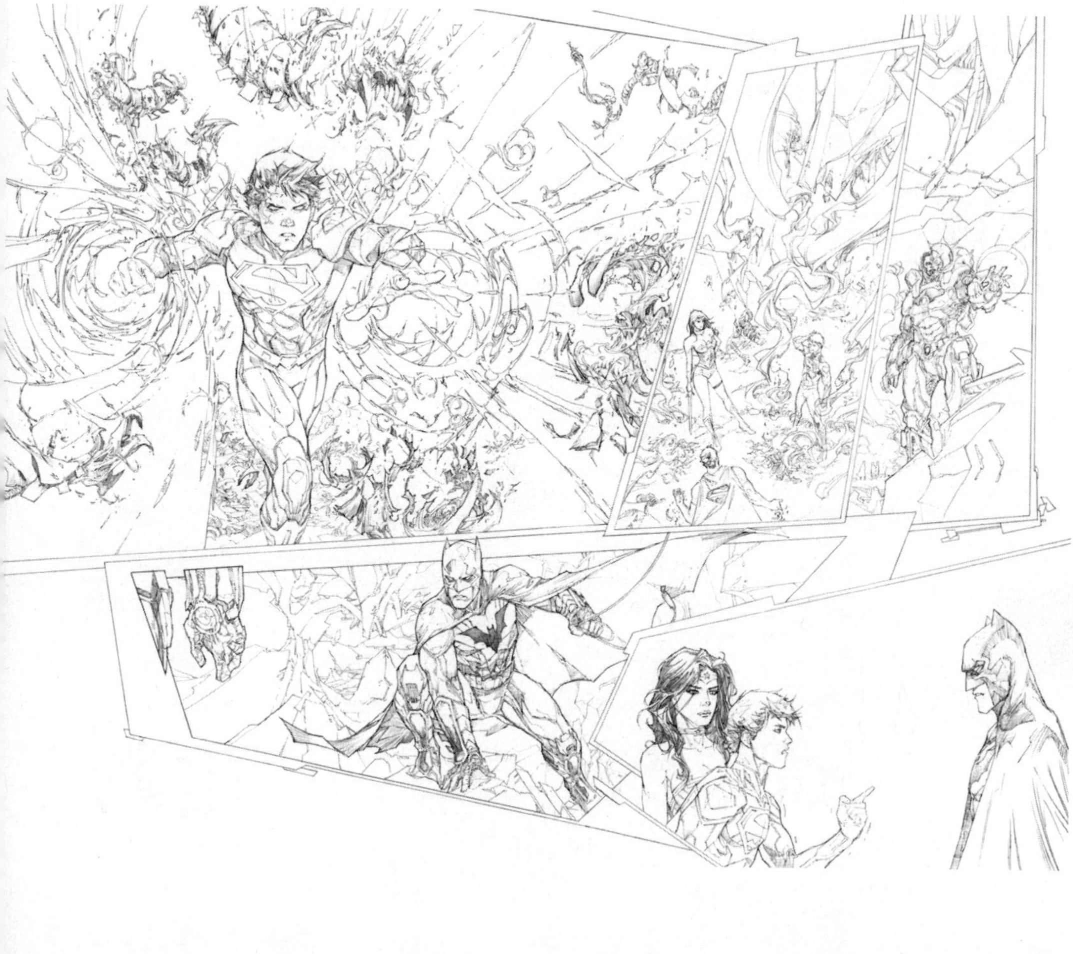

From issue #17

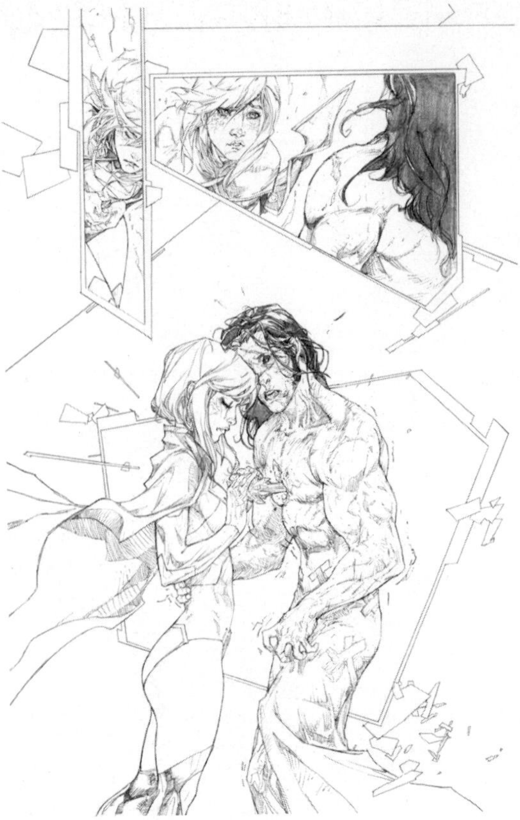

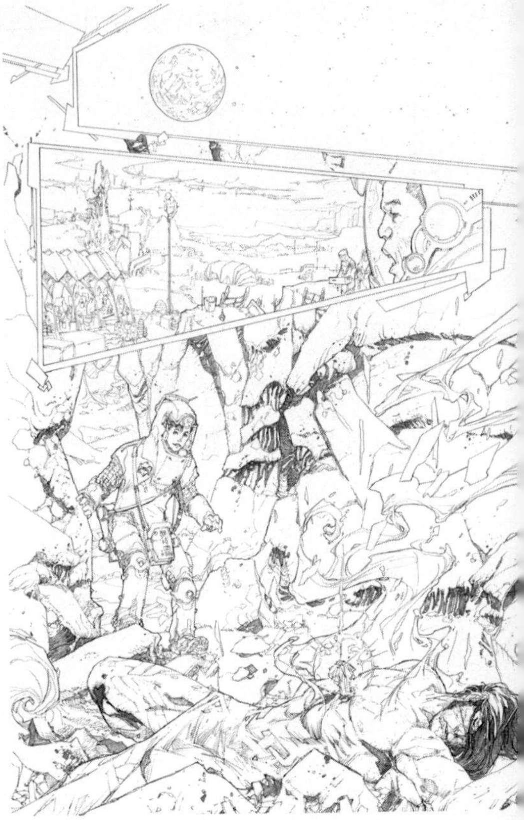

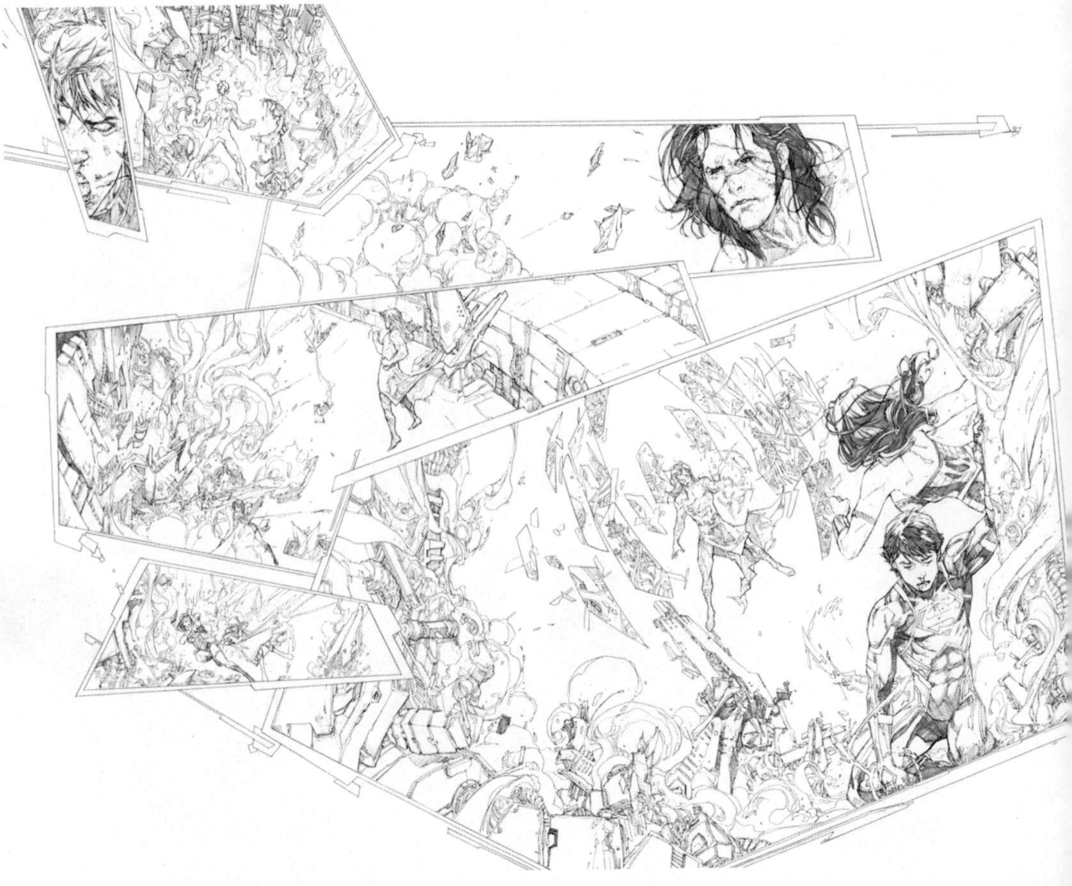

COVER PENCILS FOR ISSUE #15 BY KENNETH ROCAFORT

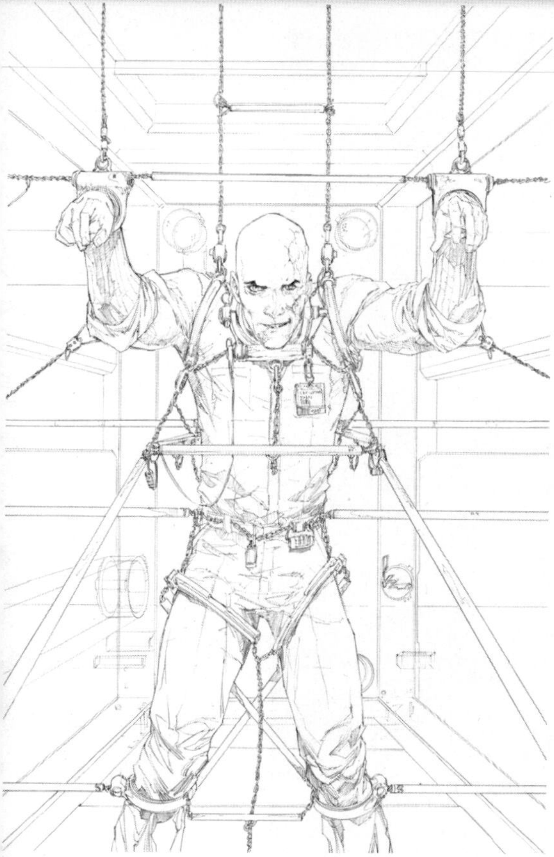

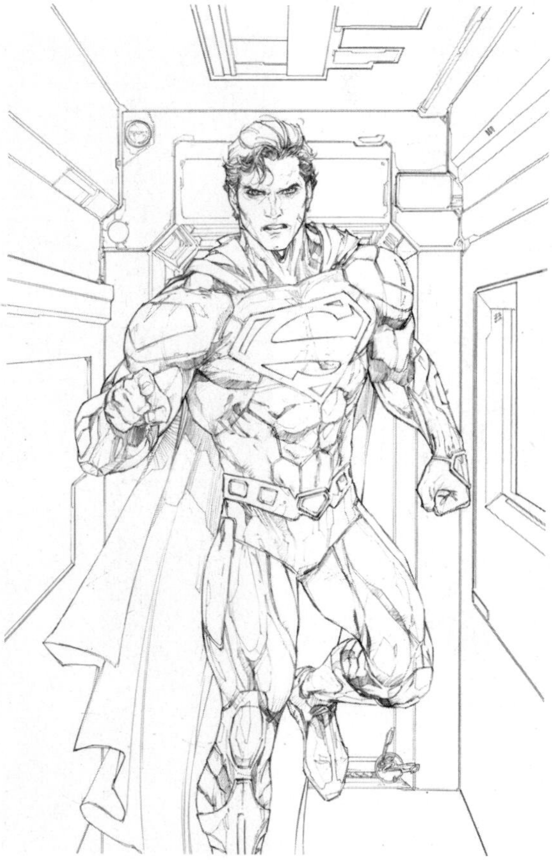

SUPERMAN
CHARACTER DESIGNS BY KENNETH ROCAFORT

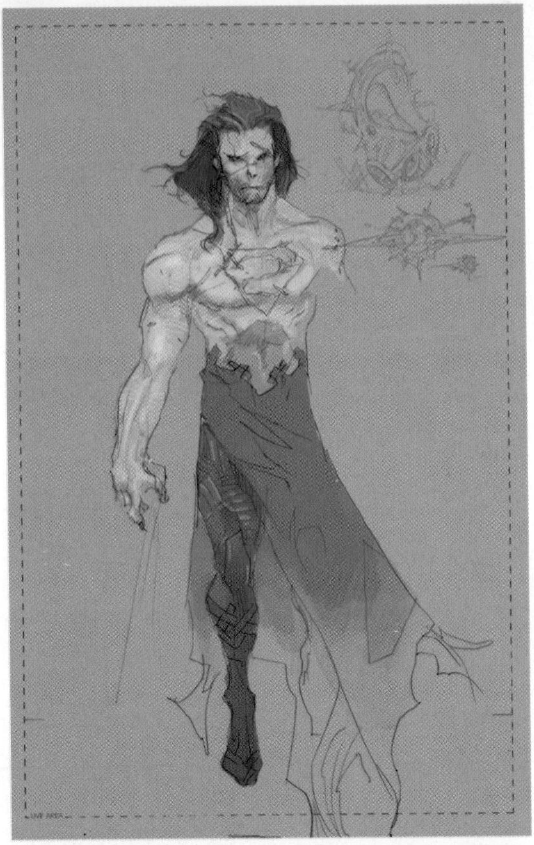

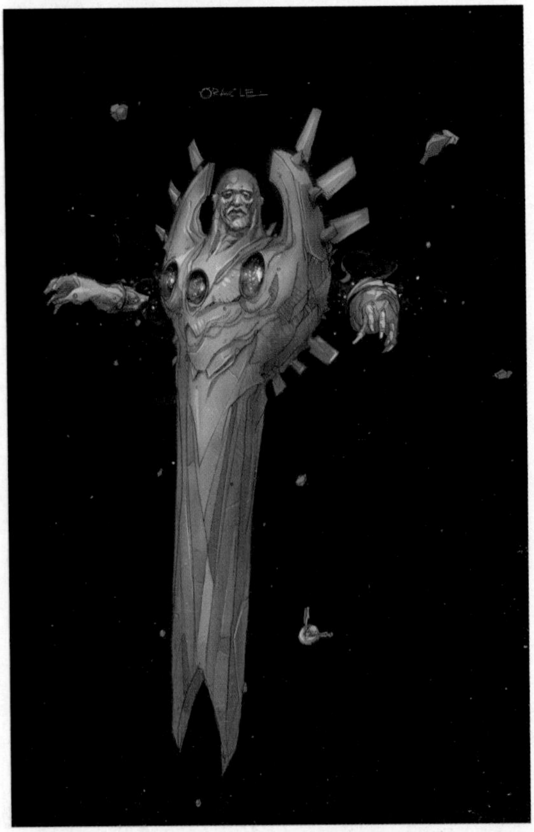